HOW GROWTH REALLY HAPPENS

How Growth Really Happens

THE MAKING OF ECONOMIC MIRACLES THROUGH PRODUCTION, GOVERNANCE, AND SKILLS

Michael H. Best

PRINCETON UNIVERSITY PRESS

PRINCETON & OXFORD

Copyright © 2018 by Princeton University Press

Published by Princeton University Press,
41 William Street, Princeton, New Jersey 08540

In the United Kingdom: Princeton University Press,
6 Oxford Street, Woodstock, Oxfordshire OX20 1TR

press.princeton.edu

Jacket image adapted from a War Industries Board (WIB) poster,
Philadelphia Council of Defense

All Rights Reserved

ISBN 978-0-691-17925-4
Library of Congress Control Number 2018936837

British Library Cataloging-in-Publication Data is available

This book has been composed in Miller

Printed on acid-free paper. ∞

Printed in the United Kingdom

10 9 8 7 6 5 4 3 2 1

For my grandchildren, Cormac, Willa, Wyoming,
Cannon, Sophia, Diyala, Sorin, and Christopher.
May they contribute to a better world in their time.

In memory of Robin Murray, a friend who changed my life,
inspired my work, and contributed to a better world in his time.

Innovations, almost by definition, are one of the least analyzed parts of economics, in spite of the verifiable fact that they have contributed more to per capita economic growth than any other factor.

—ARROW 1988, 281

CONTENTS

Figures

Maps

Tables

Boxes

THIS BOOK REPRESENTS the continuation of a journey into the world of production that began for me as the son of a labor organizer in the machine shops and factories of early postwar Spokane, Washington. During World War II, many thousands of workers built and then operated production facilities to supply the rapidly growing aircraft industry, of which the aluminum rolling mills were the largest. The workings, precision, and noises of the machines, the telltale smells of the lubricants, and the pride, humor, and camaraderie of the men were imprinted in my mind as I accompanied my dad on his rounds.

The childhood phase of my journey into the world of production involved entry through the back door, but years later, during a two-year stint on the Greater London Enterprise Board, I found myself marching through the front door. This time it was to participate in the real world of business strategy, production organization, and industrial policy.

After this experience I enjoyed a double life, one as an academic economist, the other as a participant in business and production capability development internationally. While often at work in the real world, I nevertheless continued to teach industrial organization and the history of economic thought at the University of Massachusetts, Amherst. My graduate seminar on the history of thought was a journey through the economics classics, from Smith and Ricardo to Marx, the marginalists, Marshall, welfare theory, Schumpeter, Keynes, and Samuelson's neoclassical synthesis. The twist in the course was to examine the concept of the market in each major text with respect to the implicit theory of the firm instead of conceptualizing the firm in terms of the assumptions required for a general theory of competitive markets. So began in earnest the theory side of my journey through production systems.

In 1993 I became a co-director of the Center for Industrial Competitiveness at the University of Massachusetts, Lowell, a branch of the university with a long history of partnering with engineering-driven enterprises. For the next decade I enjoyed a front-row seat in the dramatic resurgence of Route 128.

Although both Greater London and Greater Boston had similar large populations of small- and medium-sized manufacturing enterprises, the difference between the productive landscapes was stark. If I had to capture the difference between London's and Boston's regional "systems of production" in two words, I would use "technology management." The term has multiple dimensions. It is where production capability and business organization meet. It is also where successful enterprise development and government policymaking *can* meet to foster industrial innovation.

The success stories of sectoral transitions over two centuries of Massachusetts history can be told in terms of technology management capability, just as the long history of industrial decline in Britain can be told in terms of the neglect of the importance of technology management to production performance, business development, and industrial renewal. British policymakers in companies and governments have conceived of technology as external to the production process, as a material object that can be purchased in the marketplace, rather than as something internal to engineering-informed capability development, by which enterprises and regions grow and innovate. When conceived as a commodity, technology is assumed to be embodied in capital; when understood as integral, it must be seen as shaped by the establishment of productive structures and innovative processes and as part of a capability to compete in a Schumpeterian world of product-led competition. The two approaches to technology reflect alternative economic paradigms, one in which competitiveness is conceptualized in terms of markets, the other in which it is understood as embedded in productive structures.

In two earlier books I examined the historical transformations of production systems. The focus was on characterizing fundamental principles of production and business organization to understand the productive structures underlying permanent advances in regional and national economic performance. Examples included the American system of manufacturing based on the principle of interchangeability; American big business, structured to take full advantage of organizing production according to the principle of flow; the Toyota Production System, organized around the principle of multiproduct flow; and both the Emilia-Romagna entrepreneurial industrial district and Greater Boston's open-system business model, organized in terms of the principle of system integration. In each case a New Competition emerged in which the "bursting" influence of entrepreneurial activity interacted with the "shaping" influence of institutional forms (to use Schumpeter's terms) to restructure and reconfigure the competitive advantage of enterprises, regions, and nations.

In this book a different set of experiences has served as a laboratory in which to investigate economic policymaking from a production systems perspective. The great strength of standard macroeconomics is its capacity to integrate expenditure, income, and output into a single framework. This strength is purchased at a cost. Macroeconomics provides an incomplete picture of how the production side of an economy is organized and galvanized. This book offers a Schumpeterian/structural conception of entrepreneurial activity and competition over product, process, technology, and organization to replace the standard model, in which a passive firm is trapped by price competition. Historical experiences are examined to elucidate the productive structures that underlie successful innovation-focused industrial policymaking and fill the otherwise empty space between micromotives and macrobehavior that haunts the standard paradigm.

An emergent productive structures and economic governance framework is advanced in which the international performance of regional and national economies is based on socially constructed deep structural advantages that lie behind the success of networked groups of business enterprises. These I summarize in terms of a "capability triad." Low-cost productive structures are only one form of advantage, but even these are best explained in terms of capability development processes and consistency with fundamental principles of production and organization.

The emergent paradigm draws from the manufacturing system and technological innovation framework of Charles Babbage, the internal and external spatial economies of Alfred Marshall, the innovation diffusion dynamics of Allyn Young, the value-creation process and internal economies of expansion of Edith Penrose, the network economies of expansion of George Richardson, the city innovation processes of Jane Jacobs, and the social capabilities and technological progress dynamics of Moses Abramovitz.

Much work remains to be done. The research methodology applied in this book combines theory, direct observation, historical case studies, database construction and analysis, and the history of economic thought. Out of this complex and challenging methodology, my critique of the failings of what I term the "orthodox" economic paradigm inexorably emerges and has important consequence for our understanding of how growth really happens.

The journey through production systems that began in the workshops of early postwar America had another consequence relevant to this book. Upon arriving at the University of Massachusetts in 1969, I met William Connolly, who had been recently appointed to the political science department. We shared two things: we both loved playing sports, and we both had fathers who were labor organizers, Bill's with the United Automobile Workers and mine with the International Association of Machinists. Our fathers' experiences had deeply influenced our viewpoints. We co-authored a book, *The Politicized Economy* (1982 [1976]), that introduced students of political economy and American politics to a radical interpretation of the American system from a working-class perspective, and dedicated it to our fathers.

Within the academic curriculum, we criticized the lack of attention paid to the structural causes of inequality and environmental degradation, the increasing divergence between public and private rationality, and also the inadequacy of liberal market reforms. We argued that "the injustices lodged inside the American political economy could not be rectified reliably and humanely through the policies of the welfare state; attempts to do so ... would help to drive traditional liberal constituencies to the Right" (1982, v). The passage of four decades of neo-liberalism confirmed the book's critique. Nevertheless, the critical perspective suffered from the same empty space as the economic mainstream. It did not go inside the processes by which private and public agencies, working together to establish governance institutions in both domains, can construct the organizational capabilities and productive structures to advance each generation's living standards and leave the world a better place. That is the mission of this book.

The book is not an easy read because it demands unlearning what has long been taught and practiced and has been "known to be true." To assist the reader along the way, I use three interrelated arguments. The first concerns the evolution of the discipline of economics, which I see as turning away from its original concern with production to focus instead on the optimality of resource allocation and macroeconomic stabilization based on mathematical models and narrow assumptions about human behavior. Economists' "formalistic turn" has left the discipline ill equipped to understand how economies transform themselves and succeed or stay transfixed and lag behind. So my second argument is that to understand how successful growth happens we need to return to an economic framework that focuses on production, enterprise, and governance, with stabilization playing a supportive rather than a dominant role. My third argument combines this new analytical framework with a close study of historical episodes of successful and failed transformations, with a sharp focus on three core elements: the production system, business organization, and skill formation—and their interconnections as summarized in a capability triad. The interconnectedness theme has important implications for understanding how strategic policy frameworks impact economic performance. Policies that address production capability development, enterprise growth, and skill formation separately and in isolation will not be successful. A requirement for transformative policies is that they be almost seamlessly blended into the detailed mechanics of change dynamics within independently managed private firms. My real-world experiences and theoretical odyssey share a destination in Abramovitz's critique of the standard paradigm's "factors of production" approach to growth. As Abramovitz warned, and this book emphasizes, such an approach remains blind to the "interactive connections" without which there can be no understanding of productivity change and growth.

ACKNOWLEDGMENTS

TO PARAPHRASE Charles Babbage, the interior economy of factories and the principles of political economy are so interwoven that to separate the two is inadvisable. I am indebted to the countless men and women who have built and run business enterprises for opening their doors to close examination of their productive structures. It is here that one can collect the empirical evidence by which a region's place in the global economy can be characterized in terms of capabilities, governance, and skills. Unfortunately, I must thank them collectively.

On my factory visits I have had many companions through the years: Norman Best in Spokane, Washington; Robin Murray and James Rafferty in London and Cyprus; Sebastiano Brusco and Mario Pezzini in Emilia Romagna; Dieter Haas in Germany; Tea Petrin in Slovenia on visits extending over two decades; Christian Gillen, Robert Forrant, and Alan Robinson in Jamaica and Gillen again in Honduras; Giovanna Ceglie in Indonesia, along with Rajah Rasiah in Malaysia; Vlado Kreačič in Moldova; Robert Forrant and David Lubin in Massachusetts; Aiden Gough in Northern Ireland; Sukant Tripathy and William Lazonick in India; and John Bradley in Estonia, Albania, and the (island of) Ireland.

Giovanna Ceglie and the late Frederic Richard at the United Nations Industrial Development Organization created fieldwork opportunities in nations at very different levels of prosperity. Mike Gregory, Eoin Sullivan, and Antonio Andreoni at the Institute for Manufacturing of the Department of Engineering at Cambridge University opened my eyes to Charles Babbage's pioneering contribution to an economics in which production principles are integral. Research assistants Al Paquin and Hao Xie, along with Professor Georges Grinstein of the Department of Computer Science at the University of Massachusetts, Lowell, were the heavy lifters in building the database and analytical tools applied in chapter 3; Edward March, with years of industrial engineering experience, provided guidance, and Chancellor William Hogan provided financial support.

I am thankful for comments on various chapters from Robin Murray, David Lubin, Kathryn Peters, Ha-Joon Chang, Elizabeth Garnsey, Hermann Bömer, Gerhard Untiedt, Mary O'Sullivan, Michael Arthur, and Melanie Best. Frederick Guy, Jane Humphries, and Eoin Sullivan read the complete manuscript and offered warm encouragement along with constructive criticism that sharpened the text. Chapter 7 is co-authored with John Bradley, and every chapter has benefited from his insights. The integrative framework of the book has been shaped in dialogue with John over many years. Independently we had arrived at the judgement that policymaking not attuned to production and business organization will be poor, but had arrived there from different starting points: John from the omission of production in macroeconomic modeling and I from the omission of organizational capability in mainstream microeconomics.

Chapters 2 and 3 build on research I had previously published and are reproduced with permission from Elsevier. Chapter 2 is based on "Industrial Innovation and Productive Structures: The Creation of America's 'Arsenal of Democracy'" in *Structural Change and Economic Dynamics* (forthcoming, made available online September 1, 2017, https://doi.org /10.1016/j.strueco.2017.08.002) © 2017 by Elsevier Ltd. Chapter 3 draws on research from "Greater Boston's Industrial Ecosystem: A Manufactory of Sectors" in *Technovation* 39–40: 4–13 (https://doi.org/10.1016/j.techno vation.2014.04.004) © 2014 by Elsevier Ltd.

Finally, I am grateful to the seamless cross-functional team that emerged to publish my book at Princeton University Press. I have had the great fortune of guidance and support from beginning to end from Publisher Sarah Caro and Assistant Editor Hannah Paul as well as Production Editor Ali Parrington, Copyeditor Marilyn Martin, and Publicity Director Caroline Priday, all of whom combine professional expertise with a keen grasp of content. Together they illustrate a theme of the book: the importance of interconnectedness to organizational performance.

LIST OF ABBREVIATIONS

AR&D   American Research and Development Corporation

BPRC   Biodegradable Polymer Research Center

CISC   Centre for Innovation and Structural Change

CMP   Controlled Materials Plan

CNC   computer-numerical control

DEC   Digital Equipment Corporation

DFV   Double Four Valve

DoD   Department of Defense

DPC   Defense Plant Corporation

FAME   Forecasting Analysis and Modeling Environment

FIA   Federation Internationale de l'Automobile

FDI   foreign direct investment

EEC   European Economic Community

GDP   gross domestic product

GNP   gross national product

IDA   Industrial Development Authority

JIT   just-in-time

IMF   International Monetary Fund

MIA   Motorsport Industry Association

MNC   multinational corporation

MNE   multinational enterprise

MSV   Motor Sports Valley

NACA   National Advisory Committee for Aeronautics

NACE   Nomenclature Statistique des Activités Économiques dans la Communauté Européenne, or the Statistical Classification of Economic Activities in the European Community

NDAC   National Defense Advisory Committee

NPD   new-product development

OSRD   Office of Scientific Research and Development

PRP   Production Requirements Plan

PS   Production System

R&D   research and development

RFC   Reconstruction Finance Corporation

S&T   science and technology

SBIC   Small Business Investment Company

SMEs   small- and medium-sized enterprises

SOEs   state-owned enterprises

SWOT   strengths, weaknesses, opportunities, and threats

TQM   total quality management

TTWI   Toyota Training Within Industry

TWI   Training Within Industry

UML   University of Massachusetts, Lowell

vTHREAD   visual Techno-Historical Regional Economic Analysis Database

WMC   War Manpower Commission

WPB   War Production Board

HOW GROWTH REALLY HAPPENS

CHAPTER ONE

Introduction and Chapter Outline

NATIONAL AND REGIONAL experiences of rapid growth that lack easy explanations are often casually ascribed to divine intervention. Over two dozen national and regional experiences of rapid growth lacking explanation have been dubbed "miracles." These so-called miracles are unexpected and outside the scope of the conventional market-centric economic paradigm. This book brings several such purported miracles back to earth. It offers an explanation in terms of a production-centric paradigm anchored by fundamental principles of production and business organization. The capability triad is the primary organizing concept.[1] The claim is that we can learn about how capitalist economies function and malfunction from examining cases of rapid growth. The lesson is that there is no divine intervention, just a man-made conjunction of capabilities.

The Capability Triad Thesis: The Argument in Brief

In 1939 the US Army Air Corps had an inventory of 2,500 airplanes. On May 16, 1940, with the fall of France imminent, President Franklin Delano Roosevelt addressed Congress asking for appropriations to increase production, including a request for 50,000 planes within three years.[2] Eighteen months later, the newly designated US Army Air Force still had

1. I coined the term "capability triad" in a report to the Northern Ireland Economic Council (Best 2000).
2. Franklin Roosevelt, "Message to Congress on Appropriation for National Defense," www.presidency.ucsb.edu/ws/?pid=15954.

only 3,304 combat aircraft (Tate 1998). Within four years aircraft production overall totaled 100,000 planes. The American production "miracle" was not limited to aircraft. Between 1935–39 and 1944, US munitions production increased 140 times versus 7 times in Germany, and national output nearly doubled. Over the same period, the nation's labor supply available for production declined by the nearly 12 million men and women, who were absorbed into the armed forces.

What makes the experience interesting is that it involved the crafting and enactment of a development policy that successfully transformed the nation's industrial structure and doubled output in half a decade. New industries were built and others reorganized according to more advanced principles of production and organization. It was a period of unprecedented government investment in research and development (R&D), but an R&D that interfaced with production engineering in companies to develop new productive structures and scale new production processes. The diffusion of innovation processes inside and outside enterprises combined to drive the rapid growth of the American economy.

Conventional economic policymaking was suspended during World War II. Prices were frozen, and macromonetary policies were subordinated to policies geared to the development and diffusion of production capabilities in the nation's business enterprises. Special-purpose "mobilization" agencies were constructed to design and operationalize productive structures to achieve the production goals outlined in the president's vision of an "Arsenal of Democracy."

The policy focus on production capabilities and business organization takes us into uncharted territory with respect to the mainstream economics of policymaking. For example, the World War II policy focus was on the transformation of the nation's production system and the creation of a new set of productive structures to meet the president's output targets. Organizational change and technological innovation were the only means of increasing productivity at a time when increasing numbers of workers were being transferred into the armed forces.

A development policy strategy and a governance structure were designed to organize entrepreneurial activity into a force driving national growth and economic transformation. Here the government was the organizer, and business was strategically reorganized to drive the transformation of production. What were the implications for economic theory, education, and policymaking? They take us beyond the standard paradigm to an emergent political economy framework in which production, enterprise, and governance are systemically interconnected.

The standard paradigm is theoretically rigorous, but its failure to account for the drivers, processes, and enablers of transformative experiences illustrates the limits of the a priori principles to address complex interactive processes in real-world economies.[3] The role of historical experiences as a tool for theory construction and paradigm development signals a methodological divide between the standard equilibrium and the alternative systemic approach to economics and economic inquiry.

This book advances a production-centric economics paradigm that is constructed from an examination of real-world transformative experiences applying systemic observation rather than a priori reasoning to discover economic principles. The historical chapters serve as real-world laboratories for investigating patterns of change and characterizing deep structural principles of production and organization.

The historical case studies do not start from a blank page. They build on earlier work in which I characterized examinations of successful transitions in industrial leadership and economic transformative experiences in terms of a capability triad:

> Rapid growth involves coordinated organizational changes in each of three domains: the business model, production capabilities, and skill formation. The three domains are not separable and additive components of growth, but mutually interdependent sub-systems of a single developmental process. No one of the three elements of the Capability Triad can contribute to growth independently of mutual adjustment processes involving all three elements. (Best 2000, 56)

Figure 1.1 visualizes this interconnectedness.[4] This book applies and extends the thesis with new case studies and a chronologically organized supportive account of the major theoretical contributors to an emergent

3. The standard policy framework assumes a fixed production system. Business organization enters the story, but as an alternative mode of coordination to the market. Competition, regulatory, industrial, and macro/finance policies are all framed by a market-centric concept of the economy in which the economic baseline is an optimal allocation of resources. Government is conceptualized as a substitute optimizer, not an economic organizer, and economic governance is narrowly interpreted.

4. In *The New Competitive Advantage* (2001, 10) I wrote: "Interconnectedness complicates analysis and exposition. The method of analysis deployed in this book is to examine enterprise and regional capabilities from three conceptual viewpoints. We look at them consecutively from a viewpoint that highlights the production system, from a second viewpoint that focuses on business organization, and a third viewpoint that targets skill formation processes. The challenge is to develop conceptual viewpoints that capture both the defining features of each domain and the interconnections that shape and reshape them. Triple vision may be an aid!"

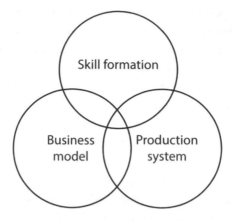

FIGURE 1.1. Capability triad.

economics in which production and business capability development are the critical dimensions of variation and integral to transformative policy frameworks.

The interconnectedness theme has important implications. Policies that address production capability, enterprise growth, and skill formation separately and in isolation will not be successful. As noted, a requirement for transformative policies is that they be seamlessly blended into the detailed mechanics of organizational change within private firms, as investigation of the alleged economic miracles shows. The instruments are not subsidies and taxes to nudge and tweak business behavior but the provision of capability development services by infrastructural agencies outside the firms. Key, too, is the incorporation of business leaders, scientists, and technology experts in the structure of economic governance and their conversion to the desirability of the transformative objectives. When firms, regions, and nations become stuck in low-productivity capability triads, the government may be the only institution that can coordinate and orchestrate holistic organizational change cutting across the three domains.

Furthermore, although enterprise development and economic governance are bound together, they are indirectly mediated by infrastructural institutions in successful transformative experiences. The policymaking spectrum extends to linking developmental infrastructures in ways that advance change within and across mutually adjusting enterprises. The term "economic governance" calls attention to ways in which financial, science and technology, and educational infrastructures can be strategically unified to foster enterprise innovation and cluster dynamic processes at both regional and national levels.

The term "economic governance" is paradigm-specific. From a market-centric perspective it is about regulating transactions not covered by detailed contracts or problems in rule enforcement.[5] In the wake of the financial, fiscal, and economic crises that began in 2008, the EU defines economic governance in terms of "coordination and surveillance of both fiscal and macroeconomic policies and the setting-up of a framework for the management of financial crises."[6] In the production-centric paradigm, economic governance is understood in terms of infrastructural institutions and organizations that galvanize capability triad innovation dynamics.

The policymaking goals go beyond standard macroeconomic stabilization targets to, for example, organize and link developmental infrastructures and processes of change to reduce regional imbalances; transition from declining to new industrial sectors; establish entirely new sectors, as in the United States during World War II; or create and grow the entrepreneurial engines and the cluster dynamic processes required to drive the transition to a post–fossil fuel economy.

The capability triad is a better way to understand how crises can be overcome and robust growth achieved. It is a way to understand how real people react (or do not react) to crises and challenges.[7] Quantitative economic analysis starts with a fixed model (or representation) of the economy as it is today and was in the past. It feeds in anticipated changes in the domestic and international policy environments and examines the impacts of such changes where the structure of the economy is often treated as effectively frozen in time.

It is possible, but not likely, that the transformative experiences described in this book can be interpreted by the economist's standard quantitative models, but despite an abundance of research, not much progress has been made. The alternative production-centric economics paradigm goes some distance toward conceptualizing the otherwise missing production side of the economy, toward capturing the interdependencies of

5. The Nobel Prize for economic sciences in 2009 was divided between Elinor Ostrom, "for her analysis of economic governance, especially the commons," and Oliver Williamson, "for his analysis of economic governance, especially the boundaries of the firm" ("Nobel Prizes and Laureates," www.nobelprize.org/nobel_prizes/economic-sciences/laureates/2009/index.html).

6. "Fact Sheets on the European Union: Economic Governance," www.europarl.europa.eu/atyourservice/en/displayFtu.html?ftuId=FTU_4.1.4.html.

7. Richard Bookstaber (2017) gets inside the concept of reflexivity to understand how real people react, or do not, to crises and challenges in a critique of standard economic theory that, in contrast, turns real people into production "inputs" and "rational economic man" to construct a paradigm in which crises are eliminated by assumption.

production capabilities, business organization, and economic governance in real-world economies and thereby toward explaining the success stories and addressing the challenge of designing and executing transformative policy frameworks. These are the claims that the book seeks to substantiate.

The paradigmatic differences go beyond a difference in the axioms to the relationship between models and complexity. The methodological approach that unites all the theorists I associate with the alternative paradigm is the priority given to observation, including case studies and empirical research, as a means of making sense of the complex relationships, institutional structures, and innovation processes of a capitalist economy. Each of the historical experiences examined in the chapters that follow is treated as a real-world laboratory for investigating and characterizing relationships, processes, and institutional forms by which principles and generalizations can be drawn for crafting policy frameworks. Each experience tells us more and subjects previous findings to review.

This research methodology creates a dilemma in terms of presentation. Which comes first, real-world case studies or the conceptual framework used in their interpretation? As noted, systemic observations influence the design of the economics framework, just as observations are chosen, interpreted, compared, and reinterpreted through it.[8] Real-world investigative research and the development of theoretical concepts combine to derive general principles and craft terms by which we observe and make sense of the complexities of capitalist economies. With this methodological caveat in mind, two real-world transformative experiences are chronicled in chapters 2 and 3 before turning to an account of the major contributors to the alternative production-centric theoretical framework in chapter 4. Chapters 5, 6, 7, and 8 apply the capability triad to the postwar economic development experiences of Germany, the United Kingdom, Ireland, Japan, and China; chapter 9 examines changes in the strategic external context for US policymaking with the success of Japan and China's export-led growth strategies. In each case, cross-country comparisons of productive structures and economic systems are used to elucidate economic governance dimensions of the production-centric paradigm.

We now turn to a brief synopsis of the chapters that follow to map the journey by which the real-world analyses and conceptual frame evolve symbiotically together. The goal is to inform policy deliberations at regional

8. Paradigm competition is the battleground for scientific advance (Kuhn 1962).

and national levels with an economics that accounts for the fundamental principles of production and business organization that underlie competitive advantage in the global marketplace.

America's Arsenal of Democracy

In chapter 2 the strategic transformation of the American production system during World War II is examined. President Franklin Delano Roosevelt's vision was to use economic power to build an Arsenal of Democracy that would help the Allies to win the war. The wartime experience serves as an extraordinary but rarely examined laboratory that permits research into the economics and governance of production.

Economic histories that focus mainly on the Federal Reserve Bank and the Treasury obscure the agencies, programs, and policies by which the nation's industrial performance advanced by orders of magnitude. Both fiscal and monetary policies were involved, but they were subservient to the transformation of the nation's productive structures.

Two agencies, among others, pioneered new methods of economic policymaking. The War Production Board (WPB) focused on the measurement, coordination, and transformation of production. Simon Kuznets, chief economist at the WPB, was the author of the Victory Program, by which economic and military strategies were coordinated. The Office of Scientific Research and Development (OSRD), at the center of science and technology policymaking, was led by Vannevar Bush, the institutional architect behind the creation of America's organizational capability to design, develop, and produce advanced-technology weapons systems. These two agencies, in effect, combined to enact a national economic development strategy to integrate mass production with technological innovation. Kuznets was awarded the third Nobel Prize in economics; Bush's *Science: The Endless Frontier* was the foundation stone for what became America's postwar science and technology infrastructure. Together, these two agencies undertook complementary policies that transformed the industrial innovation system and empowered the wartime and postwar growth of the American economy.

Implementation was led by production and business leaders immersed in the process engineering practices for applying the synchronization principle of mass-production, innovative programs to introduce participatory management practices in the workplace, and the economic governance innovations of the multidivisional enterprise. It is within this organizationally interconnected structure that a major shift in production performance was achieved and new permanent industrial planning relationships linking government, business, and universities were institutionalized.[9]

Greater Boston: A Manufactory of Sectors

Chapter 3 turns to postwar Greater Boston as a real-world laboratory to characterize the origins and complementarity of the productive infrastructures that define the region's industrial innovation system. Business enterprises in Massachusetts do not and never have concentrated on mass production. Nor have they been recognized for process engineering of high-volume assembly production processes. The region has few Fortune 500 companies, yet it leads the nation in R&D, and it has both created and lost more industrial sectors than anywhere in the world. The Massachusetts high-tech economy has the characteristics of an industrial experimental laboratory in which business enterprises, individually and collectively, are organized to pursue strategic advantage based on global leadership in early-stage technology development and rapid new business growth.[10]

The critical input for making these claims is a historical data set of economic information for real companies that includes for each its date of founding, location, employment, and products. Official data are of little help for two reasons. First, the companies are anonymous and ahistorical, and second, the classification categories lack the granularity required to capture changes in enterprise differentiation and patterns of specialization. Critical to the latter are product data screened by an engineering-based taxonomy without which the activities performed by small- and medium-sized companies in a region remain hidden.

The research included the construction of a longitudinal company and product database organized around a finely grained, technology-informed taxonomy. It offers an alternative to the market-centric paradigm that

9. The massive increase in federal R&D funding during World War II laid the institutional foundations of the science and technology infrastructure that enabled the emergence and postwar application of the principle of systems integration in the form of America's regional innovation systems.

10. Our research method is like that used in the empirical studies of revealed comparative advantage first proposed and conducted by Bela Balassa (1965). In these studies underlying comparative advantage is interpreted by the examination of traded product statistics. Instead we use measures of companies and products filtered by a finely granulated technology taxonomy to reveal underlying technological capabilities that impart competitive advantage to firms in the region.

holds technology and product definition constant and allows prices and quantities to adjust. The alternative accounts for the opposite. Firms compete by establishing a distinctive capability to develop new products and improve performance.[11]

The proposition guiding the research is that regionally distinctive production and technology capabilities are collectively and cumulatively advanced over time. Although intangible, these capabilities are embedded in the industrial processes and deep craft skills of a region and manifest in specialized groups of companies and the products they design and develop. They constitute a regional resource legacy that can be leveraged by today's companies. We seek to discover legacy technological capabilities and technical expertise that, although intangible, impart locational advantage by screening with an engineering-differentiating taxonomy.

Firms do not develop and conduct business in isolation. The population of enterprises is embedded in a regional industrial ecosystem that facilitates constant reshuffling of the region's expertise, technology capabilities, and financial resources and enables not only a single company but groups of companies to grow fast. The concept of a regional industrial ecosystem suggests an analogy to Darwin's small area in which a "manufactory of species" is active, here applied to the emergence, co-adaptation, and growth of diverse sectors. A common pattern of rapid new sector development is outlined.

The capability of Greater Boston's industrial ecosystem to foster the emergence and rapid growth of new sectors is characterized in terms of developmental infrastructures. One example is the region's place within the national science and technology infrastructure, described by Henry Etzkowitz (2002) as a triple helix linking federally funded basic research, research-intensive universities, and technologically driven enterprises. A second example is a combined private and government financial ecosystem that supported and co-evolved with the rapid growth of new high-tech firms. A third is the region's legacy of tool-, instrument-, and equipment-making small firms that have co-evolved with the production capabilities of downstream firms to pursue product-led competitive strategies. A fourth is a skill formation system funded and organized at different levels of government but collectively operating as an informal strategic industrial policy.

11. The exclusive price and output adjustment assumptions of both formal models and blackboard economics become irrelevant if no two firms supply the same product and if we assume that all firms do not have the same product development and technology management capabilities.

The Massachusetts business system has itself been transformed by an interactive dynamic localization and globalization process. When the mini-computer companies were being built in Massachusetts, the prevailing business model was one of vertical integration and integral product architecture. The opportunities for globalization shifted the pressures in favor of an open-system business model that advanced the Greater Boston's distinctive capabilities in early-stage technology development, complex product systems, and new sector creation.

Globalization meant that large investments in high tech could generate returns by leveraging technology platforms with offshore production, marketing, and sales facilities. In many cases, much of the enterprise growth in employment is out of state and offshore, and much but not all is outsourced. Nevertheless, the crown jewels of a company, its technology platform, design, and development engineering expertise as well as its early-stage manufacturing capability, remained rooted in Massachusetts. This was not simply for control or governance purposes, important as they are, but because of the region's unique industrial ecosystem, which is a nontradable resource leveraged by locally based technology-developing business enterprises. As we will see in chapter 7, the Industrial Development Authority of Ireland seized the opportunity to drive a development policy framework based on attracting such enterprises to establish production platforms in Ireland for export to Europe. It was a mutually beneficial strategy linking two regions within a single production system.

The Capability Triad: The Theoretical Legacy

Chapter 4 takes a conceptual turn, shifting attention from historical experiences to an extensive but largely ignored legacy of theoretical contributions to an economics of rapid growth and innovation dynamics. Although the dominant economics paradigm is supported by a huge base of research and knowledge, it cannot provide a consistent account of rapid growth experiences. If such accounts had fit easily within the standard framework, they would have been readily available and lessons for policymaking would have been drawn. Divine intervention would be less frequently cited to explain doubling of output in half a decade and an ability to transition to new sectors as others decline.

The strength of the mainstream is the core theory of exchange in the marketplace; the weakness is that it does not account for either productive structures or economic governance. If the goal is to understand productivity, competitiveness, transformation, and growth, it is better to start with a theory of production and work from there to understand exchange relations, but the standard paradigm does the opposite and, in the process, characterizes the sphere of production in terms of exchange relations.

Adam Smith is the starting point of both the standard market-centric and the alternative production-centric paradigms. Yet Smith's vision of economic progress was not restricted by the assumptions of constant returns to scale, unchanging technology, and universal markets of today's standard paradigm. Either diminishing or constant returns to scale have persisted as the standard model of production. Many technically creative justifications of and accommodations to the assumption of diminishing returns have been proposed, but the denial of increasing returns persisting at the core of the market-centric paradigm collides with evidence from the real world. Although both the standard and the alternative perspectives began with Adam Smith, they diverged with David Ricardo. Ricardo introduced diminishing returns to production to construct a logical theory of comparative advantage and became the exemplar of how to build a simple, timeless, closed, and elegant theoretical model of the production side of the economy.

The difficulty of incorporating increasing returns into formal models has been known since Ricardo despite the shifting of its source from land to capital to management. But all such efforts tend to collapse dynamics into a single proxy variable such as management talent, although in fact the sources of increasing returns are multiple and complex.

Charles Babbage is the pioneer of the alternative paradigm in which innovation and technological change are at center stage. Published in 1832, Babbage's *On the Economy of Machinery and Manufactures* was a conscious attempt to provide an alternative to the views of David Ricardo, the standard bearer of the political economy of his times. Babbage went beyond Smith's rhetorical pin factory to explore the interiors of the most technologically innovative enterprises of his day. The knowledge Babbage gained from systemic observation of the real world, like that of his fellow natural philosophers, laid the foundations for an emergent political economy characterized in terms of fundamental principles of production and business organization.[12]

12. Babbage's pursuit of principles of change was an application of the systemic observation approach to scientific progress being advanced by his fellow natural philosophers at Cambridge University. The pursuit of systemic-observational principles of change united the emerging sciences of evolutionary biology, geology, and astronomy. In the case of political economy, scientific investigation started with observation of production in workshops

Whereas the classic texts of the standard paradigm construct logical models by hard thinking in advance of addressing real-world complexity, Babbage approached complexity by systemic observation to characterize fundamental principles of change. His observation-based perspective continues to thrive in most scientific disciplines but is unfortunately rare in economics, particularly in the study of production, business organization, and technology.

Joseph Schumpeter paid tribute to Babbage's book more than a century after its publication as follows:

> This work which was widely used (also by Marx), is a remarkable performance by a remarkable man. Babbage ... was an economist of note. His chief merit was that he combined a command of simple but sound economic theory with a thorough first-hand knowledge of industrial technology and of the business procedure relevant thereto. This almost unique combination of acquirements enabled him to provide not only a large quantity of well-known facts but also, unlike other writers who did the same thing, interpretations. He excelled, amongst other things, in conceptualization, his definitions of a machine and his conception of invention are deservedly famous. (Schumpeter 1954, 541, cited in Hyman 1982, 121)

Babbage replaced Ricardo's law of diminishing returns with innovation-driven increasing returns to scale. Alfred Marshall's *Principles of Economics*, first published in 1890, extended Babbage's ideas into an emergent theory of industrial organization.[13] In a celebrated passage, Marshall described economies arising from an increase in the scale of production as falling into "two classes—those dependent on the general development of the industry, and those dependent upon the individual houses of business engaged in it and the efficiency of their management; that is into *external* and *internal* economies" (1920 [1890]: 266, repeated on 314; Marshall's emphasis). He wrote that external economies "result from the growth of correlated branches of industry which mutually assist one another" (1920 [1890]: 317). With the inclusion of organization and interfirm dynamics as variables, Marshall's "law of increasing returns" introduces a growth

---

and factories in which engineering practices were most innovative and change was most dramatic.

13. In Marshall's words, "The *law of increasing return* may be worded thus:—An increase of labour and capital leads generally to improved organization, which increases the efficiency of the work of capital" (1920 [1890]: 318, Marshall's emphasis).

dynamic of cumulative increasing returns later advanced by Allyn Young and Gunnar Myrdal.

Edith Penrose's *Theory of the Growth of the Firm*, published in 1959, characterizes internal economies of expansion in terms of an iterative technology capability and a market opportunity learning dynamic that drive the innovation process. Although Penrose identifies the source of value and knowledge creation within a firm, the capability development paradigm she pioneered anchors and complements the interconnectedness of engineering-focused production principles and a manufacturing systems framework as sketched by Babbage. Similarly, Penrose's concept of a technology base and her entrepreneur-driven knowledge creation dynamic are enriched by Babbage's focus on production principles.

George Richardson's theory of interfirm specialization and differentiation dynamics extends Penrose's internal capability development process to networked groups of mutually adjusting firms. Real-world examples of open-system focus-and-network, business models that have proven innovative and globally competitive, include those of Greater Boston, the "Third Italy," and Germany's *Mittelstand* (all discussed later). No longer is product and technological innovation the preserve of enterprises operating within oligopolistic market structures.

Jane Jacobs's *Economy of Cities* was published in 1969. But it was not until her work was referred to by Robert Lucas in his paper on "endogenous growth theory" titled "On the Mechanics of Economic Development" that it came to be acknowledged within the economics profession. Lucas argued that this "remarkable" book was "mainly and convincingly concerned ... with the external effects of human capital" (1988, 37). For Lucas, human capital has two special features: first, unlike physical capital, it does not suffer from decreasing returns, and, second, a higher level of human capital in an economy raises the level of productivity of everybody in that economy, not just the productivity of those whose human capital is higher.

Jacobs has a different agenda. She asks the questions: Why do cities grow? Why have today's major cities undergone a period of explosive growth? Why do some cities continue to grow over a long period, while others go into decline? She examines cities historically, giving special attention to cases of rapid growth to discover patterns of complex interactions in their most pronounced forms. She sees cities as the engines of economic advancement, providing markets, jobs, capital, and technology for themselves, the regions around them, and other cities as well.

Rather than celebrating economic efficiency, Jacobs celebrates a city's growth dynamics as expressed in the rate of addition of new goods and services. Sustained city growth is simultaneously a process of increasing differentiation of skills and an experimental process of new product development and sector evolution. In her words: "Existing divisions of labor multiply into more divisions of labor by grace of intervening added activities that yield up more sums of work to be divided" (Jacobs 1969, 58). The "intervening added activities" are described in terms of new "work" combined with multiple trials and errors linking the old to the new divisions of labor. The increasing differentiation in skills increases the opportunities for innovation and for sustained city growth.

Jacobs offers rich language such as "symbiotic nests of suppliers and their markets" (Jacobs 1984, 76) and "lateral interrelationships" to characterize Darwinian-type mutual adjustment processes. But whereas both Jacobs and Penrose extend the fundamental principle of the division of labor into ongoing differentiation processes, Penrose's capability development axioms substantiate a theory of entrepreneurial firm activity that drives the innovation process.

Jacobs is to the city what Penrose is to the firm and Babbage is to production in the emergent alternative paradigm. Each of the three theorists provides a unique and powerful conceptual framework that casts light on an otherwise hidden domain of economic life ignored at great cost in the standard paradigm. Together they expose interactive links that underlie innovation dynamics, technological change, and growth processes.

However, an economics of production, business organization, and skill formation is not sufficient to explain rapid growth experiences. The historical accounts of such experiences emphasize the strategic role of economic governance in galvanizing change within and across firms to reorganize according to world-class production and organizational principles. The governance role involves crafting a strategic policy framework that links development objectives, organizational means, and implementation measures. The capability triad is a heuristic device that unifies and integrates the interactive connections "discovered" by the theorists outlined in chapter 4. It assists policymakers to craft and coordinate infrastructures to meet the challenges of economic transformation.

Germany's Social Market Economy

Most commentary on the divergence in economic performance between the successful center and the periphery countries of the EU has been conducted in terms of market competitiveness: labor market flexibility, government regulation, and the efficiency of state versus private ownership of public utilities. Here the term "competitiveness" connotes a model of the economy in which a downward adjustment in costs and prices causes a nation's productive enterprises to become more competitive, its trade balance to improve, and its economy to grow.

In chapter 5 as well as in the following two chapters, the divergence in economic performance in three different EU states is explored in terms of business system capabilities and institutions of economic governance. The central finding is that in the core northern economies an entirely different production system has evolved from the peripheral, mainly southern, economies of Europe. The difference is revealed by the existence of a plethora of globally competitive, technologically advanced, mid-sized firms in Germany, Austria, Denmark, Finland, the Netherlands, and Sweden in contrast to a paucity in the peripheral economies.

Germany is the most successful large economy in Europe. The German business system does not fit either conventional theoretical models[14] or the historical experience of other industrialized countries. Known as the *Mittelstand*, a population of small and medium-sized, largely family-owned business enterprises, constitutes a business model that predates German unification in the nineteenth century and has persisted through the political revolutions of the twentieth century up to the present. Today more than three million small and mid-sized enterprises—that is, companies with fewer than 500 employees and annual sales of less than €50 million—together employ over 70 percent of German workers and generate roughly half of the country's gross domestic product (GDP) (Frenkel and Fendel 1999).[15]

The numbers of small- and medium-sized enterprises (SMEs), however, are not the issue; it is what they do. Specifically, it is the prevalence of enterprises with production capabilities geared not only toward a distinctive and well-engineered product but toward new product development, technology management, and continuous innovation. These are the organizational capabilities that enable enterprises to engage in Schumpeterian competition, to pursue strategies aimed at superior product, process,

14. Models such as that produced by the neoclassical theory of the optimizing firm and the assumption that all firms have immediate access to the same technologies and production functions.

15. Frenkel and Fendel (1999) classify firms as follows: micro enterprises (up to 9 EEs), small enterprises (10–99), medium enterprises (100–499), and large enterprises (500 or more EEs). They report that one in 500 was large in Germany and one in 140 in the United States and that the contribution of medium-sized enterprises to turnover was 24.4 percent in Germany and only 13.9 percent in the United States in 1992.

technology, and/or organization. They are the organizational requirements of entrepreneurial firms that enable them to create value, increase productivity, and support high-paying jobs and upon which enterprise and regional and national competitive advantage depend.

The case study of Germany draws upon and resonates with the characterization described in chapter 3 of the productive structures that constitute the regional industrial ecosystem of Greater Boston. In both economies we find localized networked business systems in which firms focus on core capabilities and form partnerships for complementary capabilities. But the adjustment dynamics among firms that make up the *Mittelstand* are not characterized by high rates of enterprise population churn, as in Greater Boston.

There are differences, too, with respect to economic governance functions. In the German economy, the regional government's stewardship role is pronounced, widespread, and linked to the federal government's production-centric model of macro/financial policymaking. From the structural competitiveness perspective, success in economic development results from combining the right production perspective with policymakers who refrain from destabilizing the macro economy. Erratic macro/financial policymaking undermines the preconditions for the successful development of the production system. At the same time, the notion that development is generated as a direct result of macro/financial policy cleverness is wishful thinking.[16]

The concept of economic governance calls attention to three levels of economic stewardship: those within the enterprise and within both regional and national government. The unified triadic competitiveness structure of the German economy is not unique in the EU. It distinguishes the articulated capability triads of the much smaller social market economies of the Nordic countries from the fragmented capability triads of the peripheral economies of the EU and the United Kingdom.

The German economic governance model has three distinctive and mutually reinforcing characteristics missing in the United Kingdom. First, the balance between central and regional economic governments is organized to capture the benefits of operational decentralization combined with national-level strategic policymaking for economic performance. The

16. Awareness of the limits of neoliberal macro and fiscal stabilization policies as development policy in the IMF was announced by IMF economists in a series of articles in the mid-2010s (Ostry, Loungani, and Furceri 2016, 38–41).

central government legislates the standard development infrastructure, both intangible and material, by which regional governments can craft localized economic policy. The German nation's science and technology infrastructure, along with its vocational education system, corporate governance laws, and its financial institutions, provides inputs into regional strategic policymaking. Regional governments have the power to convene and thereby build the interrelationships among enterprises, agencies, and agents required to have the crew on board to manage both the flight and the landing safely.

Second, Germany built a dual educational system to create a skilled labor force and provide technical expertise on the scale necessary to transform the nation into an industrial power by the late nineteenth century. The history of Germany's vocational training had its origins in the guild system, whereby craftsmen organized the process of qualifying to become a journeyman and progressing to a master. It evolved through a series vocational training acts from 1869 up to the present time.[17]

Third, the German model of macro/financial policymaking is production-centric. Macroeconomic stabilization policymaking is subservient to the establishment of the capability development measures needed to advance production performance. Erratic macro/financial policymaking undermines the preconditions for successful development in all regions. As noted, the notion that development of production capabilities is generated as a direct result of macro/financial policy guile is absurd.

Capability Triad Failure: The United Kingdom

In chapter 6 we apply the capability triad concept to the industrial experience of the United Kingdom. Although it was the first country to undergo an industrial revolution, it was not successful in maintaining its leadership. Economic historians tell us that by the mid-nineteenth century US manufacturing productivity in terms of labor hours was nearly twice that of the United Kingdom, and by the turn of the century Germany was the leader in the emerging electrical and chemical industries, the leading sectors of the second industrial revolution. The United Kingdom has never overcome a substantial productivity gap in manufacturing.

17. "Vocational Training 'Made in Germany': Germany's Dual System of Vocational Education and Training," www.gtai.de/GTAI/Content/EN/Invest/_SharedDocs/Downloads /GTAI/BLG/blg—most-wanted—dual-vocational-training-in-germany-pdf.pdf?v=4.

Could it have been different? The capability triad takes us inside the production system to examine mutual adjustment processes linking production capabilities, business organization, and economic governance. The decline of British industry is traced to capability triad fragmentation at a time in which other nations were pursuing development frameworks fostered by articulated support infrastructures.

The starting point is production. Three branches of the UK car industry are examined: the traditional road-car companies, the Formula 1 race-car cluster, and the production units of foreign-owned enterprises. The first could have led a transformation in UK industry to meet international performance standards but failed to do so and collapsed in the 1970s. The failure over decades to acknowledge, reorganize, and transition to productive structures based on fundamental principles of interchangeability, flow, and system integration is the single reason for the historic low performance standards and low productivity of much of British industry.

The second and third sectors are also interesting but for different reasons. They are globally competitive but do not have a macro-scale impact on business development and operate independently of the national industrial ecosystem. The scale of the racing car cluster known as Motor Sports Valley is too small to have a macroeconomic impact. With respect to high-volume affiliates of foreign multinational enterprises, the production facilities are extensions of their home-base capability triads. Unlike production facilities, capability triads and economic governance systems cannot be imported or exported.

The car industry looms large in UK industrial history owing to the potentially positive impact of performance capability on the nation's component supply base and machine tool sectors (tooling, instruments, and equipment making). Both subsectors are important because of the contribution of a technically skilled supply base to a rapid ramp-up of growth opportunities and that of a precision engineering machine tool industry to the new product development and technology management capabilities of all final goods producers. In these roles the specialist component and machine tool sectors perform an infrastructural role to enable a nation's business system to engage in product-led competition. The failure of UK car companies to organize according to the principles of interchangeability and flow had the opposite effect on the nation's component and machine tool sectors, which had little reason to meet the ever more demanding precision engineering performance standards of their functionally equivalent sectors in the United States and Germany.

A nation's skill formation system is equally integral to building and maintaining the nation's structural competitive advantage. A highly skilled labor force is a productive resource to the nation's business enterprises. It enables product-led competition, innovation, and the rapid growth of emergent sectors. Examples of German and US historical experiences are described in which government policymakers have constructed educational institutions and undertaken timely and strategic investments in sync with the quality and quantity of skills demanded by innovative, repositioning, and growing enterprises and complete sectors.

The experiences of rapid growth highlight the critical importance of strategic frameworks that recognize the mutual interdependencies of production capabilities, business system performance, and skill formation institutions. The historic failure of the United Kingdom to address its skill formation shortcomings, combined with industrial decline, consigned a growing proportion of workers to structural unemployment or underemployment in the 1980s and 1990s and more recently to the gig economy, recently described as a growing "precariat."

The deep structural sources of innovation and productivity are hidden from view by the theory and measures of technological progress and by the "factor" productivity of the standard paradigm that has informed British economic policymaking. In fact, governments in the United Kingdom have undertaken more industrial strategies than anywhere else in the world, but they have all failed to address the interdependencies that link production, business, and governance to unified intangible infrastructures. The final section of chapter 6 backs the claim with examples of policymaking that, by commission or omission, either failed to arrest industrial decline or failed to identify opportunities to do so.

Ireland: A Divided Economy

Ireland, with a much smaller economy than that of the United Kingdom, provides a historical experience that permits a comparative examination of development policy frameworks. Following a failed period of economic protectionism betweem 1932 and 1960, the Industrial Development Authority, established in 1949 by the Irish government, designed and implemented an industrial strategy that attracted many of America's leading information technology and life science companies to make Ireland an export platform to service the European marketplace. These multinational enterprises (MNEs) established branch plants organized around world-class manufacturing practices for volume manufacturing.

The Irish government combined a set of enabling tax and financial incentives with the creation of educational and transportation infrastructural investments to implement the strategy.[18] The foreign enterprises proved to be engines of growth that propelled employment growth from under 1.4 million in the 1980s to over 2.0 million in the early 2000s. This was and remains an extraordinary success story in which the nation was transformed from one of the poorest to one of the richest in Europe.

However, no one foresaw the post-2007 unfolding of events. In record time a property bubble burst, a vast construction industry collapsed, and the nation's banks, which had acquired massive international debts, were suddenly insolvent and their obligations transferred to Irish taxpayers. The Irish Stock Exchange general index, which reached a peak of 10,000 points in April 2007, fell to 1,987 points in February 2009. There was an abrupt return of the centuries-old tragedy of Ireland: mass outmigration.

In chapter 7 we examine Ireland from a perspective of dynamic capabilities to better understand both the country's success and its subsequent economic crash. The lessons learned from the successful growth experiences in the earlier chapters are distilled to examine the Irish boom. The journey takes us inside the organizational dynamics of enterprises and development policy frameworks on both sides of the border between Ireland and Northern Ireland, which remains part of the United Kingdom.

We start with a striking and perhaps distinctive feature of Ireland's economy exposed by the Great Recession. Ireland is a nation of two economies that internally mirrors the EU split between core and periphery economies. Although the core economies have been relatively resilient, the peripheral economies have suffered. The foreign-owned high-tech economy of Ireland has been largely unaffected, while the indigenous business and production system has suffered a decline in activity similar to that experienced by peripheral economies of Europe.

The business and production systems of both the indigenous and foreign elements of the economy are examined. A study of border counties of Ireland and Northern Ireland reveals isolated entrepreneurial firms but virtually no interfirm cluster dynamic processes and enabling infrastructures that foster the enterprise and regional production capability development upon which competitive advantage depends.

18. It should be noted that the availability of generous EU development assistance, in terms of Structural Funds, greatly facilitated the later stages of the "real" Celtic Tiger advance. Yet, in the words of John Bradley, "It is sobering to reflect that the cost of the bank bail-out of recent years greatly exceeded the totality of Structural Funds received over the period 1989–2013" (Bradley 2013).

Clusters are important in part because emergent cluster processes offer governments a range of instruments for shaping entrepreneurial activity within business systems without risking the creation of a co-dependent business culture, which has become an unfortunate feature of industrial policy and business organization on both sides of the Irish border. An examination of Ireland's clusters of foreign high-tech branch plants reveals the same absence of entrepreneurial firm and cluster-dynamic processes critical to domestic entrepreneurial firm emergence, growth, and proliferation. The capability difference between foreign and the indigenous business units is that, with few exceptions, only the branch plants of MNEs operate world-class production facilities.

However, production capabilities alone do not make an entrepreneurial firm. Both the foreign and indigenous sides of Ireland's business system lack new product development and technology management capabilities. This finding transcends the division in Ireland's national development policy framework between foreign and indigenous business and production systems.

New Production Systems: Japan and China

The last quarter of the twentieth century witnessed a fundamental change in the global context with the emergence, first, of the rapid-growth Japanese economy followed by the four "tiger" economies of South Korea, Taiwan, Hong Kong, and Singapore and, second, of the Chinese export-driven rapid-growth economy. Both rapid-growth experiences are examined in chapter 8 from a production-centric perspective. Japan's success came from building a production system that established new performance standards in cost, quality, and time. The new system is organized around the principle of multiproduct flow and a continuous improvement model of work organization. The new business organization supported a competitive advantage in new product development, technology management, and incremental innovation capabilities. Strikingly, the new production capabilities enabled Japanese enterprises to use America's advanced-technology innovation capability in pursuit of product-led competition. American mass producers were organizationally ill equipped to convert the nation's advanced science and technology infrastructure to commercial applications.

China, in contrast, constructed a policy framework that included attracting foreign direct investment (FDI) in the form of global production networks organized by foreign-headquartered enterprises. The strategy fostered the offshoring of manufacturing by US multinational enterprises. The offshore production facilities of US corporations located in China replaced the onshore manufacturing of the same companies.

A measure of the magnitude of the transition is the increase in the percentage of China's foreign trade (exports plus imports) to GDP from 10 percent in 1978 to 67 percent in 2006. The pace of transformation in economic activity across a nation of nearly 1.4 billion people remains virtually incomprehensible. Its impact on economic activity in the rest of the world can no longer be ignored.

America's Fragmenting Capability Triad

Chapter 9 examines the postwar evolution of the US economy starting with the consequences of the establishment of America's Arsenal of Democracy. The nation's production system was permanently transformed by the creation of an industrial planning system and a national science and technology infrastructure. The interrelationships linking the nation's production and business systems and institutions of economic governance were permanently altered.

President Eisenhower's "Farewell Address to the Nation" famously warned of the unwarranted powers of a military-industrial complex that threatened democratic institutions. At least in the case of Greater Washington's economy, Eisenhower's warning has been borne out. It is a regional economy based on the postwar establishment of a government-contract business culture dominated by about a half-dozen permanent prime contractors (Ceruzzi 2008).

America's postwar policymakers have not responded to the challenge to the nation's manufacturing base of the emergence of Japan, the four "tigers," and China. The manufacturing employment share of the US economy has declined steadily, from nearly 25 percent in 1970 to 9 percent in 2011. Although America's leadership in science and technology and in regional innovation systems such as those of Silicon Valley and Greater Boston remains, the threats to manufacturing capabilities put America's industrial future at risk.

What can a busy person who invests time in reading these chapters learn? Economic growth, development, and good job creation are shown not to depend on divine intervention. The cases explored are not miraculous episodes of unusual economic beneficence. Nor are they the result of especially deft manipulation of macrofinancial policies instruments. Instead they can be understood in terms of an analytical framework with a sharp focus on three core elements—production system, business organization, and governance—and their interconnections. Interconnectedness is pivotal for understanding how strategic policy frameworks impact economic performance and how building on them is essential for successful policy. The lesson of this book is to highlight the importance of thinking in terms of the capability triad.

CHAPTER TWO

The Creation of America's Arsenal of Democracy

Orators, columnists, professors, preachers, and propagandists performed magnificently with the theme that World War II was a war between two competing ideologies. But whatever inflamed people's minds in warring countries, victory was on the side of the heavier armed battalions. The conflict became one of two systems of production.

—CHARLES SORENSEN, CHIEF ENGINEER,
FORD MOTOR COMPANY, 1956

Introduction: War Mobilization Strategy and Structure

It took Japan's attack on Pearl Harbor on December 7, 1941, for American politicians to abandon over two decades of isolationism and address the challenge of Germany's armaments buildup and expansionary ambitions. The gap in military preparedness is suggested by the fact that America had only 400,000 men under arms, a total that would increase to 12 million by 1943.

In a message sent to Congress in January 1942, following the declaration of war, President Roosevelt announced the Victory Program to win World War II. Roosevelt's vision was to build an Arsenal of Democracy and win the war by massively outproducing the Axis powers.[1] The corollary was that military options were dependent on the nation's capabilities

1. The "Arsenal of Democracy" rallying cry was first used by Roosevelt in a radio broadcast on December 29, 1940. At that time it was a call to supply the Allies (Great Britain, the Soviet Union, and China) with American armaments to be used against Nazi Germany and Japan.

to produce and deliver the requisite munitions in the quantities, at the time, and to the places needed. The operational details of the Victory Program, as announced by the president, did not yet exist but included as essential items the production of 60,000 airplanes in 1942 and 125,000 in 1943; 8 million tons of merchant shipping in 1942 and 20 million in 1943; 45,000 tanks in 1942 and 75,000 in 1943; and 55,000 anti-aircraft guns to be produced by 1943.

What makes the World War II US policymaking experience interesting is how rapidly the Arsenal of Democracy vision became a real industrial system. Its unmatched performance can be measured by comparing national rates of expansion in munitions production over the period from 1935–39 to 1944: it was 7 times in Germany, 10 times in the Soviet Union, 15 times in Japan, 22 times in the United Kingdom, and *140 times in the United States* (Goldsmith 1946; emphasis mine). Furthermore, the United States alone produced guns and butter; guns were not produced at the expense of the civilian standard of living (Overy 1995; Edelstein 2001). The GNP nearly doubled in the same period (Higgs 1992; see also Field 2008).[2]

When the United States entered the war, the powers and responsibility to meet the production targets set by the president and expected by military planners fell to the WPB.[3] Roosevelt created the independently managed WPB by executive order on January 16, 1942, with authority to control production priorities and procurement policies (Janeway 1951, 296; Lacy 2011, 71). The WPB's broad mandate gave it economic powers over military procurement. At the same time, the nation's business units remained under private control. The production system was subject to WPB governance, but it remained a private enterprise system.[4]

2. Higgs (1992, 45) compares various estimates. Official government sources estimate that real gross national product (GNP) increased from an index number of 100 in 1939 to 172.5 in 1944 (US Bureau of the Census 1975); to 192.5 in 1944 (US Council of Economic Advisors 1990); and to 172.4 in 1944 (Kendrick 1961).

3. To organize production growth of the magnitude and composition required for war, President Roosevelt created a dizzying array of emergency mobilization agencies beginning in 1939. By executive orders, the president created a group of specialist, mission-focused but complementary emergency mobilization agencies to supplement existing government departments. The emergency agency model was to recruit industry experts and academic specialists into temporary government service. The main idea was to maintain civilian control over the governance of the war economy.

4. The United States had a strong anti-trust tradition that limited industrial power and controls over the rest of the economy, including suppliers and raw material producers, and an ideological and political context that was strongly opposed to and suspicious of both central military and central economic power. According to Cuff, "Washington required a

Although the WPB's economic policies have not been an object of re-search by economists, they have been examined by military historians, business historians, and military preparedness/operations science experts.[5] Military historians interpret the development of the Victory Program as an exercise that demonstrated the contribution of the WPB statisticians, led by Simon Kuznets, to the integration of national income and product accounts and their application to military strategy. Business historians focus on the transfer of accounting practices for planning, coordinating, and controlling decentralized business units to the WPB. Both were crit-ically important, but the WPB's contributions to production transforma-tion and industrial innovation were equally important yet largely unac-knowledged. In fact, US wartime economic experience is a real-world laboratory for exploring both the contested and the multifaceted concept of industrial policy and the workings of advanced capitalist systems.

The strategic background of US wartime industrial policy was an ob-jective assessment of the strengths and weaknesses of the Allies and the Axis powers. The unpopularity of US involvement in World War I was followed by two decades of isolationism and left the nation ill prepared to confront the might of the German military machine. The United States suffered a serious gap in both conventional armaments and technologi-cally advanced weapons. But it had a secret weapon that gave it a strate-gic advantage. In the words of Roosevelt in his Message to Congress on June 10, 1941: "With our national resources, our productive capacity, and the genius of our people for mass-production we will ... outstrip the Axis powers in munitions of war" (cited in Overy 1995, 220).

America's strategic advantage lay in having access to the design and production of well-constructed, standardized weaponry that could be produced in huge volumes in quick order. No one doubted the unrivaled capability of German engineering to design and develop technologically advanced aircraft and weapons. But, in the words of Richard Overy: "The pursuit of advanced weaponry came at a price. Instead of a core of proven designs produced on standard lines, the German forces developed a be-wildering array of projects. At one point ... there were no fewer than 425 different aircraft models and variants in production.... The German

---

plan that could combine central, civilian control with decentralized, operating responsibil-ity to both large-scale corporate enterprise and military organizations" (1990, 111).

5. The Planning, Programming, and Budgeting System paradigm of the Department of Defense (DoD) originated with the WPB's Controlled Materials Plan (Cuff 1987). See chapter 9.

army was equipped with 151 different makes of lorry, and 150 different motor-cycles" (1995, 247).[6]

A differentiating feature of the American strategy was to capture potential synergistic benefits from the judicious linking of mass production and technological innovation in contrast to the pursuit of technological superiority without regard to production principles. While American leadership fully appreciated the German advantage in design engineering and technological innovation, German leadership did not fully appreciate America's advantage in process engineering and mass production.[7]

The US strategy required building a production system that linked technological innovations in weapons with the production capability to absorb and integrate technological change. It meant embedding technological innovation into the nation's production system in ways that leveraged without compromising mass production. Making it work required the active and interorganizational engagement of engineers, managers, workers, and scientists.

The policymakers' challenge was to create an economic governance system to manage the establishment of the productive structures that could drive mobilization. It involved the establishment by executive order of independently managed emergency mobilization agencies to work jointly with statutory departments. Their purpose was to engage business management, workforces, and the engineering and scientific communities in creating enterprises and sectors and restructuring existing ones to implement the Arsenal of Democracy vision.

Simon Kuznets, chief economist in the WPB's planning division, was the author of the Victory Program, by which economic and military strategies were integrated and production targets were scheduled. The OSRD was at the center of science and technology policymaking. It was led by Vannevar Bush, the architect of America's advanced-technology weapons industries. Kuznets and Bush, in effect, combined their efforts in order to enact what became a national strategy to integrate mass production with technological innovation. Much later, in 1971, Kuznets was awarded the third Nobel Prize in economics; Bush's report to the President, *The Endless Frontier* (1945), was the clarion call to what became America's postwar science and technology infrastructure. Together the WPB and the OSRD

6. "Superiority," a short story by Arthur C. Clarke, brilliantly captures the diabolical consequences of the pursuit of the perfect weapon, as Paul Krugman called to my attention. www.mayofamily.com/RLM/txt_Clarke_Superiority.html

7. Hermann Göring, while head of German armed force production, famously quipped that all America could produce was razor blades (Overy 1995, 248).

Simon Kuznets, 1901–1985.
Source: Harvard University Archives, HUV 2380.1.

were the agencies that led in the design and administration of integrative policies that transformed the American production and industrial innovation system.

The argument is that the WPB was, in effect, the lead development agency in charge of integrating the entire chain of industrial innovation, from basic research in the academic laboratories to employee involvement and work organization on the shop floor. Many links were connected to this chain, but at the center was a mass-production system capability that coordinated the vertical supply chains and the horizontal innova-

Vannevar Bush, 1890–1974. *Source:* Courtesy MIT Museum.

tion chains.[8] The demand and supply sides of technological innovation were administratively interfaced to form an integrated interorganizational capability development process on a national scale.

8. See Klein (2013) and Koistinen (2004) for details of and references to agencies tasked to creation and transformation missions in specific sectors. For rubber, see the roles of Compton and Killian in Tuttle (1981) and Klein (2013, 410–11). Ante (2008) describes Georges Doriot's role in transforming the quartermaster general's application of science to production for every item required by military personnel.

Productive Structures of Industrial Innovation

Implementation of the strategy involved an industrial policy designed to advance the development of three complementary productive structures. They were created not by an invisible hand or by central planning but purposefully by an industrial policy agenda that organizationally integrated and diffused rapid technological and production innovation.

The first productive structure was the integration of science and industry to design, develop, produce, and deploy new technologically advanced products (e.g., radar systems, penicillin). The second was the diffusion of mass-production principles to build and ramp up new organizationally complex products/plants/industries (e.g., aircraft, ships) and to convert existing factories to new products (e.g., cars to jeeps) and to extend mass production principles throughout supply chains. The third was the design, administration, and implementation of a participatory management philosophy and skill formation to foster workforce involvement in job design, quality improvement, and new technology introduction. Each of these structures is examined using case studies that take us inside the real-world economics of production, business, work, universities, and industrial organization to examine how US industrial policy transformed the nation's industrial innovation system.

THE INTEGRATION OF SCIENCE AND INDUSTRY

To address Germany's huge technology lead in weapons systems, President Roosevelt created and put MIT's Vannevar Bush in charge of the OSRD in May 1941 with the mandate to administer the design, development, and production of technologically advanced weapons systems (Zachary 1999). Bush reported outside the military command structure directly to the executive office. He designed and orchestrated a triangular organizational architecture, later described as a triple helix (Etzkowitz 2002), interlinking the governmental, academic, and industrial spheres to leverage the distinctive capabilities of each for rapid and strategic industrial innovation and production.

Thus began the establishment of an industrial system that combined government-sponsored, mission-oriented scientific and technological research with technology-driven, engineering-intensive enterprises. The science and technology infrastructure supplied knowledge leveraged by the technology management capabilities of enterprises.

Massive resources were committed to create America's advanced-technology weapons industry. Between 1941 and 1945, the OSRD directed 30,000 researchers and oversaw the development of some two hundred innovative weapons, including sonar, radar, the proximity fuse, amphibious vehicles, and the Norden bombsight, all considered critical in winning the war (Zachary 1999; Etzkowitz 2002). Total federal R&D expenditures increased over fifteen times (in 1930 dollars), from $83.2 million in 1940 to $1,313.6 million in 1945 (Mowery and Rosenberg 1993, 39–40).

However, the campaign to rapidly develop new technology depended on the integration of scientific knowledge with applied research, practical engineering expertise, and production know-how. The latter was available only in manufacturing enterprises/systems with technologically adaptable and efficient production processes. For example, an OSRD-sponsored partnership linked British radar knowledge with Raytheon, a small engineering-driven US enterprise, to ramp up magnetron tube output. Raytheon engineers designed and constructed a "novel way to boost production ... by assembling them out of laminated sheets instead of carving them laboriously out of solid blocks" (Rosegrant and Lampe 1992, 84). Output increased from one hundred to two thousand magnetrons per day. Thus began Raytheon's rapid growth and the Boston region's postwar leadership in microwave technology, a core capability that contributed to a series of new companies and combined with other technologies to generate a sequence of new sectors after the war (Rosegrant and Lampe 1992).

The case of penicillin was a more complex project involving international triangular relations with spectacular consequences. Here, too, Bush's OSRD identified and seized the opportunity to build production capabilities, this time in collaboration with the WPB (Lax 2004).

The reality was that more soldiers would die from infection than from munitions. Penicillin was first produced in a laboratory for medicinal purposes in 1938 by scientists at Oxford University, but with kitchen-tool methods on such a small scale that treating a single person would exhaust the total output. UK government laboratories and drug companies were too preoccupied or otherwise unwilling to fund experiments in the unproven technology. Subsequently, on July 2, 1941, two of the frustrated scientists, Howard Florey and Norman Heatley, arrived in the United States with two academic papers and a few mold spores in search of laboratory facilities and funding for experimental research, fermentation techniques, and production methods to develop and produce penicillin. They were invited to the US Department of Agriculture's huge Northern

Regional Research Laboratory at Peoria, Illinois, to replicate their Oxford experiments. After the successful production of penicillin bacteriostatic material from a mold culture seeded by the spores they had brought from Oxford, further experiments were conducted drawing on the Peoria laboratory's distinctive capabilities in fermentation methods, particularly deep fermentation techniques.[9]

While Heatley stayed in Peoria to brew a higher-yield penicillin, Florey undertook a round of visits to US drug companies, hoping to persuade one or more of them to pilot industrial techniques to extract a quantity of mold sufficient to conduct clinical trials for five patients (Lax 2004, 227–32). Research scientists at Merck and Company, E. R. Squib and Sons, Charles Pfizer and Company, and Lederle Laboratories showed interest but nothing more. Florey reported that he felt like "a carpet bag salesman trying to promote a crazy idea for some ulterior motive" (Lax 2004, 236).

Fortuitously, the OSRD's Committee on Medical Research and Development was chaired by Dr. Alfred Newton-Richards, who knew Florey to be a brilliant scientist. The OSRD's mission was to conduct research on scientific and medical problems relating to national defense, and Newton-Richards wasted no time. He invited the heads of research of the drug companies to attend a meeting with Vannevar Bush on October 8, 1941, to set a course for penicillin research and development. Also included was the Department of Agriculture's chief mycologist. The outcome of the meeting was an agreement in which the government granted exemption from anti-trust laws and the companies agreed to conduct experiments in bulk production methods and share research and production information. As at the US Department of Agriculture labs at Peoria, the US government took patent rights.

When on March 14, 1942, in New Haven, Connecticut, the first patient was treated for streptococcal septicemia with US-made penicillin, half of the total supply produced at the time was used on that one patient. By June 1942, just enough US penicillin was available to treat ten patients.

Although the scale of output was still small even by clinical trial standards, the proof of concept for bulk production methods was proceeding rapidly and successfully at Merck and Pfizer. The WPB gave financial assistance not only to the first drug companies to produce penicillin (Abbot Laboratories, Merck, Pfizer, Squibb, and Winthrop Chemical Company),

---

9. An agreement was signed that any patent rights from the cooperation "will be obtained under the usual Department of Agriculture procedure and will be assigned to the Secretary of Agriculture" (Lax 2004, 228).

but also to twenty-one other chemical and pharmaceutical firms (Lax 2004, 282). In effect, the WPB created a mass production industry virtually overnight, and in July 1943 it drew up a plan for the mass distribution of penicillin stocks with the goal of having an adequate supply available by the time the Allies invaded Europe. They succeeded in achieving this goal. The production of penicillin in the United States jumped from 21 billion units in 1943 to 1,663 billion units in 1944 to 6.8 trillion in 1945, and its cost dropped dramatically, from priceless in 1940 to $20 per dose in July 1943 to $0.55 per dose by 1946.[10]

The wartime creation of the US synthetic rubber industry played a critical role in the Arsenal of Democracy as well. When Japan seized Malaya and the Dutch East Indies, cutting the United States off from virtually all its usual sources of natural rubber, the US government invested in fifty-one new synthetic rubber plants, enough to supply the entire industry (Tuttle 1981).[11]

Technological innovations in magnetron tubes, penicillin, and synthetic rubber production all contributed to the emergence of new industrial sectors. Yet, however important, they would hardly register in employment or armaments output. But the production of aircraft, ships, tanks, munitions, and aluminum would, and here, too, similar output growth rates and performance standards were achieved. America's leadership in the principles of mass production informed the architecture of newly created manufacturing plants and the reorganization of existing plants to convert to armaments.

THE DIFFUSION OF MASS-PRODUCTION ENGINEERING PRINCIPLES

The successful integration of technological innovation and mass production trumped Germany's scientific and technological advantage in new weapons systems. No industry illustrates the system integration challenge

10. For their work on creating the wonder drug of the twentieth century, Fleming, Florey, and Ernest Chain, with Florey the leader of the Oxford group, were awarded the Nobel Prize in 1945; unfortunately for Heatley, no more than three can receive the same award. A few years later, Florey gave much credit to US chemical firms. "Too high a tribute cannot be paid to the enterprise and energy with which the American manufacturing firms tackled the large-scale production of the drug," he wrote. "Had it not been for their efforts, there would certainly not have been sufficient penicillin by D-Day in 1944 to treat all severe casualties, both British and American" (Lax 2004).

11. Innovations in deep-tank fermentation by chemical engineer Margaret Hutchinson Rousseau contributed to the bulk production of both penicillin and synthetic rubber.

and the success of government leadership in building an industry better than does aerospace.

In May 1940 President Roosevelt announced plans to make 50,000 military aircraft per year, which was more than existed in the entire world at the time.[12] In 1939 the US Army Air Corps had fewer than 800 aircraft and 20,000 men; Germany had 4,100 aircraft and 500,000 men (Zachary 1999, 103). By 1944 the United States produced 96,000 airplanes—sixteen times the output of 1940 and nearly double Roosevelt's goal of 50,000. Employment in the industry increased from 30,000 to 2.1 million, and aerospace became America's largest industry.

The government's success at overseeing the creation of an industry employing over two million in a half a decade had two complementary components. The first was the application of mass-production methods to what had previously been a job-shop mode of industrial organization. The second was the creation of an integrative aerospace science and technology infrastructure. Each component is examined below.

Mass production

In the early days of World War II the Army Air Force's aviation program was stalled by slow production methods.[13] Aircraft were virtually hand-crafted; simply ramping up the existing production system would not win the war.

For mass-production methods, the WPB knew where to go. It turned to Charles Sorensen, Henry Ford's chief engineer.[14] When Sorensen was taken to the B-24 Liberator bomber plant of Consolidated Aviation in San Diego in November of 1940, the plant was struggling to build one plane per day. He spent the night drawing up plans for a factory that he boasted could produce one B-24 per hour (Sorensen 1956, 281). He relished the opportunity to apply mass-production principles to aircraft production:

[T]his was the biggest challenge of my production career.... It took eight years to develop Ford mass production system, and eight more

12. "On 16 May 1940, with the fall of France imminent, President Roosevelt delivered an address to Congress calling for a supplemental appropriation of nearly a billion dollars and the manufacture of 50,000 aircraft a year for the armed forces (36,500 of them for the Army Air Corps). Eighteen months later the newly designated Army Air Force still had only 3,304 combat aircraft (only 1,024 overseas), and 7,024 non-combat aircraft, of which 6,594 were trainers" (Tate 1998).

13. Officially United States Army Air Corps, the statutory forerunner of the United States Army Air Force.

14. Henry Ford had had a stroke and was a sick man (Sorensen 1956, 271–72).

Charles Sorensen, 1881–1968. *Source:* From the Collections
of The Henry Ford. Portrait of Charles Sorensen, 1918.
Photo ID. 84.1.1660.P.O.1046.

years before we worked up to a production of 10,000 cars a day. Now,
in one night, I was applying thirty-five years of production experience
to planning the layout for building ... the largest and most complicated
of all air transport and in numbers never thought possible. (282)[15]

Sorensen added, "I knew I had the solution, and I was elated by the certainty that the Germans had neither the facilities nor the conception for
greater bomber *mass production*" (Sorensen 1956, 282, emphasis added).
A contract for $200 million was signed with the Army Air Force and the

15. See chapter 8 for a technical description of mass production by Taiichi Ohno,
the chief engineer and architect of the Toyota Production System. No one understood it
better.

Aircraft Section of the WPB to build the world's largest manufacturing structure for the mass production of B-24 bombers.

It took nineteen months from approval of the project in February 1941 until the completion of the mile-long structure and the first acceptance of B-24s completely assembled at Willow Run, between Ypsilanti and Belleville, Michigan, in September 1942 (Sorensen 1956, 286). The same month, celebrating its achievement, Franklin and Eleanor Roosevelt toured the plant (Sorensen 1956, 292).

The next year Willow Run produced 8,428 bombers and achieved Sorensen's boast of one B-24 per hour. Moreover, Roosevelt's target of 50,000 military aircraft was met the same year.[16] In the six-year period from 1940 through 1945, American firms built 295,959 aircraft.[17] By the end of the war, the aviation industry had become America's largest producer and employer, employing two million workers (Tassava 2008).

Sorensen's own account of establishing the Willow Run production line underplays the process-engineering challenges that had to be addressed and met across the industry. According to an Air Force document published in 1947, it required a "revolutionary approach to the basic methods of production" (Lilley et al. 1947, 54).[18] The document describes in detail the cumulative innovations by which high-volume production capabilities were pioneered. It is a collective innovation story of a whole industry that grew and transitioned by means of an accumulation of hundreds if not thousands of process improvements that were rapidly diffused across hundreds of factories. The World War II production "miracle" was not a consequence of divine intervention or government planners.

16. As Tassava has written, "Overall, American aircraft production was the single largest sector of the war economy, costing $45 billion (almost a quarter of the $183 billion spent on war production), employing a staggering 2 million workers, and, most importantly, producing over 125,000 aircraft" (2008). Data elsewhere are summarized across nations by Overy (1995).

17. Annual production of US aircraft totaled 3,611 in 1940, 18,466 in 1941, 46,907 in 1942, 84,853 in 1943, 96,270 in 1944, and 45,852 in 1945 (Office of Statistical Control, Army Air Forces, 1945, table 79), https://ia802505.us.archive.org/5/items/ArmyAirForcesStatisticalDigestWorldWarII/ArmyAirForcesStatisticalDigestWorldWarII.pdf.

18. Germany's strategy was to use its technological leadership to produce a range of new advanced aircraft designs. The strategy failed as aircraft production stagnated between 1939 and 1942. In 1939 the United States produced 2,141 aircraft to Germany's 8,295, but by 1943 the United States produced 84,853, over 13,000 more in a single year than the 71,774 that Germany produced between 1939 and 1943 ("World_War_II_aircraft_production," https://en.wikipedia.org/wiki/World_War_II_aircraft_production). In the words of Overy, "The failure of almost the whole range of new aircraft designs forced the Luftwaffe to stick with older proven models." Not only did the effort fail; it drained skilled labor and material from the production of old models (1995, 269).

The production transformation was captured by the *synchronization* of cycle times. According to Ohno (1988 [1978], 22), "Cycle time is the time allotted to make one piece or unit .... [It] ... is determined by production quantity; that is, the quantity required and the operating time." The earliest application of the concept of synchronization of cycle times to a complete production line was in January 1914 in the production of Ford's Model A at Highland Park, Michigan.[19] For the first time, in the words of Sorensen, "The flow of parts and the speed and intervals along the assembly line meshed into a perfectly synchronized operation throughout all stages of production" (1956, 132).

The output rate of 10,000 Model A cars a day, each with some six thousand distinct parts, required putting sixty million parts in motion day after day. It was done neither by sophisticated scheduling nor by a production planning department but by production engineers establishing a common cycle time for the production and delivery of every part (for more see chapters 6 and 8 in this book and Best 2001 for a full discussion).[20]

The challenge Sorensen undertook at Willow Run was to build a production system to produce B-24 bombers at the rate of one per hour. It meant putting in motion some 30,000 different parts and a total of 1.55 million parts in all (Overy 1995, 240). Although the B-24 had five times as many distinct parts as the Model A, the daily output of twenty-four was a small fraction of 10,000 per day.

But this is not the whole story. It is important to note that Ford's breakthrough performance was achieved by a highly experienced group of engineers and a focused organizational structure that it had taken some eight years to develop and another eight to get up to 10,000 cars per day. Although the Willow Run factory was built on this legacy, it, like Highland Park's assembly line, was one link in a long and complex production chain that linked a vast supplier network of enterprises producing, in the case of the B-24, some five times as many different parts and an even greater multiple of total parts, all synchronized with the rhythm of the final assembly line.

19. It is not a coincidence that Ford announced an increase in its minimum wage from $2 to $5 on January 5, 1914 (Sorensen 1956, 132).

20. It was a decentralized scheduling system that worked as if by an "invisible hand." Ford's rules were to keep material in motion and to eliminate waste. These rules produced the effect of equalizing cycle times even without the concept. The tendency of perfect markets to produce the allocative efficiency rule of $P = MC$ is an analogy from neoclassical economic theory. Producers' actions are consistent with the rule even though their actions are guided by maximizing profits and not allocative efficiency.

The extension of the Ford system to aircraft during World War II entailed an added complexity. Ford's specialty was process engineering. Ford engineers did not design and develop the sophisticated advanced-technology weapons required for war, which were changing rapidly. For this reason, the design of the B-24 bombers was frozen, as captured in a Department of Defense report: "The primary obstacle to mass production was the fact that aircraft designs changed continually as requirements changed and as the lessons of combat were absorbed. Such design instability presented no problems to a job shop but was anathema to an assembly line, where interruptions for redesign and retooling brought production to a standstill" (Shiman 1997, 9).

The designs of the technologically advanced weapons with which the B-24 bomber was equipped were continuously upgraded. For weaponry, the Willow Run assembly line was networked with Army Air Force air depots. The work these centers performed included the addition of armor, guns, and communications and target-finding equipment.[21] The air depots were also specialized. For example, B-24s were fitted with antisubmarine radar systems at air depots in Middletown, Pennsylvania; Spokane, Washington; or Ogden, Utah (Shiman 1997, 10). Equipped with radar, the long-distance-flying B-24s kept the Atlantic supply lines open.

The number of government-operated Army Air Force depots increased from four to eleven during the war. There were a total of twenty-eight government and airline modification centers in operation at some point during the war, largely operated by the airlines, which could use the maintenance facilities they already possessed for the work. These modification centers linked the aircraft and engine production lines with the R&D labs that designed and developed the technologically advanced weapons systems and the specialist engineering firms that produced them (such as Raytheon for radar systems). The purpose was to combine the unchanging design requirements of aircraft mass production with the incessant technological changes in weapons developed by scientists as a result of the demand for specialized weapons from the military.

---

21. The Army Air Force depots mediated the OSRD and NACA administered weapons research activities in university laboratories, with the weapons delivery systems administered by the War Production Board and the War Manpower Commission. As Shiman writes, "The Army Air Corps did not operate its own manufacturing facilities; it relied on industry for all of its procurement. However, it did operate its own air depots, which were mostly intended for supply, maintenance, and repair" (1997, 4).

Creation of an aerospace science and technology infrastructure

The aircraft design drawings that Sorensen obtained from Consolidated Aircraft embodied decades of aeronautical engineering R&D performed by the industry. The National Advisory Committee for Aeronautics (NACA) was the only such permanent agency before World War II, when, in contrast to Germany, the United States had only a tiny science and technology (S&T) infrastructure for the aircraft industry (Klein 2013, 101). NACA, established in 1915, administered a single laboratory, the Langley Memorial Aeronautical Laboratory, established in Langley, Virginia, in 1917, but it depended heavily on émigré expertise as aeronautical engineering had not yet been established in engineering departments. In 1939 George Lewis, NACA director of Aeronautical Research, toured aeronautical installations in England, France, and Germany. The Germans were eager to show him their new aeronautical research facilities, and "Far from concealing anything, they seemed to gloat over their accomplishments ..." in spite of the prospects of war (Hartman 1970, 16). In 1940 NACA located its second R&D facility, Ames, near Stanford University and the aircraft manufacturing companies on the West Coast to focus on aircraft aerodynamics; the third, an engine research laboratory, was in Cleveland, Ohio, due to its ready accessibility to the manufacturers of aircraft engines (Hartman 1970, 22).

The Ames Aeronautical Laboratory, later renamed the Ames Research Center, quickly established itself as an aerodynamics research center with around eight hundred employees by the end of the war. In the words of Hartman: "Much of the research effort at Ames during the war had been spent in assisting the military services and aircraft companies in developing aircraft having a maximum of performance and military usefulness" (Hartman 1970, 111).

Likewise, university aeronautical research and education was limited. MIT led the way in developing aeronautical education and research labs. In 1913 Jerome C. Hunsaker was hired to teach aeronautical engineering in the Department of Naval Architecture. A wind tunnel was built the same year. The Charles Stark Draper instruments laboratory was founded in 1935 to provide graduate students with experience in guidance and control systems. The Department of Aeronautical Engineering was established in 1939, with Hunsaker as the first head of the department. The same year, the Wright Brothers Wind Tunnel began operation. During the war, Hunsaker was the chairman of NACA.

The department rapidly expanded to meet wartime needs. Three laboratories opened during World War II: Flutter Research, Vibrations Measurements, and Structures. In 1942 Draper's laboratory, renamed the Confidential Instrument Development Laboratory, began R&D work on military guidance and control systems. Stanford and the California Institute of Technology were also establishing basic research capabilities, and the nation's biggest aircraft companies were located nearby in Southern California.

By the end of the war, the centrality of air power drove defense policy. While the production of aircraft declined precipitately, greatly expanded research activity came to rule the industry. In fact, the aerospace industry employed about one-fifth of all American scientists and engineers engaged in R&D from the early postwar period up until 1985 (Bugos 2001). Ames Research Center, a national laboratory, remained a hub of early postwar aerospace research, but the research funding shifted from government labs to private subcontractors. Frederick Terman, the father of Silicon Valley, persuaded Lockheed Aerospace Company to set up a research facility in the newly opened Stanford Industrial Park in 1956, and its new Missiles and Space Division was added a year later (Saxenian 1994, 24). By 1964, Lockheed Missiles and Space employed 12,000 in Santa Clara County (Saxenian 1994, 178); Ames Research Center employed 2,300 the same year (Hartman 1970, 515). As airframes became platforms for taking electronic equipment aloft, avionics firms emerged specializing in the systems engineering and the integration of electronics and aerospace. These two industries were the drivers of California's emerging high-tech economy, and the region's engineering departments were transformed in the process.

As shown in table 2.1, the expansion of the shipbuilding industry was on nearly the same scale as that of aerospace (Janeway 1951, 246–47; Lane 1951). Created by the Maritime Commission, the Liberty Ship Program designed and developed the Liberty vessel for mass production. Between December 1941 and December 1944, output per manhour increased by about 40 percent annually, a rate nearly fifteen times the average of 2.4 percent for the economy between 1909 and 1941 (Rapping 1965).[22] The

22. Rapping's study was one of a large volume of learning curve literature at the RAND Corporation and in economics journals (Asher 1956). The most referenced is Kenneth Arrow's "The Economic Implications of Learning by Doing," in which the term "rational expectations" was introduced as an improvement over "perfect foresight," with attribution to Muth (Arrow 1961). The original learning curve paper by Wright (1936) noted the de-

Frederick Terman, 1900–1982. *Source:* Stanford University Archives.

growth in output of tanks, guns, and ammunition was similarly staggering (Shiman 1997).

creasing cost and increasing productivity link to output expansion in the production of a
new model aircraft. Unfortunately, the literature attributes learning to experience but does
not attempt an explanation of the sources of learning. Instead, learning is defined in terms
tractable to a neoclassical production function and measured by achieved volume.

Table 2.1. Indexes of American Manufacturing Output, 1940–1944 (1939 = 100)

Sector	1940	1941	1942	1943	1944
Aircraft	245	630	1,706	2,842	2,805
Munitions	140	423	2,167	3,803	2,033
Shipbuilding	159	375	1,091	1,815	1,710
Aluminum	126	189	318	561	474
Rubber	109	144	152	202	206
Steel	131	171	190	202	197

Source: Milward (1979, 69).

PARTICIPATORY MANAGEMENT
METHODS AND PRACTICES

Following the German invasion of France, Roosevelt used World War I legislation on June 24, 1940, to re-create the NDAC, with seven members, "for the coordination of industries and resources for the national security and welfare," to prepare for the transition to a war economy. William Knudsen, president of General Motors, was appointed commissioner of industrial production, and labor leader Sidney Hillman was appointed commissioner of employment.[23]

When the NDAC morphed into the WPB, Roosevelt created the War Manpower Commission (WMC) with responsibility for the recruitment, placement, and training of labor, and Hillman was appointed as chairman (WMC 1945, 4). The armaments buildup was already underway, and the numbers gaining employment were staggering. By August of 1940, 80,000 new workers, most unskilled, had been drawn into the mushrooming shipyards, the aircraft plants had absorbed 50,000, and 18,000 skilled operatives had been channeled into the machine tool industry (Janeway 1951, 160). But this was just the beginning.

The initial challenge was to address the production targets, given the buildup in the armed forces, which would eventually cumulatively total 14 million (WMC 1945, 5).[24] Surprisingly, the big issue was not one of a civilian labor shortage. The gap created by the exit of men aged 20–44 from the civilian labor force to military service was in fact covered by previously unemployed men and the recruitment of women and of men under 20 and over 44 (Long 1944, 53).[25]

23. The multiple administrative stages in the evolution of the NDAC into the War Production Board can be found in Janeway (1951, 296).

24. See also Koistinen (2004) and Klein (2013).

25. Unemployment of 8 million in 1940 was reduced to 670,000 in 1944, plus an additional 10.5 million jobs were filled by new entrants to the labor force. By 1945 almost 19

The more pressing manpower planning challenge was skills. In other words, how to develop and match the skill sets of the labor force with those required to run factories being converted to weapons production as well as rapidly expanding and newly created weapons industries. A Training Within Industry (TWI) program was established within the WMC with a mandate to develop a national skills training system that could educate the labor force in the requisite skills in order to convert, build, and operate the factories at ever-increasing capacity and to do so with nearly immediate effect.

The design of the TWI program was informed by two lessons the directors derived from history. The first was a negative lesson from World War I. In the words of Paul McNutt, second chairman of the WMC: "The training methods developed at that time had not taken root in many industrial establishments. They had failed to convince management to make use of training techniques to increase production. This time the work had to go deeper into the consciousness of management" (WMC 1945, x).

The second was a positive lesson from the interwar period. Hillman appointed as directors four senior leaders of training programs on loan from major industrial enterprises. Three of the four also had government experience from World War I.[26] As human resources leaders in successful companies in the interwar period, the TWI directors brought practical experience in the new management methods and labor skills required not only to operate programs but to convert them to mass-production systems. The implementation of mass-production principles was fostering new roles for managers, supervisors, and workers.

The key to the strategy, structure, and ultimate success of the TWI program is signaled by the preposition "within." It reflects a distinction between "knowing what" and "knowing how" (Ryle 1949; Loasby 1999).[27] The knowledge of "what" and "why" is necessary but not sufficient to achieve breakthrough advances in production. It needs to be combined

---

million American women (including millions of black women) were working outside the home (Tassava 2008). Overy puts the total number of women who took up employment at 14 million (1995, 241)). Output and productivity did not suffer; instead, both were increasing at historic rates (Evans 1947; Rapping 1965).

26. C. R. Dooley at Westinghouse, Standard Oil, and Socony-Vacuum Oil; Walter Dietz at Western Electric; M. J. Kane at GE and AT&T; and William Conover at US Steel, Western Electric, and Lycoming Manufacturing.

27. "Knowing that" is knowledge of facts, relationships, and theories and can be divided into "knowing what" and "knowing why." "Knowing how," in contrast, is the ability to perform the appropriate actions and includes skill in both performance and awareness of when and where this skillful performance is appropriate (Loasby 1999, 51).

with the knowledge of "how" to transform inputs into outputs. For example, scientific and engineering knowledge of the conversion of petrochemicals into plastics is not the same as how to do it; the know-how is a necessary but distinctive category of knowledge that is easily overlooked.[28]

The distinction is captured in the words of C. R. Dooley, director of TWI:

> If there is any single thing that could be stated as "what TWI has learned," it would be that "the establishment of principles, and even getting acceptance by managers, alone have practically no value in increasing production." "*What* to do" is not enough. It is only when people are drilled in "*how* to do it" that action results. (WMC 1945, xi, emphasis mine)

The focus on "know-how" explains the TWI's perception of the scientific management paradigm as a barrier to the establishment of the skills required to meet the production capabilities necessary to win the war.[29] To quote a TWI report:

> Work in the field of scientific management had been going on since the turn of the century. All of this work, however, was done by professionals. Except for suggestion schemes, there had been no attempt to stimulate individual workers or their immediate supervisors or in fact, any persons except trained engineers in the improvement of methods until the Job Methods program was started. (WMC 1945, 223–24)

The TWI program stressed the importance of on-the-job skills training not only for workers but for supervisors. And it required a managerial perspective that advanced employee involvement in a range of problem-solving activities now associated with continuous improvement and high-performance work systems. The Japanese term *kaizen*, translated as "continuous improvement," is consistent with the content of the TWI skills-training methods.

---

28. This kind of knowledge plays little or no formal role in mainstream economics, central planning boards, or the scientific management paradigm. According to Loasby, "All three ignore the kind of knowledge which is crucial to the performance of a person, a firm, an industry, an economy (and even an economist!)" (1999, 51).

29. Sorensen writes, "One of the hardest-to-pin-down myths about the evolution of mass production at Ford is one that attributes much of the accomplishment to 'scientific management.' No one at Ford ... was acquainted with the theories of ... Frederick W. Taylor" (1956, 41).

Taiichi Ohno, the recognized father of the Toyota Production System, credits Ford with the employee-involvement managerial revolution. In Ohno's words: "Standards should not be forced down from above but rather set by the production workers themselves" (Ohno 1978; trans. 1988, 98). Ohno's claim needs to be corrected. It was the TWI program, not Ford, that drove the employee-involvement managerial revolution. Ford concentrated standards-setting, problem-solving, and learning functions in his process engineers; they were not pushed down to the workers (see chap. 6).

Ford achieved the three-part performance standards of cheaper, better, faster later celebrated by the Toyota Production System but by making each factory specific to a single product and by freezing product design.[30] Workers in the Ford system enjoyed the benefits of an order of magnitude increase in productivity and wages, but they were not called upon to improve methods.

The mass-production system simplified the training of workers and supervisors to meet the challenge of turning millions of unemployed and millions that had never worked at a factory into a productive labor force. The lean management philosophy at Ford was created naturally as a by-product of pioneering the mass-production system. But much of American manufacturing was not organized according to the new principles.

Ford's flow system was a production engineering paradigm for characterizing the skills that could most rapidly advance the nation's armaments production capabilities. The assembly line of the B-24 bomber, for example, had required synchronized advances in production along a supply chain of, as noted, 30,000 different parts. Delivery delays would derail the whole system. Workforce skills in bottleneck analysis methods are critical to converting companies from batch production methods to the sequential process layouts of mass production. Likewise, workforce quality management skills reduced the costs of inspection and the likelihood of defective parts undermining the integrity of the final product. Workers skilled in methods improvement increased the capabilities of companies to efficiently introduce new products and new technologies into production. New-product development and technology-management capabilities are links in the innovation chain by which R&D could be converted into technologically advanced weapons.

30. Ford wrote: "We believe ... that no factory is large enough to make two kinds of products" (1926, 82).

For maximum effectiveness, TWI administrators tailored skills-training content to the generic requirements of suppliers to the established mass producers, companies transitioning from job shop and batch production systems to mass production, and flexible producers supplying multiple products. Most such establishments did not have a staff of process engineers and many did not have the luxury of making only a single product.

The genius of the TWI directors was to characterize the generic workforce skills that could rapidly develop the nation's production capabilities and to design a training system that would get buy-in from supervisors as well as the workforce to teaching and learning the new skills. Supervisors were the gatekeepers, and the skills-training program needed their active buy-in. Moreover, it needed supervisors to become teachers to coach work teams and to train the workforce in job methods, problem solving and continuous improvement skills. Consequently, the consciousness or the mindsets of supervisors was the immediate target of the TWI program. The means of meeting the WMC's national manpower training mandate was to engage supervisors as teachers and convert factories into learning organizations. But supervisors needed the tools in the form of teaching methods.

The TWI directors and staff designed group teaching methods and programs whereby workers would learn through example from their own practices; the teachers would be their supervisors. To quote the TWI report again:

> The real job had to be done *by* industry, *within* industry. Industry's own men collected, standardized, streamlined, and developed techniques for industry itself to use on a volunteer basis. The four TWI programs, Job Instruction, Job Methods, Job Relations, and Program Development, are methods of group instruction whereby plant people learn through practice on their own current problems to use these specific 4-step methods, so simple that each is printed on a pocket card. (WMC 1945, 6, emphasis mine)[31]

Academic specialists were called upon to assist in designing the four TWI programs. For example, the Job Relations program started with a January 1941 question Commissioner Hillman asked of the National Academy of Sciences: "What can be done to increase knowledge and improve understanding of supervision at the work level?" It was forwarded

---

31. In the words of C. R. Dooley, director of TWI: "Education and organization are ... the tools with which America must shape her destiny" (WMC 1945: xii).

to Lawrence Henderson, chairman of the National Research Council's Committee on Work in Industry and director of the Fatigue Laboratory at Harvard University. This led to the enlistment of F. J. Roethlisberger and John B. Fox of Harvard University and L. J. O'Rourke of the Civil Service Commission to work with TWI's Walter Dietz and staff to address the "human relations problems of handling men." A research methodology was devised that combined surveys, case studies, and test trials to create the best possible teaching and learning program before rolling it out nationally (WMC 1945, 204; Robinson and Schroeder 1993, 40).

The field organization for all four TWI programs consisted of twenty-two district offices, each of which was created with a staff largely borrowed from industry. Eventually the paid staff, both at headquarters and in the districts, totaled four hundred. Another six hundred became advisors and consultants at headquarters and on district panels. But both the training and the creation of trainers were based on the program's "multiplier principle." The concept was to "develop a standard method, then train the people who will train the other people who will train repeated groups of people to use the method" (WMC 1945, x).

It worked according to plan. Paul V. McNutt, chairman, of the WMC, claimed that during the war "23,000 industrial men and women ... were prepared as TWI trainers and ... [supervisors] did the actual training in supervisory skills which resulted in almost 2,000,000 certifications for supervisors in over 16,000 war production plants and essential services" (WMC 1945: x, 6; see 44ff. for case studies).

The revolution in management philosophy that inspired TWI's extraordinary success was rarely acknowledged in the postwar United States. The story of the postwar transfer of the TWI program and manuals by the Japanese Department of Labor and its continued centrality to the success of Japanese management philosophy and work organization is told by Robinson and Schroeder (1993). It was studied and copied directly by the postwar Japanese Department of Labor before it was implemented to establish the work organization and skills training system at the heart of the Toyota Production System.[32] TWI was the prototype of

32. After the war the Japanese Ministry of Labor hired American trainers with the shutting down of the WMC to introduce TWI methods throughout Japanese industry. Toyota labelled their system TTWI (Toyota Training Within Industry). The TWI manuals themselves became the basis for the codification of the new continuous improvement model of work organization, a pillar of what is variously labeled the Toyota Production System, lean manufacturing, and world-class manufacturing. Meanwhile, in the United States, reversion to the old model of work organization took place (Ohno 1988 [1978], 100).

what became the total quality management philosophy by which Japan established industrial leadership in the quality revolution of the 1980s and 1990s. The story of its return to the United States, including the manuals, with the establishment of Japanese plants in the United States in the 1970s is told by Donald Dinero (2005).[33]

The Application of the Flow Principle to Victory Program Macroeconomic Planning

The economic statisticians who constructed the tabulations that informed the Victory Program were ingenious at discovering, assembling, combining, and creating data and sources of data for macroeconomic measurement.[34] Kuznets's colleagues Stacy May and Robert Nathan constructed tables of material requirements and estimates of full employment production, respectively. They did so within an organization that understood and had experience in production engineering. The production men were also knowledgeable about the changes in management mindsets and factory organization required to implement the principle of flow and achieve the resulting productivity gains. They were not economists. But the Victory Program written by Kuznets was a planning document consistent with the requisite production-level structural changes they alone fully understood.

The economic statisticians' concept of ambitious but feasible growth was informed by process engineering and the practical knowledge of organizational change within a single plant, along vertical supply chains, and at the national output level. Stacy May's tabulations involved real-time updating of production activities throughout the industrial economy to track these developments. Shortages in critical materials had national

33. Others have treated the equally important contribution of unions to undertaking the establishment of new production facilities and the reorganization of existing ones in record time. See Norman Best (1990, chap. 4) for an insider's account of the International Association of Machinists' role in establishing the Trentwood Aluminum Rolling Mills in Spokane, Washington, during the war years. Charles Sorensen (1956), a one-time member of the Patternmakers Union, offers an account of the mutual respect among himself, Walter Reuther, head of the United Automobile Workers, and Philip Murray, head of the Congress of Industrial Organizations. Unfortunately, his views were not shared by Henry Ford, who relied instead on the infamous views of Harry Bennett. For a history of the war years as the time in which trade unions finally got recognition from the mass production industries, see Lichtenstein (2002).

34. According to Paul A. Samuelson and William D. Nordhaus, "While the GDP and the rest of the national income accounts may seem to be arcane concepts, they are truly among the great inventions of the twentieth century" (1995, cited by Landefeld 2000).

attention. No single concern was more important in the economic calcula-
tions undertaken by the WPB economic statisticians. It was, in effect, an
economics of effective supply management that incorporated the economics of factory production and mirrored Keynesian economics of effective
demand.

The combined production engineering and national accounting expertise at the WPB is critical to understanding how the rapid growth targets of the Victory Program were both set and achieved. There is a striking parallel between the emphasis of the Victory Program on the criticality
of bottleneck policy analysis to realizing macroeconomic growth potential
and the focus of production engineering on identifying and eliminating
bottlenecks to increase throughput efficiency at the enterprise level.

The economic statisticians used national income and product accounts
as part of an exercise to discover and identify bottlenecks to national production capacity. This was critical; it identified where policy could be targeted to have system-level impact. The implementation question was how
to remove bottlenecks, and in what order. The idea was not simply to remove a single bottleneck but, as in process engineering, to create methods
to operationalize policy instruments to identify and remove successive
bottlenecks to system performance enterprise by enterprise. Each relax-
ation of the primary bottleneck creates a new primary bottleneck in an
endless succession. It required the extension of bottleneck analysis into
management thinking and work practices to embed the output expansion
capability in the nation's production system.

This was a major responsibility of the WPB. The core of the Victory
Program was the dependence of the projected time path of production
expansion on policies and measures to anticipate and tackle bottlenecks
with targeted measures in raw materials, machine tools, and industrial
facilities. But whereas bottlenecks were easily identified in enterprises by
the buildup of inventories, the economic statisticians had to rely on a vast
collection of data measuring output capacities against raw materials, required industrial facilities, and the time required to address and overcome major bottlenecks. Successful bottleneck elimination policies called
for substitute materials in the case of rubber and increased aluminum
plants in the case of aircraft production, of copper production for ammunition, of electricity for energy-intensive processes, and of mining for strategic raw materials.

The policy instrument was to apply bottleneck analysis to the flow of
production at the national level. It was an analysis designed to anticipate the production requirements necessary to achieve the output targets

required to meet military needs but ultimately set by the president. The estimates of large increases in potential production were greatly appreciated by the military planners but not the timing; they always wanted them sooner without appreciating the interconnectedness of production supply chains. But the supply projections by the economic statisticians were informed by production engineering realities, and in this also informed an evidence-based analysis of the rate at which productive potential could be increased and the sensitivity of that rate to early identification and removal of bottlenecks.[35]

The focus on investment in industrial facilities and machine tools in the Victory Program was a means of driving home the point that the maximum level of production could be achieved only by setting the right targets and synchronizing production schedules at the systemwide level. To set goals too high would create bottlenecks in the system, generate imbalance and waste, and slow the rate of growth that could be achieved. It was this relationship between the rate of growth and potential growth that informed the nation's Victory Program and with such a convincing logic that it was accepted as the policy of the nation, which the military ultimately, if reluctantly, accepted. As an empirical estimate of the rate at which the productive potential could be increased, it empowered the WPB's economic statisticians to set the dates at which the output targets could be met and military operations undertaken. Thus the WPB was at the center of the struggle over civilian versus military control of procurement schedules, industrial policy, and military strategy.

Financing the Invisible "Industrial Empire"

The defense crisis began with the surrender of France in May 1940 and the bombing of Great Britain. Industrial expansion became the United States' "Problem Number 1" (William Knudsen, quoted in White 1949, 159), both to supply Great Britain and to build an armaments industry there. In the

---

35. The factory reorganization and skill formation programs of the WPB and the TWI program of the WMC (see above) were critical to the application of the fundamental production principle of flow underlying mass production. Moreover, work organization reforms that integrated planning and doing at the shop-floor level, accompanied by the restructuring of plant layouts according to the logic of process integration rather than functional departmentalization, had a profound impact on the flexibility of production to absorb new technologies. Such factories could pull new technologies, just as the nation's greatly expanded science and technology infrastructure was creating new technologies. The combined push and pull underlie the enhanced technology management capabilities at the levels of both enterprise and the national economy.

beginning, the problem was money, that is, where to get the capital to finance the expansion.

The seemingly insurmountable challenge was met by public-sector entrepreneurship in the form of an organizational innovation in the relationship between finance and industry. During World War II, two-thirds of expenditures for industrial facilities were directly financed by the government (White 1949, 156; Jones and Angly 1951). Economic policymakers went outside the market system to create a leasing mechanism to negotiate the industry-government divide. The Defense Plant Corporation (DPC) was created in 1940 as a subsidiary of the Depression-era Reconstruction Finance Corporation (RFC), "with such powers as it may deem necessary to aid the Government of the United States in its national defense program" (White 1949, 161). It could act only on the request of the Federal Loan Administration and with the approval of the president.[36]

The leasing mechanism was a means by which facilities financed and owned by the government could be operated by private companies. The result was the creation of what has been labeled a "vast industrial empire" by White (1949, 158) and described as an "enormous industrial empire which most economists have never heard of" by Gordon (1969, 230).

This financial instrument was used to build and equip new factories and mills that were leased to private companies to operate. From its inception in August 1940 through 1945, the DPC disbursed over $9 billion on 2,300 projects in forty-six states and overseas. At the time of its dissolution on June 30, 1945, the DPC owned

between 10 and 12 per cent of the total industrial capacity of the nation. At that time the corporation owned approximately 96 per cent of the capacity of the synthetic-rubber industry, 90 per cent of magnesium metal, 71 per cent of aircraft and aircraft engines, and 58 per cent of the aluminum metal industry. It also had sizeable investments in iron and steel, aviation, gasoline, ordnance, machinery and machine

36. The rules governing the RFC's Depression-era financing of industry were modified in May and June of 1940 to enable subsidiaries of the RFC to finance and own defense plants, and to lease them to private industry (White 1949, 161). The authority was requested by the Federal Loan Administration in the person of Jesse Jones and granted by the Senate Banking and Commerce Committee. The authority was to be used only in cooperation with the NDAC, the predecessor to the WPB. The RFC established a range of sector-specialist subsidiaries besides the DPC, such as the Metals Reserve Company, Rubber Reserve Company, Petroleum Reserves Corporation, and the Defense Homes Corporation, and disbursed more than $20 billion ("Brother, Can You Spare a Billion? The Story of Jesse H. Jones," www.pbs.org/jessejones/jesse_ww2_2.htm; see also Jones and Angly 1951 and Fenberg 2011a).

tools, transportation, radio, and other more miscellaneous facilities. (White 1949, 158)[37]

The problem for academic economics is not simply that the existence of the industrial empire is unknown. The bigger problem is that denial of its existence creates glaring errors in macroeconomic measurements of the economy. In the words of Gordon, "A little-known $45 billion treasure chest of plant and equipment which the U.S. Government ... purchased for the use of private firms ... has never been counted as part of the private U.S. capital stock" (1969, 221). To quote him again, "Conventional statistics on private investment by manufacturers completely ignore almost 60 per cent of the wartime expansion of privately operated facilities" (226). He continues that such "glaring errors ... are important enough to raise serious questions about the validity of production function studies of the U.S. economy which extend before 1948" (221). The hidden industrial empire illustrates the broader theme that the omission of an economics of production from the discipline of economics contributed to what Gordon describes as a "statistical dark age on which practically no information exists" (231).

Reflections on Theory and Policy

World War II was a period of policymaking experimentation and government intervention, much as was the Great Depression that preceded it.[38] But although the Great Depression inspired an emerging Keynesian macroeconomic demand management perspective, the successful policy regime of the wartime American economy, intended to create and grow new industries and transform existing industries to meet unprecedented performance targets, did not inspire a new supply-side production development perspective within the economics profession.[39]

37. White cites the *Report on Audit of Reconstruction Finance Corporation and Affiliated Corporations: Defense Plant Corporation*, 80th Cong., 1st sess., House Document 474 (Washington, DC, 1947), IV, 36.

38. Paul Samuelson (1944, cited in Bernstein 2001, 73) quipped, "[T]he last war was the chemist's war ... this one is the physicist's. It might equally be said that this is the economist's war." The extraordinary prestige of economics was exemplified by the creation of the Council of Economic Advisors within the Executive Office of the President with the passage of the Full Employment and Stabilization Act of 1946.

39. See chapter 9 for a partial exception in which wartime material resource planning systems became institutionalized within the military industrial complex, but implications for the assumptions required by market-centric economic theory have been largely ignored.

Unfortunately, the World War II complementarity of Keynesian demand management with supply-side measures to advance production and technological capabilities has been as if airbrushed from standard economics. The omission of production in postwar macroeconomic theory coincided with a return of orthodoxy to the a priori-generated theory of a self-organizing market economy.[40]

Roosevelt set in motion the creation of a vast research-intensive university system to build a national science and technology infrastructure. But it was not the first time a president had turned to engineering education to strategically advance the nation's production system. As described in chapter 9, Thomas Jefferson had established the nation's first engineering college at the Army Academy at West Point, and Abraham Lincoln had passed the Morrill Land Grant education act, which created universities offering engineering education in every state.

An important lesson is that both theory and policies undertaken are required to analyze and understand how the supply side of the economy works at any particular time. This is because economies are not subject to natural laws independent of organizational context, as presumed by market fundamentalism. Three productive structures were critical to explaining the production performance of the US wartime economy, and each was strategically shaped by government policies and instituted programs. Moreover, the US economy was transformed permanently and thereafter operated according to different "laws of motion." For example, the science and technology infrastructure that created America's first high-tech sectors became the basis for the emergence of regional innovation systems, such as Boston's Route 128 and Silicon Valley. The triple-helix productive structures of these regions fostered the creation of populations of science- and technology-driven enterprises that before the war had been limited to large enterprises that could fund internal research laboratories. Economic theory, in contrast, has not evolved to account for permanent changes in productive structures.

The lessons have not been universally ignored. Ironically, while the economic governance lessons of World War II were not integrated into mainstream economics, they were incorporated into policymaking, institutional design, and practices to drive rapid-growth success stories elsewhere in

---

40. John Kenneth Galbraith writes: "In 1936, it was not only wrong but professionally unwise to reject Say's Law. It was a litmus by which the reputable economist was separated from the crackpot" (1981, 65). Following Keynes's critique of Say's Law, the neoclassical production function and optimum allocation theory became the postwar litmus tests for assessing theoretical economic research.

the world. Japan's Toyota Production System, as noted, did not originate in Japan; the principles and methods that inform just-in-time (JIT) production, total quality management (TQM), and *kaizen* (continuous innovation), which are described in chapter 8 and in Best (1990 and 2001), were all put into place to drive US industrial growth during World War II. The economic statisticians Kuznets, Macy, and Nathan created production measurements of key industrial inputs designed to highlight bottlenecks at the macroeconomic policy level, analogous to the production engineer's targeting of inventory buildup to focus process innovations at the enterprise level.

Postwar US engineering priorities within production went elsewhere, and the principle of flow was "unlearned." In Ohno's words: "Ford's successors, however, did not make production flow as Ford intended. They ended up with the concept 'the larger the lot size, the better.' This builds a dam, so to speak, and stops the flow at the machining and stamping processes" (Ohno 1978, 100; Best 1990, 147ff.).

An equally important lesson revealed by US experience in World War II and "forgotten" in postwar policymaking is reinforced in all of the following chapters: the production capability development and technology diffusion processes depend on the level of skill formation at the operational as well as the advanced engineering levels. In chapter 8 we examine the negative consequences for America's competitive performance of the curtailment of the government's wartime TWI teaching and learning program while it was simultaneously imported by Japan and incorporated as a key element in that nation's strategic development policy framework, implemented by the Japanese Ministry of Labor and diffused by the Japanese Union of Scientists and Engineers (Best 1990, 156ff.; Robinson and Schroeder 1993).

Ironically, as America abandoned the concept of a strategic development policy framework, Japan applied the lessons of its power to shape a nation's competitive structural advantage. The long-term consequences of the postwar shift to market fundamentalism for the standard of living in America due to the decline of large-scale production and loss of manufacturing employment are increasingly impossible to ignore as more nations have followed Japan's example of crafting strategic development policy frameworks.

CHAPTER THREE

Greater Boston's Industrial Ecosystem

A MANUFACTORY OF SECTORS

NEW ENGLAND HAS BEEN highly successful at creating and growing new sectors during two time periods in its industrial history. The first, and the basis for establishing American industrial leadership, was dominated by what was referred to by British engineers and the leading contemporary British economist Alfred Marshall (1920 [1890], 257–58) as the American system. It was characterized by the world's first machine-tool industry based on the production principle of interchangeable parts (Roe 1937, Rosenberg 1963, Hekman 1980, Best 1990). The second was the post–World War II period in which a successive range of new sectors have emerged and grown in the Greater Boston area. In between these two phases, Massachusetts lacked the industrial innovation capability to create and grow new sectors (Dorfman 1983, Tödtling 1994, Glaeser 2005). Like Rip Van Winkle, it slumbered.

Today Greater Boston has a regional competitive advantage in early-stage technology development, rapid business growth, and new sector formation. Most accounts attribute the region's industrial innovation to business opportunities for technology transfer created by federally funded scientific research conducted by famous local universities. But the linear, science-push, technology transfer model of opportunity creation and industrial innovation is not the whole story. It obscures the dynamic processes by which innovation opportunities are created and exploited.

I propose an alternative industrial ecosystem approach to innovation, the creation of opportunities, and sector emergence that draws on systems thinking and evolutionary metaphors. The idea of an industrial ecosystem evokes an economic analogy to Darwin's habitat acting as a "manufactory of species" but applied to the emergence and growth of high-tech sectors (1979 [1859], 110).

Darwin wrote of the "constant tendency ... in the economy of nature" toward divergence in the character of species, a divergence that is most pronounced in any "small area" where species "come into the closest competition" (1979 [1859], 398). Competition, in our metaphorical Darwinian economy, is not over the cost of production as conceptualized in neoclassical economic theory. Rather, it suggests technological competition among heterogeneous firms and sectors. Whereas sex and random mutations are the sources of genetic variation in the natural world, experiments by technology-led enterprises provide the immediate sources of increasing technological differentiation, industrial innovation, and sectoral growth dynamics in Greater Boston's population of high-tech companies. As one firm differentiates and exploits an opportunity, it exposes opportunities for other firms and nudges them into action, and as they themselves differentiate, they pass forward the opportunity-creation process.

Opportunity creation involves multiple agents who drive a combined process of increasing technological differentiation and integration (Best 2001; Blundel 2013). The business enterprise, in this interpretation, is the entrepreneurial agency in which opportunity discovery and distinctive capability development meet and mutually condition one another (Penrose 1959). The degree of success depends on the technical capabilities, expertise, and past achievements of both the enterprise and the region. Thus opportunity discovery, at the enterprise (micro) level, and opportunity creation at the region (macro) level, are mediated and enhanced by the process of increasing technological differentiation in the region.

In the case of Greater Boston, the population of SMEs, in turn, is embedded within a Schumpeterian "shaping" institutional environment in which new and repositioning firms can grow rapidly to take advantage of emerging opportunities (Schumpeter 1947, 153). But the region's shaping environment is not external to the population of firms; instead, it is an interinstitutional assemblage, including the enterprises, that functions as a regional industrial experimental laboratory. As a metaphorical laboratory, it contains the requisite complementary activities, scientific and technical expertise, and financial and other resources that can be rapidly assembled and integrated by entrepreneurial agents into innovation process networks that, as described below, institutionalize the region's dynamic integration capability.

The focus on the industrial ecosystem complements the business ecosystem literature (Moore 1993; Adner 2012). Both emphasize network linkages. But whereas the business ecosystem concept highlights the business model as a recipe for business managers, the industrial ecosystem concept draws attention to a region's business model as a variable of economic and theoretical enquiry. Here the biological metaphor is not that of an evolutionary theory of the firm (Nelson and Winter 1982) but rather that of capability-differentiating enterprises as agents within a complex regional coadaptive system (Garnsey 1998; Johnson 2001; Iammarino 2005; Beinhocker 2007).

Although this book adapts Darwin's natural ecosystem and species differentiation concepts to regional economic growth, ironically Darwin himself cited a historical understanding of technological change as an illustration of evolutionary methodology that could fruitfully be used by natural historians: "When we regard every production of nature as one which had a history ... nearly in the same way as when we look at any great mechanical invention as the summing up of the labour, the experience, the reason, and even the blunders of numerous workmen ... how far more interesting ... will the study of natural history become!" (1979 [1859], 456). The evolutionary system described in this chapter builds on empirical studies of engineering evolution and sector growth dynamics informed by a panel data set of over three thousand Massachusetts high-tech firms and their products classified by a fine-grained technology taxonomy. But instead of "even the blunders of numerous workmen," we might say "even the failures of numerous experiments."

The chapter is organized as follows. The next section examines the nineteenth-century origins of specialized engineering expertise and evolved technology threads manifest in present-day companies. The third section examines the transformative effects on the region's productive structure of the wartime federal government-led, technologically advanced weapons industry. The much-expanded basic research capacity of the region's universities combined with the applied research strengths of the region's engineering enterprises to design, develop, and produce a range of weapons in record time, as described in chapter 2.

The fourth section maps the postwar consequences for Greater Boston's business and industrial organization. For the first time, the region's business enterprises of all sizes could engage in and manage innovation chains that linked basic, applied, and developmental research with new product development and production process activities. As more SMEs pursued focus-and-network strategies, a mutually reinforcing open-system business model emerged with collective system integration capabilities. The core external relationship of the high-tech enterprise is participation not in supply-chain networks but in the multilevel coordination of innovation process activities to pursue technological leadership. National government–sponsored mission-driven R&D fostered and interacted with Greater Boston's population of technologically differentiated high-tech enterprises to establish a regional industrial ecosystem with a competitive advantage in the creation and rapid growth of new technology-driven sectors.

The fifth section presents examples of rapid growth sectors, including perhaps the most important, the region's differentiated but articulated business development finance sector. The chapter concludes by relating the approach pursued here to other recent developments in the literature and reflects further on the Darwinian methodology.

Descent with Modification: Engineering Expertise and Specialist Technologies

America's early industrial leadership can be traced to the establishment in New England of a machine-based, as distinct from craft-based, manufacturing system to meet the uniformity requirements of interchangeable parts (Thomson 2009, 54–65). The American system of manufacturers, the expression used by British engineers to capture the uniqueness of American production in the mid-1800s, was based on the principle of interchangeability. The idea was to assemble each musket, for example, from interchangeable parts, all of which met uniform size requirements. It involved characterizing a sequence of activities required to make each part by specialist machines. It was the basis for the emergence and growth of a community of machinists skilled in product engineering and the emergence of a machine, tooling, instrument, and equipment-making regional capability (Meyer 2006).

The creation of a large community of machinists and the proliferation of machine shops became a unique regional productive resource in the form of precision engineering and machining capability. The endless pursuit of ever smaller tolerances involved the creation of instruments that opened new technological domains, as illustrated in figure 3.1. The predominately mechanical period spanning the nineteenth century gave way to an electromechanical era beginning at the turn of the past century, then to electronics and on to today's opto-electronics or photonics era. The capability to measure and manufacture at ever-smaller size dimensions shown on the vertical axis preceded the transition to opening new

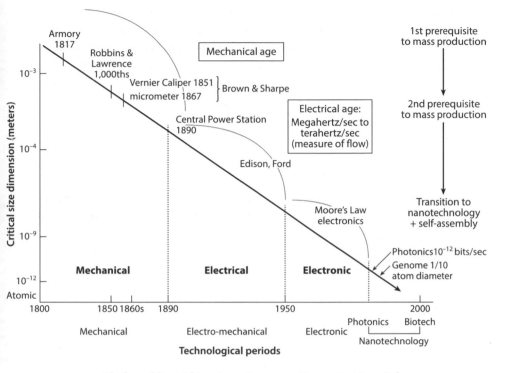

FIGURE 3.1. The law of diminishing sizes, 1800–2000. *Source:* Best (2001), fig. 5.2, 133.

technological domains to production as illustrated along the horizontal axis of the figure. In each succeeding technological period mechanical engineering advanced, underwent change, and combined with electrical, electronic, information, and opto-electronic engineering expertise from 10^{-3} in early nineteenth-century machine shops to 10^{-12} in the age of nanotechnology (Best 2001, 131–40).

The increasing diversity of technical expertise created opportunities for novel application in virtually all existing and emerging sectors in the form of new technology combinations, new production processes, and new product applications. Again, analogies from natural science can be suggestive: "Every technology has traceable ancestry" (Ridley 2009) and "to create is to recombine" (Jacob 1997, 1163). Jacob, a geneticist, adds: "Novelties come from previously unseen associations of old material."

This chapter draws on vTHREAD, a Techno-Historical Regional Economic Analysis Database in which the letter "v" stands for "making visible." The database uses a finely granulated engineering taxonomy to organize and classify a national longitudinal sample of 55,000 high-tech companies and their products. vTHREAD enables sectors to be linked to their many products and extended products through detailed coding; eighteen sectors extend to 280 major product codes and 3,000 further refined product codes. See Best (2003a); Best, Paquin, and Xie (2004); and Best (2006).

The applications of vTHREAD to Greater Boston's high-tech companies reveal traces of engineering expertise and specialized technology that track back to the region's early industrial history. A series of examples of specialist engineering and technology expertise that link the distant past to the present follow.

TURBINE TECHNOLOGY

The nation's first scientific engineering experiments were designed to increase the energy-generating capacity of the turbine blades that powered the Lowell textile mills on the Merrimack River. They were conducted by the British-born engineer James B. Francis (Francis 1871 [1855]; Hekman 1980; Layton 1992). Francis turbines were installed at Hoover Dam in the 1930s and power Cruachan Power Station in Scotland, constructed in the 1960s, and the Chinese dams in Xiaowan, Jin Ping II, Nuo Zha Du, Xi Luo Du, and Li Yuan, constructed between 2005 and 2008. The Francis turbine remains the most commonly used water turbine in use a century and a half after its introduction in a Lowell textile mill, where it can still be observed today.

In the postwar era, most design and development of US jet-engine turbines was conducted in GE's plant in Lynn, Massachusetts, and in Pratt & Whitney's Hartford, Connecticut, facilities. A historical company genealogy does not currently exist to track the concentration in the design and development of jet-engine turbines to early water-turbine experiments. But perhaps deep craft skills combined with engineering expertise in turbine technology contributed a know-how thread to the complex pattern of the region's technology knowledge base in systems engineering (Loasby 1999, 58). The length of this genealogy would connect hundreds of generations of novel applications as successive sectors emerged and declined. Today the region is home to the government-sponsored Wind Technology Testing Center, which is equipped to test turbine blades longer than a football field.

CHEMICAL ENGINEERING

The origins of the Greater Boston region's unique chemical engineering skill base can be directly traced back to the region's textile industry. The thread begins with the establishment of the Lowell Textile Institute by mill owners to provide technical education and conduct research. Faced with competition from other regions, the mill owners pursued a strategy of transitioning from natural to synthetic fibers. This required engineering expertise and was accomplished by establishing a chemical engineering staff, curriculum, and research capability at the institute.

The accumulated technical knowledge of synthetic fiber and chemical engineering expertise contributed to the emergence of the nation's leading plastics cluster (Best 2001, 111–12). The Lowell Textile Institute was renamed the Lowell Institute of Technology, with the country's largest plastics engineering department, a department that today graduates roughly eighty students per year. The faculty is recruited entirely from PhD programs in chemical engineering.

Reincarnated as the University of Massachusetts, Lowell (UML), the same institution became host to the National Science Foundation–sponsored Biodegradable Polymer Research Center (BPRC) in 1993. The BPRC is a partnership of industrial scientists and government laboratory and university researchers to carry out exploratory and applied research on biodegradable polymers as an alternative to the petrochemical feedstock in the plastics industry (see Best 2001, 246–48). UML's deep roots and skill base in chemical and plastics engineering have created innovation opportunities and industry partnerships in a range of high-tech applications for biodegradable materials in medical devices and photovoltaic and renewable energy technologies.

OPTICS

An optics technology thread links present-day companies in Massachusetts to the early days of precision machining and the age of amateur astronomers. The American Optical Lens Company, established in 1832, continued to operate at its Southbridge factory into the present century. Its sunglasses were worn on the moon by Commander Neil Armstrong and used by the crew of Apollo 11 in 1969. The O. C. White Company, a manufacturer of microscopes, was established in 1894 and still operates in Three Rivers, Massachusetts.

These two companies are not major employers today. But the region's technological capability in optics has remained a locational advantage to the present time. During the Cold War years, Itek, founded in 1957, designed and manufactured the world's most sophisticated satellite reconnaissance cameras. The company's name was a phonetic contraction of "information technology." Its scientists and engineers also developed the first computer-aided design system and explored optical disk technology, both of which contributed to the entry of specialist firms and the emergence of new sectors in the region (Lewis 2002).

In a technology-mapping exercise covering the Lowell area, we found a large group of photonics, imaging, and optics companies (Best 2003a). For example, McPherson, established in 1953 and currently with fifty employees, supplies the world's science labs with optics tools for precision measuring instruments; its spectrographs fly in space rockets and allow scientists to record and search out ancient events in the universe. Barr Associates Inc. was established in 1971 and grew to employ 350. It designs and manufactures infrared optical filters that operate from a wavelength of less than 200 nanometers out to the far infrared (to 35 microns). A mission to service the Hubble space telescope integrated an instrument that contains twenty-five optical filters designed and manufactured by Barr Associates. Several other Lowell-area companies operate in optics, imaging, and X-ray technologies for various industrial sectors and government customers.

Today's successful companies and technology miniclusters at the contemporary end of the long optical technology threads may not be aware of their debt to the astronomer hobbyists who originally advanced lens-grinding capabilities in the region in pursuit of a more distant glimpse into the universe. Nevertheless, it is a locational advantage that is not lost on photonics companies around the world: over 16 percent of Massachusetts's operating units in photonics are foreign-headquartered firms. During the Internet equipment-making boom, the Merrimack Valley region of Massachusetts was called "photonics valley" because of the concentration of firms that designed and supplied the technology products for the backbone of the fiber-optic networks (Best 2003a, 11–12).

Cascade Communications, the leader in the establishment of the new combined network switching equipment industry, was founded in 1990. It was quickly followed by a large group of companies illustrating the differentiation process in figure 3.2. Although most were later acquired or otherwise exited the industry, collectively these and associated firms developed a Massachusetts regional capability in Internet protocol products and services required to move data, voice, and video over public networks, seeking to meet the equipment needs of the new telecommunications service providers.

However, the long historic reach of specialist technology threads and engineering expertise was not sufficient to maintain leadership in the growth of new sectors in the interwar period. It was primarily in the Midwest that an entirely new model of business organization emerged to take

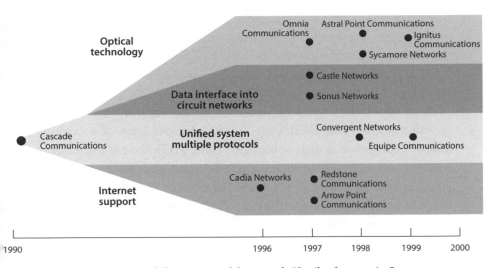

FIGURE 3.2. Technology differentiation of the Cascade "family of companies," 1990–2000.
Source: March 2003.

full advantage of the opportunities of economies of speed and scale, first
in transportation and later in mass production and mass consumption
(Chandler 1977).

The rise of the modern managerial enterprise established the scale
and organizational architecture necessary to exercise market power and
create profit margins in order to conduct R&D internally (Schumpeter
2008 [1942]). The small- and medium-sized business model of Massachusetts, in contrast, was well-suited to the short production runs of capital goods, and the region's R&D was conducted primarily in universities.
Scientific research and regional industry were not organizationally interconnected except in isolated cases.

A Yankee in Washington: The Origins of the Postwar
Science and Technology Infrastructure

As we saw in chapter 2, the story of the embrace of science for strategic
military purposes in America leads straight to Vannevar Bush, hailed as
the "man who won the war" by *Time Magazine* and the "Engineer of the
American Century" by biographer G. Pascal Zachary (1999). Bush was
also the architect of the nation's science and technology infrastructure,
which transformed industrial innovation in postwar America.

Bush was uniquely attuned to the complexity of issues surrounding
university-industry collaboration and technological innovation. He had

been a co-founder of small engineering-led firms, one of which became defense giant Raytheon. His academic role spanned science and engineering research and administration. He had been the dean of Engineering at MIT and was the holder of numerous patents, including one for the invention of a mechanical calculator/computer.

Most importantly, as a long-time MIT insider Bush was immersed in the controversies and debates surrounding various types of university-industry collaboration and, at the same time, MIT's unique institutional commitment to accessible engineering education, fundamental scientific research, and industrial development (Lécuyer 1998). What made MIT unique was its institutional capability simultaneously to pursue and manage all three potentially divergent goals.

But MIT's model was at risk in the pre–World War II years. The sources of funding for basic research were pitifully small and contracting. Receipts for MIT's Technology Plan, designed to build closer industry-university relations for basic research, mission-oriented research, and product development research, declined from $424,090 in 1919–20 to $27,621 in 1926–27 (Etzkowitz 2002, 45; see also Davis and Kevles 1974 and Owens 1990).

Appointed by President Roosevelt to create and lead the OSRD in May 1941, Bush and his team targeted specific weapons system requirements, set the terms of reference, administered and monitored, but did not conduct research or manage operations. Basic research was to be performed by scientists and engineers at university-administered laboratories in close association with production engineers in technology-oriented enterprises.

Autonomy in the academic sphere was critical to mobilize the commitment and energy of European émigré scientists who alone possessed deep knowledge of German science and technology. The institutional effects of the government's recast and substantially expanded interrelationship with the scientific community was captured in the words of James Conant, president of Harvard University and a member of the OSRD Committee:

> I shall never forget my surprise at hearing about this revolutionary scheme.... Scientists were to be mobilized for the defense effort in their own laboratories. A man who we of the committee thought could do a job was going to be asked to be the chief investigator; he would assemble a staff in his own laboratory if possible; he would make progress reports to our committee through a small organization of part-

time advisers and full-time staff. (Conant 1970, 236, quoted in Zachary 1999, 115; see also Etzkowitz 2002, chap. 4)

The whole project depended on the applied research and practical engineering expertise of engineering-intensive enterprises. Bush and his OSRD colleagues drew on existing university-industry partnerships and engineering community networks to identify the requisite expertise and technological capabilities. MIT, the largest university recipient, signed seventy-five OSRD contracts for a total of over $116 million (Mowery and Rosenberg 1993, 39–40).

When military victory was in sight, President Roosevelt commissioned Bush to write a report on the lessons learned in the war effort for the mobilization of science for the pursuit of peaceful goals, including economic growth. The result was *Science: The Endless Frontier; A report to the President on a Program for Postwar Scientific Research* (Bush 1945). This extraordinary document signaled the new era in which public investment in science would institutionalize a strategic policy framework for American industrial innovation leadership. Bush's wartime triangular organizational architecture was implicit.

Dubbed the age of Big Science, this new era involved the creation of a national S&T infrastructure centered on a vastly extended research-intensive university system complemented by mission-specific Federally Funded Research and Development Centers or national laboratories (Nelson 1993; Etzkowitz 2002). Over seven hundred such national laboratories have since been established. These nonprofit, federally contracted centers offer salaries outside civil service pay scales, are administered by nongovernment agencies, and can be located anywhere in the United States. Legally, they cannot engage in the manufacture or production of hardware. For this they need industry partners. Consequently, national along with university laboratories are localized research nodes linking America's multilevel, geographically distributed science and technology infrastructure.

The federal government's S&T infrastructure penetrates deeply into the Greater Boston economy. The first national laboratory in the Boston area was the MIT-administered Radiation Laboratory. At its wartime peak, it employed over four thousand scientists and engineers in over fifteen acres of floor space in Cambridge; Rosegrant and Lampe write that the Radiation Laboratory went on to develop over 150 systems "that applied the versatile microwave technology to a dizzying array of applications" (1992, 84). Lincoln Laboratories, established in 1951 following the Soviet

Union's detonation of an atomic device in 1949, succeeded the Radiation Laboratory. In 1958 the MITRE Corporation, a nonprofit corporation, was established and originally administered by MIT to focus on systems engineering and was located on Route 128 next to Lincoln Laboratories at Hanscom Air Force Base. Over time MITRE came to administer four national laboratories and employ over seven thousand scientists, engineers, and support staff, 65 percent of whom have advanced degrees (MITRE Corporation, 2008). Today MITRE has dozens of branches around the nation and the world, mostly co-located with military bases.

Thus both wartime and early postwar Greater Boston became home to a large accumulation of R&D resources and technological capabilities. In fact, the establishment of a national science and technology infrastructure and a regional concentration of industrial technological capabilities and engineering expertise in Greater Boston were interactive elements in a complementary and mutually reinforcing dynamic pivoting around MIT.

MIT's contribution, used to great effect by Bush, was a consequence of a long-established culture that lies at the center of the region's innovation system. Established by the Morrill Act of 1862,[1] MIT was from the 1880s an engineering university closely allied to industry but whose institutional culture, curricula, and research programs have been suffused, not without intense debate and counterpressures, by the ideal of open science (Lécuyer 1998). Involvement of the region's leading universities ensured a powerful voice for open research (David 1998). As we shall see in the next section, academic pressures for open science facilitated access to the nation's S&T infrastructure by firms of all sizes and thereby the transition to an open-system business model with positive feedback effects on the creation and enactment of innovation opportunities. Other regions were not so fortunate; entirely different business systems and polities emerged in regions lacking a vibrant educational culture of open science. The case of Greater Washington's "iron triangle" is examined in chapter 9.

Transition to a High-Tech, Open-System Business Model

The potential impact on business and economic development of the region's unrivaled concentration of public R&D resources was illustrated by the minicomputer industry. At its peak in the early 1980s, DEC (Digital Equipment Corporation) employed 124,000 globally and spearheaded

1. For more on the Morrill Act, see chapter 9.

the establishment of the region's minicomputer industry. Overall, a half-dozen Massachusetts minicomputer giants employed more than 200,000 globally at the industry's peak in 1985.

Nevertheless, the minicomputer industry exhibited a fatal flaw that led to its early demise in Massachusetts. Its contraction was not the result of a lack of innovation by the leading companies. In fact, the companies involved were ferocious innovators. Rather, the industry lost out to a rival business system. The weakness was technology management at the collective level. The region's minicomputer companies individually pursued a vertical integration business strategy in contrast to the open-system or focus-and-network business model of Silicon Valley (Grove 1996). Sun computers, for example, were designed with common interface rules and operating system source code to plug in microprocessors from Intel, IBM, Motorola, or AMD; disk drives from Seagate or Quantum; memory chips from Hitachi or Samsung; printers from HP or Xerox; and word processing applications from competing vendors. This, in turn, set in motion the industrial ecosystem dynamics described above.

The minicomputer companies of Massachusetts were great system integrators at the level of the individual enterprise. DEC, for example, designed, produced, and bundled all the major computer components but within a *closed*, centralized product architecture. Design was concentrated in a single company rather than an *open* product architecture in which design was decentralized and diffused across multiple specialist component producers. The customer could not mix and match hardware and software components such as printers and word processing programs.

Engineering system integration was critical to both regional business models. The difference was that the Massachusetts companies did system integration at the enterprise level and the Silicon Valley companies did system integration at the regional level. The considerable individual technological strengths of the Massachusetts companies turned into a sector-wide innovation deficit and individual-level commercial weakness. They were vulnerable to the rival open-system business model that emerged first in Silicon Valley, which exhibited superior industrywide innovation performance. Moreover, the business capability to organize supply-chain networks associated with mass-production consumer products is not in Greater Boston's organizational DNA.

Consequently, between 1985 and 1992 the industry that had driven the regional economy collapsed. The end of the Cold War brought a simultaneous decline in the defense industry, and the region's industrial future appeared bleak. The precipitous collapse of the minicomputer industry echoed, on a sharper scale, the much slower decline in textiles and footwear, the region's previous large-scale industries.

However, contrary to expectations, Massachusetts remained technologically entrepreneurial. R&D performed as a percentage of GDP rose from 5 percent to 8 percent between 2001 and 2008 and between 2011 and 2014 settled at between 5 and 6 percent, the highest in the nation.[2] The state's per capita income remained near the top in the nation.

The companies and sectors driving industrial renewal were obscure. The innovators did not fit Schumpeter's dictum: "What we have got to accept is that ... the large scale establishment ... has come to be the most powerful engine of ... progress" (2008 [1942]: 106). They were not giant enterprises funding R&D laboratories from scale economies and oligopolistic profits (Chandler 1977). Instead the outlines of a population of innovative high-tech SMEs that had emerged over the postwar decades began to come into view.

The term "high-tech" was first used in the late 1960s to describe the science-based companies and government-sponsored laboratories along Boston's Route 128, a perimeter road completed in 1951 to facilitate the flow of traffic around the city. In the words of a contemporary observer: "It is not clear whether the name [high-tech] derives from the high technologies flourishing in the glass rectangles along the route or from the Midas touch their entrepreneurs have shown in starting new companies ... maybe both" (Lieberman 1968, 139). Lieberman attributed the success of an estimated 690 such entities on Boston's "Golden Semicircle ... to 'uniqueness' of the average company's technology ... and the availability of government contracts during the early years" (1968; see also Roberts 1991).

It was within the Route 128 corridor that early-stage technology development combined with the rapid growth of enterprises to foster the so-called Massachusetts miracle. Although originally dubbed "The Road to Nowhere," Route 128 was soon signposted "America's Technology Region" (Earls 2002, 7). The number of research-based companies located in seventeen industrial parks along the Route 128 corridor grew rapidly to an estimated 574 in 1965 and 1,212 in 1973 (Rosegrant and Lampe 1992, 130). By the mid-1980s there were nearly 3,000 high-tech companies in Massachusetts, a number that has continued to approximate the popula-

2. Data are from the *Index of the Massachusetts Innovation Economy* 2011, 32; 2012, 26; and 2016, 35. For 2016 see www.masstech.org/sites/mtc/files/documents/2016_Index /MAInnovationEconomy_2016.pdf.

tion of all business units in Massachusetts that engage in R&D and design and develop next-generation technologies (CorpTech, various years;
Best 2003a). The Mass High Tech Directory had roughly twice the number by the 1990s, but they included many that did not develop, as distinct
from use, high-tech products and services. Many have been recipients of
federal technology development programs. For example, the region leads
in the take-up of Small Business Innovation Research grants (*Index of the
Massachusetts Innovation Economy*, various years).

The high-tech enterprises that emerged in the Greater Boston area
are not conventional SMEs. Each is an individual unit within a localized
population of enterprises that collectively form an open-system business
model. Many do applied science, and most engage in early-stage technology development. Few sell consumer products in retail markets. All seek
to establish a distinctive technological capability under conditions of technological uncertainty and rapid technological change. They are collectively innovative, not because the firms own laboratories independent of
production operations but because most SMEs design and conduct experiments as part of ongoing operations.

At the core of the open-system business model is the competitive
focus-and-network strategy as individual firms focus on core capabilities
and network for complementary capabilities. But the system also has a reverse network-and-focus feedback dynamic: as more networks are formed,
opportunities are created for new entrants to specialize in niches and
plug into existing networks.

While companies focus on technology development, they coordinate
extended innovation process chains that can include direct and indirect
access to government-funded and university-conducted basic research. In
this way the interorganizational relations organized within and by each
firm are a microeconomic variant of the triple helix of triangular interrelations involving industry, academia, and government that were established to design, develop, and create technologically advanced weapons
during World War II.

Thus for the first time a localized population of SMEs emerged in
which each member could partner with others, as needed, to engage all of
the multiple activities along the innovation process chain (Kline 1985). As
some opportunities for innovation are selected and others culled in the
competitive process, the region's technical knowledge base is deepened,
technologies are further differentiated, and new opportunities for innovation are created for innovation elsewhere in the population of enterprises.
The cumulative and collective result is an industrial ecosystem at the core

of which are thousands of technologically differentiated enterprises placing bets on their vision of, and capacity to produce, next-generation technologies. As needed, companies coordinate their research, development, production, and funding activities in the form of innovation process chains that cut across companies, government and university research labs, education institutions, technical communities, and financial institutions.

The potential for diverse technologies to create innovation opportunities has long been recognized as a consequence of "unplanned confluences of technology from different fields" (Kostoff 1994, 61; see also Schumpeter 1934, 65, and Jacobs in chap. 4 of this book). From this perspective, a population of technologically differentiated enterprises, unlike any single firm, offers the potential of a technological full house (Gould 1996), with a variety and range of research- and production-related activities that can foster creativity, fill gaps, replenish the knowledge pool, link needs to research, and incite an unplanned confluence of technologies.

The result is a never-ending systemic process of the creation, closure, and renewal of niche opportunities. Niche opportunities emerge in the form of promising but as yet unexplored technological possibilities (Best 2001, 74–79). Figure 3.2 illustrates a series of niche opportunities pursued by new entrants into the telecommunications network-switches sector that emerged in Greater Boston to build the Internet infrastructure (elaborated in the next section). Eventual enterprise winners and emergent growth sectors are unknowable in advance. But the great diversity of technological experiments by focused and specialized enterprises expands the pool of potential candidates for successful innovation and thereby the possibilities of sector emergence and regional technology consolidation.

The enterprise population dynamics are pivotal to the sectoral transition process. The open-system business model counteracts the tendency toward technological lock-in associated with big, once dominant firms that fail to reorganize to take advantage of new technologies or to recognize nascent market opportunities (Christensen 1997). Loasby argues that competing visions among firms are necessary to an evolutionary or experimental economy; in contrast, "competing visions within firms, unless very carefully managed, and limited in scope, cause trouble" (2000, 11; see also Maskell 2001, 928).

The next section presents a series of rapidly growing sectors that have both benefited from and regenerated the region's unique industrial ecosystem. They collectively draw from and regenerate the region's comparative advantage in early-stage technology development and complex product systems (Best 2001, 140–43; Prencipe, Davies, and Hobday 2003).

Examples of New Sector Growth

This section presents examples of rapid-growth high-tech sectors identified by interrogation of the database vTHREAD (see above) to Greater
Boston's high-tech companies from 1990 to 2003/4. The enterprise demo-
graphics of the rapid-growth sectors follow a general sequential pattern.
First, a successful innovating company is immediately followed by a group
of technology-differentiated companies in the same expanding market.
Second, another group of established companies in closely related technologies begins a process of repositioning into the growing market. Many
of these firms offer products in two or more standard classification codes.
Third, intersector opportunities are created for technological convergence.
Fourth, growing firms drive a reshuffling process by which the region's productive resources, including expertise, assets, and facilities, are released
from declining sectors and absorbed by growing sectors, as illustrated for
software and telecommunications in Greater Lowell in tables 3.1 and
3.2.[3] The tables show the number of companies in the vTHREAD sample
of companies headquartered in the adjoining townships of Lowell, Chelmsford, and Westford that offered products in software or telecommunications sometime over the period 1997–2004, the year each was founded,
and the number of employees for each year. It reveals a population of
co-located companies with high rates of entry, a few of which grew rapidly
while most remained small.

Fifth, leading companies headquartered outside the state are attracted
to the region, often by acquiring a small local company. In fact, sixty-nine
of the two hundred largest employers in Massachusetts are headquartered out of state (examples include IBM, HP, Microsoft, J&J, and Cisco
Systems). Moreover, as shown in figure 3.3, roughly 8–9 percent of the
state's approximately three thousand high-tech business units are foreign-
headquartered (see Best, Paquin, and Xie 2004).

MEDICAL DEVICES

Medi-Tech, a small R&D company founded by inventor Itzhak Bentov
in the 1960s, developed a steerable polyethylene balloon catheter for the
nonsurgical opening of clogged arteries in 1978. A year later, Boston Scientific was established to acquire Medi-Tech and turn it into a market
leader in promoting the new procedure of inserting stents nonsurgically.

---

3. Greater Lowell includes the townships of Chelmsford, Lowell, and Westford.

Table 3.1. Software Industry Churn (Greater Lowell, Massachusetts, 1997–2003)

Company name	Year formed	Base year 1997	1998	1999	2000	2001	2002	2003
Frontier Software Development Inc.	1984	50						
Carberry Technology	1989	10						
Electronic Book Technologies Inc./Carberry	1989	10						
Voicetek Corporation	1981	120	175					
Statistics Unlimited Inc.	1986	5	5					
Connolly International Ltd.	1991	25	25					
Gartner Group Learning	1987	N/A	66					
ProMetrics Software Inc.	1982	10	85	10				
Adra Systems Inc.	1983	180	190	65				
Gulf Computer Inc./LangBox Division	1994	200	200	100–249				
Gulf Computer Inc.	1979	200	200	200			Exit	
Gulf Computer Inc./Spartacus Technologies	1981	200	200	100–249				
GeoTel Communications Corp.	1993	N/A	115	200				
Mehta Corporation	1991	N/A	85	75				
Spacetec IMC Corporation	1991	N/A	76	76				
Utility Systems Inc.	1987	11	11	11	11			
Software Solutions of America Inc.	1979	6	6	6	6			
Quester Software Services Inc.	1977	3	3	<10	<10			
Silinsh Software	1984	1	1	1	1			
Fundvest Inc.	1983	N/A	2	2	2			
ONTOS Inc.	1985	60	60	60	40	40		
EDS-Scicon Inc.	1984	N/A	N/A	70	100	100		
Quallaby Corp.	1996	N/A	N/A	N/A	N/A	90		
Iris Associates Inc.	1984	96	160	350	350	350	500	
Harmon Technologies Inc.	1985	N/A	N/A	10	10	10	10	
Global Telemedix Inc.	1995	N/A	N/A	N/A	16	16	16	
NextPoint Networks Inc.	1996	N/A	N/A	N/A	50–99	N/A	300	
e-StudioLive Inc.	1971	N/A	N/A	N/A	N/A	N/A	50	

[illegible]	[illegible]	16	17	16	17	17	14	14
A.P. Software	1987	1	1	1	1	1	1	1
Visual Solutions Inc.	1989	10	10	10	10	10	10	10
Crown Systems Inc.	1980	6	6	6	6	6	6	6
SoftLinx Inc.	1980	20	30	30	30	30	40	40
Nonprofit Management Systems	1983	3	3	3	3	3	3	3
Lerman Associates	1985	2	2	2	2	2	2	2
Trix Systems Inc.	1994	23	12	12	13	16	17	17
Davox Corp.	1981	N/A	300	300	300	398	400	470
NetScout Systems Inc.	1984	N/A	140	190	220	220	364	355
Lincoln & Co.	1978	N/A	N/A	10	10	10	10	10
Quickturn Design Systems Inc./Advanced Simulation Division	1993	N/A	N/A	39	45	45	45	45
MatrixOne Inc.	1994	N/A	N/A	200	350	366	500	600
Duxbury Systems Inc.	1976	N/A	N/A	N/A	13	13	13	15
Datawatch Corp.	1985	N/A	N/A	N/A	230	230	175	98
Zuken USA Inc.	1983	N/A	N/A	N/A	N/A	N/A	500	500
Tariva Inc.	1991	N/A	N/A	N/A	N/A	N/A	14	14
Digital Voice Systems Inc.	1988	N/A	N/A	N/A	N/A	N/A	20	20
Asset Technology Group	1991	N/A	N/A	N/A	N/A	N/A	3	3
Universal Software Corp.	1992	N/A	N/A	N/A	N/A	N/A	140	140
Viridien Technologies Inc.	1997	N/A	N/A	N/A	N/A	N/A	60	Exit
Hyperwave Information Management Inc.	1997	N/A	N/A	N/A	N/A	16	N/A	N/A
Vikor Inc.	1999			N/A	N/A	N/A	45	14
Brix Networks	1999			N/A	N/A	N/A	N/A	66
EnrichNet Inc.	1999			N/A	N/A	10	10	Exit
Provanum Co.	1999		**Entry**	N/A	N/A	3	3	
Financial Systems Architects	1999			N/A	N/A	14	14	10
Mission Critical Linux Inc.	1999			N/A	N/A	75	75	8
IBEX Process Technology Inc.	2000				N/A	N/A	9	18
Amperion Inc.	2000				N/A	N/A	1	Exit

Source: Best (2003a, table 3).

Note: N/A = not available.

Table 3.2. Telecommunications Industry Churn (Greater Lowell, Massachusetts, 1997–2004)

Company name	Frmd	1997	1998	1999	2000	2001	2002	2003	2004
M/A-COM Inc.	1958	SUB	SUB	SUB	SUB	SUB	SUB	3325	3325
ZipLink, LLC	1960	N/A	COM	COM	54	85		OoB	
Quallaby Corp.	1996	N/A	N/A	SOF	SOF	SOF	110	110	65
Lockheed Martin Microwave-FSI	1964	240	240				Acquired		
ITK International	1984	103	200				Acquired		
California Microwave/Microwave Networks	1987	100	100				Merged		
Microwave Radio Communications	1987	140	150	150			Merged		
Ascend Communications/Core Systems	1990	170	922	922			Acquired		
Tektronix Inc./BTT Division	1989	80	90	90	98	98	98	50–99	Merged
Optronics International Corp.	1968	190	80	80	100		MA		
e-Studio Live Inc.	1971	N/A	N/A	N/A	18	55	52	23	MA
AXIS Communications Inc.	1984	N/A	MA		55	55	50	MA	23
Davox Corp.[a]	1981	185	300	300	300	398	400	470	460
Biscom Inc.	1986	42	50	70	60	66	60	60	60
Openpages Inc.	1990	N/A	N/A	N/A	N/A	140	70	50	50
Intraplex Inc.	1987	Unk	Unk	53	N/A	N/A	N/A	N/A	N/A
UNIFI Communications Inc.	1990	MA	600	500	Unk	Unk		OoB	
Acacia Networks Inc.	1995	N/A	N/A	60	60	60		Out of Contact	
OrderTrust Inc.	1995	N/A	N/A	N/A	N/A	200		OoB	
Avici Systems Inc.	1996	N/A	30	80	N/A		MA		

Company	Founded	Q1 1997	Q1 1998	Q1 1999	Q1 2000	Q1 2001	Q1 2002	Q1 2003	Q1 2004
Integral Access Inc.	1996	N/A	N/A	N/A	N/A	105	150	149	Unk
ArrowPoint Communications Inc.	1997	Entry	N/A	40	80	Unk	Acquired	Acquired	Merged
Nortel Networks/Network Access	1997	Entry	N/A	66	Unk	115	250	250	371
Sonus Networks Inc.	1997	Entry	N/A	N/A	115	70	745	497	93
Captivate Network Inc.	1997	Entry	N/A	N/A	N/A	N/A	70	93	93
NetNumber Inc.	1997	Entry	N/A	N/A	N/A	103	N/A	29	29
Convergent Networks Inc.	1998		Entry	N/A	N/A	100	300	Unk	405
Sycamore Networks Inc.[b]	1998		Entry	N/A	100	30	460	460	50–99
Brix Networks[c]	1999			Entry	N/A	500	100	50–99	50–99
Unisphere Networks Inc.	1999			Entry	N/A	Unk	750	Acquired	Acquired
Crescent Networks	1999			Entry	N/A	N/A	66	14	OoB
Cratos Networks	1999			Entry	N/A	N/A	66	OoB	OoB
WaterCove Networks Inc.	2000				Entry	N/A	100	110	110
Storigen Systems Inc.	2000				Entry	N/A	30	65	66
Narad Networks Inc.	2000				Entry	N/A	125	149	50
Creative eTECH Inc.	2000				Entry	N/A	140	140	149
SnowShore Networks Inc.	2000				Entry	N/A	60	60	45

Source: Best, Paquin, and Xie (2004, table 4).

Notes: Q1 1997, Q1 1998, Q1 1999, Q1 2000, Q1 2001, Q1 2002, Q1 2003, Q1 2004, CorpTech. N/A = not listed in CorpTech; MA = other Massachusetts towns, suggesting that a relocation took place; Unk = listed by CorpTech but employment unknown; Merged = merger of multiple units within a corporation; OoB = out of business.

[a] Davox Corp industry code changed from TEL to SOF (photonics) in 1998.

[b] Sycamore Networks industry code changed from TEL to PHO (photonics) in 2004.

[c] Brix Networks industry code changed from TEL to SOF (computer software) in 2003.

Technology category

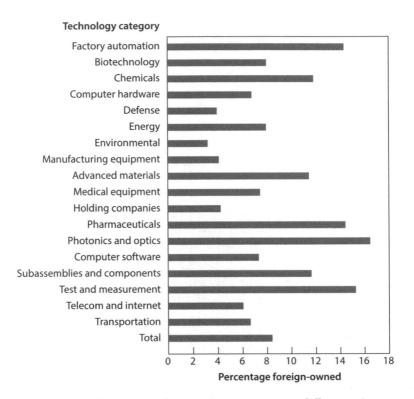

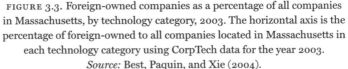

FIGURE 3.3. Foreign-owned companies as a percentage of all companies in Massachusetts, by technology category, 2003. The horizontal axis is the percentage of foreign-owned to all companies located in Massachusetts in each technology category using CorpTech data for the year 2003.
Source: Best, Paquin, and Xie (2004).

Peter Nicolas, a co-founder, had previously run the medical products division of Millipore, a purification engineering company founded in 1954. Boston Scientific went on to establish the industry standard for drug-eluting coronary stents, a second breakthrough innovation. The steerable catheter and drug-device combination attracted imitators for a variety of applications. Both contributed to Boston's leadership in a new sector-defining concept known as minimum-invasive therapy.

Within less than three decades, Massachusetts went from a very small presence in the national medical-device industry to one of the top three. Boston Scientific grew steadily to over 14,000 employees by 2004. But by the same year we identified 177 companies classified as medical-device firms; another 105 companies not classified as medical-device companies that made medical-device products; and 21 foreign-headquartered companies with divisions or facilities in Massachusetts. We estimated a total of 71 of these domestic and foreign companies had more than 200 employees (Best 2005 and 2006).

INTERNET SWITCHING EQUIPMENT

The manufacture of telecommunications equipment is not new to the region. The location in the 1930s of AT&T's 2 million-square-foot manufacturing site in North Andover established a large-scale telecommunications switching and transmission equipment production site north of Boston. Known as the Merrimack Valley Works, the plant built circuit-switching equipment to optimize massive volumes of voice traffic over the traditional Bell telephone system.

The facility did not adapt to Internet-driven technology and was closed in the late 1990s. The closure, however, did not signal the end of telecommunications technology expertise in the region any more than the demise of the giant minicomputer companies had meant the end of computer technology expertises. Instead the region became the site of a large group of new, fast-growing companies specializing in the design and development of the Internet telecommunications hardware and software transmission infrastructure (see fig. 3.2). But instead of one giant switch-making company, a large, technologically differentiated cluster of communications-network companies emerged. They specialized in combining legacy circuit switching with digital packet-switching hardware equipment and embedded software systems.

The region's rapid technology consolidation in industrial network switching equipment both attracted and was reinforced by the entry of foreign telecommunications systems companies such as Siemens, Alcatel, and Nortel as well as Cisco Systems, the Silicon Valley newcomer. All acquired production locations along Interstate 495, the second highway circling Boston.

ENTERPRISE SOFTWARE TOOLS

The equipment makers were not the only enterprises in the region's rapidly growing telecommunications industry. A closely related software tools group underwent similar differentiation and transformation dynamics. In fact, roughly the same number of network communication software tools companies as equipment makers was formed in the 1980s and 1990s

(Best 2016). These companies were growing in sync with the expanding network communications equipment companies.

The communications software tools companies are part of a large regional cluster of enterprise software tools companies. Software tools companies are functionally analogous to the machine tool companies of the region's industrial past. Then, as now, tools companies diffuse technological innovations across multiple downstream sectors.

The broader category of information technology was the fastest-growing Massachusetts industry in the 1990s. Between 1989 and 1996 Massachusetts software companies, output, and employment nearly tripled: the number of companies increased from 800 to 2,200, revenues from $3 billion to $7.8 billion, and employment from 46,000 to 130,000 (Rosenberg 1999).

BIOTECH

Official biotechnology R&D employment in Massachusetts was 34,366 (of a total Massachusetts biopharma employment of 66,053), which narrowly exceeded that of California, the only other state with a comparable concentration (MassBio 2017, 3). In a comparison of the leading sixteen US life-science clusters, Boston ranked first in five of six indicators (employment, science and engineering graduate students, funding by the National Institutes of Health, R&D expenditures, and research facilities) and second in venture capital funding (Jones Lang Lasalle 2011, 16).

The emergence and rapid growth of the biotech industry in Massachusetts is a story of dynamic intersector opportunity-creation effects with information technology, nanotechnology, and medical devices. For example, the region's expertise in computer science was a critical input into bioinformatics. But the computational requirements needed for genome sequencing are an order of magnitude higher than for circuitry design. Furthermore, the genomics and proteomics revolutions have created demands for self-assembly fabrication techniques for nanoscale medical devices and biopolymer materials to deliver drugs.

The application to life sciences is new, but an important source of the competitive advantage of the region's biotech industry resonates with another analogy from evolution in the natural world: "descent with modification" (Darwin 1979 [1859], 450–51). As noted, Massachusetts companies have been at the leading edge of driving down critical size dimensions since the historical origins of the machining and tooling industries based on the application of the production principle of interchangeability in the nineteenth century. In the words of Jim Vincent (chair and CEO of Biogen Inc.) and Henri Termeer (chair and CEO of Genzyme Corp.): "Many of the tools revolutionizing the pharmaceutical discovery and development process—genomics, bioinformatics, and combinatorial chemistry— have been invented and continue to flourish in this region" (Vincent and Termeer 2000, A15). They add: "It is no wonder that a number of the world's major pharmaceutical companies have chosen to locate research and development facilities in the Boston area."

Business Development Finance

Technological innovation and business finance innovation co-evolved in the establishment, growth, and regenerative capability of Greater Boston's high-tech economy.[4] It is in the money market that the economic projects are assessed, development is financed, and the "system of future values first appears" (Schumpeter 1934, 125; Best 1990, 121–22; Perez 2002; Janeway 2012). The evolution of Boston's uniquely differentiated financial system was a consequence of timely responses to innovation opportunities generated in the real sectors.

Two important financial adaptations accompanied the surge of Greater Boston's population of high-tech enterprises in the 1950s. The first came from the Bank of Boston, the region's largest bank at the time. Informed by Schumpeter-inspired entrepreneurial research, the Bank of Boston pursued an aggressive campaign to lend against the security provided by the value of federal contracts and receivables (Frankel, Fulman, and Howell 1988). In 1958 the federal government passed the Small Business Investment Company (SBIC) law enabling private investment companies to leverage investment dollars by borrowing from the federal Small Business Agency. By acquiring an SBIC license, a bank could own stock and make venture capital investments for the first time since the 1930s; the Bank of Boston seized the opportunity and grew expertise in venture investments (Rosegrant and Lampe 1992, 120–21).

The second financial adaptation was the first emergence and rapid growth of a specialized public venture capital industry, which began with the founding of the American Research and Development Corporation

4. I am grateful to David Lubin for sharing his insider knowledge of Boston's uniquely differentiated financial ecosystem.

Ralph Flanders, 1880–1970.
Source: Courtesy U.S. Senate Historical Office.

(AR&D) in 1946 (Ante 2008; Rao and Scaruffi 2013). AR&D was the first financial enterprise dedicated to the venture capital concept of spreading the risk of failure across a group of emerging investment opportunities. It was founded by Georges Doriot (the oft-cited father of venture capital), with Karl Compton, president of MIT, and Ralph Flanders, president of the Federal Reserve Bank of Boston, in 1946 (Ante 2008). Dubbed the perfect marriage, AR&D invested $70,000 for 70 percent of DEC in 1957. When AR&D liquidated its investment fifteen years later, DEC was worth $400 million.

AR&D, following the Bank of Boston, was the entrepreneurial leader in the creation of a large business development finance industry in Greater Boston. Today Massachusetts and California are roughly equal in venture capital investment per capita, a level that is four to five times that of the other leading technology states (*Index of the Massachusetts Innovation Economy* 2011, 44).

Venture capital has multiple Schumpeterian functions, as illustrated by the activities of AR&D. The first is to search for and evaluate successful experiments. Doriot and his staff had intimate knowledge of the projects and people involved in science and engineering research in universities and national laboratories in the region. The second is to manage a growth dynamic, integrating the supply of and demand for investment funds. AR&D complemented federal sponsorship of basic research and proof of concept with the private finance of early-stage technology development (Branscomb and Auerswald 2002). This involved organizing the region's university endowments, the emerging mutual fund industry, the insurance sector, and wealthy families to collectively meet the financial needs of risky but promising high-tech start-ups. Third, AR&D participated in the governance of companies in which it invested. In the case of DEC, its board of ten directors included five AR&D staff.

The venture capital industry has served yet a fourth Schumpeterian function: strategic industrial regeneration. The region's financial system recycles resources from past successes into new ventures. The real growth sectors described above recycle technological resources from past ventures into new ones. In both ways, resources generated in yesterday's growth and today's maturing sectors are recycled into tomorrow's growing companies and emerging sectors.

Spencer Ante's biography of Georges Doriot is also a history of the contribution of Ralph Flanders (Ante 2008). It may be the best book yet written on the real story of Greater Boston's conversion from a region struggling with declining traditional industries to its transformation into a region with a global advantage in the emergence, creation, and growth of new high-tech sectors. It is a story of how four leaders with different kinds of expertise teamed up together before, during, and after World War II to self-consciously design and implement a combined private and public policy framework to build an entirely new model of regional technological and industrial development: Flanders, a mechanical engineer who became head of Jones and Lamson Machine Tool Company and later a prominent senator; Merrill Griswold, president of Massachusetts Investors Trust; MIT President Karl Compton; and Doriot, a Harvard Business School professor and wartime military officer with a Schumpeter-like understanding of the links connecting finance, innovation, and technology development with business development.

Skill Formation and Multilevel Government

Enterprise or governmental policy initiatives to make the transition to more advanced models of technology management or technology domains (see fig. 3.1) will be undone without the requisite skill base. Regional growth processes are limited by the supply of engineering and scientific personnel available to staff rapidly growing firms. Mutual adjustments between technology-advancing enterprises and skill formation institutions, internal and external to the enterprise, are integral to growth dynamics.

An example is the development of electronics and the minicomputer industry in Massachusetts during the "Miracle Years." A remarkable feature of the Miracle Years (1978–1986/7) was the responsiveness of the education system to the skill requirements of the rapidly growing firms. As shown in figure 3.4, the number of BS degrees in electrical engineering conferred by Massachusetts universities and colleges increased from around 700 in 1982 to nearly 1,700 in 1988.

The expansion in a region's "production" of engineers is a costly process. A ballpark estimate for a stepwise increase of 1,000 engineering graduates was $50 million annually in the 1980s (Best 2001, 155–56). Although this number is a small fraction of the increased output in the state, it was a big number for the public educational institutions that expanded their engineering programs.

Only government has both the funds and the legitimacy to implement educational restructuring and investments on the scale involved. Nevertheless, the state government was not the leader but rather a third partner in the implementation of an informal manpower development plan. The rapidly growing technology-driven firms and the engineering deans were the active partners in designing and implementing the expansion.

Technology-driven firms had resources but lacked skilled labor; local universities had students but lacked resources. To address the mismatch, the Massachusetts High Technology Council sponsored a meeting of the founders of many of the region's leading high-technology firms and the chancellors of higher education institutions. In what became known as the "2 percent solution," the firms agreed to provide 2 percent of their annual R&D budgets to educational institutions in exchange for an agreement by the educational institutions to expand their engineering programs. The firms acted on their agreement. Much of the funding came in the form of equipment. Engineering faculty in Massachusetts's regional engineering programs were the first to be equipped with minicomputer workstations.

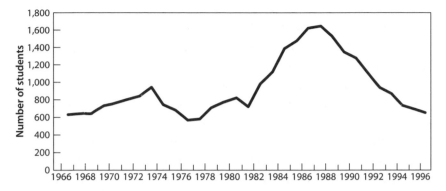

FIGURE 3.4. Electrical engineering graduates in Massachusetts, 1966–1996.
Source: Data supplied by John Hoy, president, New England Board of Higher Education.

As a manpower planning exercise, the limited number of firms that drove the economy during the Miracle Years simplified coordination of the demand for and supply of skilled labor. The result was a step increase in both engineering graduates and the technical skill base of the region. Technology-driven firms, educational institutions, and government funding partnered to provide the skill base required to fuel the growth and development of America's first high-tech regional innovation system. Against the costs to the public were the benefits not only to the students involved and the hiring firms but also to the region's economy. The high-tech labor pool did not disappear with the minicomputer industry; it became a productive resource enabling the emergence and rapid subsequent growth of a series of high-tech sectors.

But the education investment challenge did not stop here. Complementary skill formation at the intermediate and lower skill levels was equally important to expand the pool of potential college entrants in engineering and the sciences. Claudia Goldin dates the American "high school movement" to the period between the 1890s and 1920s. The male high school graduation rate, which stood at 10–15 percent of the cohort born in 1890, rose to nearly 50 percent for those born after World War I (1998). This spectacular transition accompanied the rise of mass-production industries in America and the manufacturing productivity revolution of the 1920s. Relying on empirical research by John Kendrick (1961), David and Wright (1999) point to an annual leap in manufacturing output per man-hour from 1.5 percent in the first decade and a half of the twentieth century to 5.5 percent in the 1920s.

The upgrading of skills across the labor force made it possible to diffuse the new production system and technological capabilities associated with the electrical revolution across much of the manufacturing sector. All three elements of the Capability Triad were reintegrated at a more advanced level of production capabilities. The 1920s witnessed the transition to the multidivisional model of business organization captured by Chandler's history of the business enterprise (1961, 1977). The new business model created a managerial hierarchy with the organizational capability to extend the principle of flow to new product applications. The development of mass-production capabilities depended on the invention of distributed electric power, which made it possible to conceive of the manufacturing challenge as one of equalizing cycle times (see chap. 2).

In these ways, local and state government financing of the high school movement was a powerful indirect industrial policy. It not only advanced the skills of those who worked in manufacturing and managed the new managerial enterprises. It also created a huge pool of students that made it possible to expand engineering and science education at the college level.

Discussion and Conclusions

The 1990s witnessed a diverse range of theoretical breakthroughs involving the integration of space into economic doctrine. As we shall elaborate in greater detail in the next chapter, Nobel Prize winner Paul Krugman applied increasing returns to Marshall's localization concept of specialist suppliers to create models of industrial specialization that transformed trade theory (1991, 2008). Nobel Prize winner Robert Lucas (1988, 38) attributed the endogenous growth revolution to Jane Jacobs's (1969) concrete examples of knowledge spillover effects from new ideas created by group interactions in cities. Complexity theorists cite Adam Smith's invisible hand metaphor as an early illustration of complex adaptive systems (Johnson 2001; Beinhocker 2007). Michael Porter's cluster perspective inserted the physical proximity of world-class rivals between the microeconomic and macroeconomic worlds of neoclassical theory to explain the competitive advantage of nations (1990). Economic geographers challenged social scientists to address evolutionary and complexity thinking (Martin and Sunley 2007; Ter Wal and Boschma 2011).

Controversies over the role of place in economic theory were followed by a burst of empirical research across disciplinary boundaries to characterize spatial knowledge spillovers and externalities that complement the research presented here. For example, Frenken, Van Oort, and Verburg (2007) combine official sectoral data with sophisticated statistical methodologies to analyze the regional growth effects of sectoral relatedness and diversity within the Netherlands. Owen-Smith and Powell (2006) apply patent data to social network analysis to compare collaborative relationships and regional variations in the form of innovative activity in the Boston and Bay Area biotechnology clusters. The same research methodology is employed by Meder, ter Wal, and Cantner (2010) to characterize innovator networks and regional knowledge bases in three European regions, and Casper (2013) examines knowledge spillover theories in two California biotech regions. Patent data are classified by finely granulated and periodically updated technology taxonomy codes that offer a major advantage over standard but comprehensive industrial classification systems. Thomson's comprehensive history of technological innovation across fourteen major industries in antebellum America illustrates the indicative potential of patent data (2009).

This chapter has introduced a Schumpeterian entrepreneurial function to the localization literature and a spatial/evolutionary dimension to Schumpeter's entrepreneurial agency. For Schumpeter, entrepreneurial activity is "getting a new thing done" (Schumpeter 1947, 151). Greater Boston offers a record of accomplishment for getting things done in the form of creating and growing new firms and sectors. Critically important, getting new things done entails creating new knowledge and releases expert resources to detect new entrepreneurial opportunities (Penrose 1959; Jacobs 1969). The system integration capability of the open-system business model extends the concept of dynamic capability from the property of a firm to that of an industrial ecosystem. Teece (in Teece, Pisano, and Shuen 1997, 516) defined dynamic capability as "the firm's ability to integrate, build, and reconfigure internal and external competences to address rapidly changing environments."

Breaking away from and offering something new in comparison with Schumpeter, this chapter has applied Darwin's evolutionary principles to suggest the importance of regions or habitat to systemic industrial innovation. This shifts the focus from the entrepreneur's perception of or response to opportunity, important as both are, to ways in which enterprises within a regional industrial ecosystem detect opportunities and a regional industrial ecosystem itself creates opportunities for innovation. The intellectual history of the evolutionary principle of increasing technological differentiation within a localized population involves both political economy and natural science. To quote Darwin: "The advantage of diversification in the inhabitants of the same region is, in fact, the same as that of the division of labour in the organs of the same individual body—a subject so well elucidated by Milne Edwards" (1979 [1859], 158). Henri

Milne-Edwards was a naturalist who applied Adam Smith's division of labor in industry to the organs of the body. Matt Ridley (2009, 12) adds: "Darwin promptly re-applied it to the division of labor amongst specialized species in an ecosystem."

Greater Boston is instructive for what it can tell us about the systemic processes by which a population of technologically differentiated high-tech firms mutually and iteratively discover, create, and enact innovation opportunities. The Greater Boston industrial knowledge-creation system works because companies of all sizes can conduct experiments and pursue technological innovations in a region with an assemblage of legacy technology assets and engineering expertise, multilevel science and technology funding, an independent educational community committed to the ideal of open science, and a financial sector with Marshallian "intimate knowledge" of emerging entrepreneurial activities.

Unlike natural habitats, the region's industrial ecosystem combines purposeful institutional design with bottom-up, self-organizing processes; in this it is a socially instituted ecosystem. Using different language, Dosi draws a similar distinction between "environmental selection of mutations" and the "selection of the 'mutation generating' mechanisms" (1982, 156). According to Ridley, "Dirigisme has a place ... in the regulation and operation if not the design of institutions" (2009, 12). The purposeful design dimension, in this case, is subtle. The constitution and relationships of Greater Boston's industrial ecosystem are the consequence of historically complex co-adaptive processes that create entrepreneurial opportunities in both the private and the public sectors. The supply of entrepreneurship itself is expanded in response to the systemic creation of opportunities and the ready access to the diverse range of expertise required to create and grow a business enterprise. While the winners drive transitions, the failing firms and declining sectors contribute as well. As described above, the decline of the minicomputer industry released cutting-edge IT expertise, assets, and facilities for reassembly by new and repositioning firms conducting experiments in pursuit of incipient opportunities in emerging sectors including Internet-related telecommunications and biotech informatics.

Greater Boston's regional economy is a real-world laboratory for characterizing the system dynamics of industrial innovation. It is a complex regenerative industrial ecosystem the secrets of which are revealed only by closely grained empirical research.

CHAPTER FOUR

The Capability Triad in the History of Economics

One of the primary assumptions of the theory of the growth of firms is that "history matters"; growth is essentially an evolutionary process based on the cumulative growth of collective knowledge, in the context of the purposive firm.

—EDITH PENROSE, *THE THEORY OF THE GROWTH OF THE FIRM*, 1959

WITH TWO EPISODES of economic transformation considered from a production-centric perspective under our belts, this chapter brings us back to economic theory but indeed not economics or theory as students today will know them. This chapter puts together a procession of important but seemingly disparate thinkers. Many would not be considered either political economists or experts in production, but they are revealed to have shared a methodological stance and a keen interest in the dynamics of change, both of which caused them to bring production into an alternative economics. With growing confidence, we use our survey of ideas to build an economics that can be used to strip away the mystification of episodes of rapid growth and understand them not as miracles but as the intended outcomes of purposeful actions informed by a production-centric policy framework: the capability triad.

Although the real world of production has been transformed beyond recognition since the Industrial Revolution, the theory of production within the standard economic paradigm has remained locked in place. It is inseparable from a theory of exchange and at the core of the difference between the capabilities (or production-centric) and the individual choice (or market-centric) paradigms. The recognized flaw in the mainstream account has long been the inability until recently to cope with increasing returns, and even then their general neglect of a phenomenon that is rampant in the real world.

The Unmet Challenge of Increasing Returns

The algebraic production function of today's textbooks is implicit in the verbal accounts of the "law of diminishing returns" applied to agriculture by the French physiocratic school preceding the publication of Adam Smith's *Wealth of Nations*. For David Ricardo, the diminishing returns to land inspired a theory of income distribution. Rents, wages, and profits are both the costs of production and the return to landowners, labor, and the "undertaker," the contemporary term for men of business.

Charles Cobb and Paul Douglas's "A Theory of Production," published in 1928, was the culmination of a long history in economic thought. The theoretical elegance of the nearly two centuries–old concept that became the neoclassical production function is beyond reproach.[1] The neoclassical production function is at once a theory of both production and income distribution, and it also unifies decision-making in production with individual rational choice theory. It is almost as elegant and synthesizing as $E = mc^2$. No wonder it became integral to mainstream economics.

On its own terms, the standard paradigm is mathematically elegant and logically unassailable. Expenditure, income distribution, and output are integrated into a conceptual framework in which the total returns to the "factors of production" in rents, wages, and profits exactly exhaust the total output of the economy and both are equal to total spending. The mathematical elegance, however, depended on the assumption of increasing marginal costs of production, which clashed with the economies of scale in the age of mass production. Increasing returns violated the assumptions required for an equilibrium theory of competitive prices upon which mainstream economics based its claim to scientific validity. The problem of integrating increasing returns into mainstream economics has long been recognized.[2] The stumbling block was the threat posed to the assumptions of perfect competition.

---

1. The German Johann Heinrich von Thünen applied differential calculus to productivity theory and was likely the first to solve economic optimization problems that decades later defined the marginalist revolution of the 1870s (Humphrey 1997, 61).

2. For a review of major contributions, see Best (1990, chap. 4) and Shackle (2010).

With perfect competition, demand and supply in the marketplace would adjust to a level of output at which price equaled the marginal cost of production across the economy. This is precisely the rule by which Smith's "invisible hand" achieves the optimality rules upon which the science of economics was framed. Without rising costs of production, the level of output and prices in the economy has no reason to converge with the optimality rules.

John Hicks made the classic statement of what was at stake in *Value and Capital*, one of the great books in the history of economics:

> It has to be recognized that a general abandonment of the assumption of perfect competition ... must have very destructive consequences for economic theory. Under monopoly the stability conditions become indeterminant; and the basis on which economic laws can be constructed is therefore shorn away....

> It is, I believe, only possible to save anything from this wreck—and it must be remembered that the threatened wreckage is that of the greater part of general equilibrium theory—if we can assume that the markets confronting most of the firms with which we shall be dealing do not differ very greatly from perfectly competitive markets.

> At least, this get-away seems well worth trying. We must be aware, however, that we are taking a dangerous step, and probably limiting to a serious extent the problems with which our subsequent analysis will be fitted to deal. Personally, however, I doubt if most of the problems we shall have to exclude for this reason are capable of much useful analysis by the methods of economic theory. (Hicks 1939, 83–85)

Hicks's escape was to rescue the assumption of perfect competition by asserting rising costs of the management of production as the source of diminishing returns. In his words: "The only reason why marginal costs should increase is the increasing difficulty of controlling an enterprise, as its scale of production grows" (1939, 83). In a parallel literature, the assumption of diminishing returns to management became the starting point for the mainstream theory of the firm (Coase 1937).

In mainstream theories of economic growth other solutions have been offered. Theories of growth start and end with the production function. Solow's growth model converted the Ricardian assumption of diminishing returns from land to capital (1957). The "new growth theorists" of the 1980s claim to have escaped the Ricardian assumption. One does so by assuming that human capital and technological knowledge are one and the same (Lucas 1988). The perception of the problem of economic development as the underaccumulation of capital, in which capital is assumed to embody technological progress, was the basis for World Bank–funded large-scale investment projects. Easterly (2001) argues that they failed. A second variant consists of innovation-based growth models but assumes that new innovators will replace old innovators, all of which operate according to a diminishing return-to-scale production function (Aghion and Howitt 2006).

Paul Krugman is the latest in this tradition but with a novel twist. His Nobel Prize lecture in 2008 was titled "The Increasing Returns Revolution in Trade and Geography." Earlier he had written, "In International economics, what this meant from Ricardo until the 1980s was an almost exclusive emphasis on comparative advantage, rather than increasing returns, as an explanation for trade" (Krugman 1991, 6). His claim is not to have resolved the contradiction but to assert that certain economic topics such as international trade and regional economics require increasing returns and that specific mathematical models can be constructed to address them without violating mainstream economics. Krugman breaks with diminishing returns but not the standard paradigm.

In Krugman's words, written at another time:

> At base, mainstream economic theory rests on two observations: obvious opportunities for gain are rarely left unexploited, and things add up. Or as I sometimes put it, $20 bills don't lie in plain view for very long, and every sale is a purchase. When one sets out to make a formal mathematical model, these rough principles usually become the more exact ideas of maximization (of something) and equilibrium (in some sense). (Krugman 1995, 74–75)

Why did the increasing returns revolution in development economics, trade theory, and economic geography not come earlier? The reason progress did not come sooner, we are told, is that "these fields were left untilled because the terrain was seen as unsuitable for the tools at hand" (Krugman 1995, 67). Proof meant the creation of "tools" consistent with the "economist's formula," axioms of "self-interested individuals," and "things add up" (1995, 74–75). For Krugman any gap in comprehensiveness must wait for a breakthrough mathematical application of the two timeless principles. The delay is a price of scientific progress: "A temporary evolution of ignorance, a period when our insistence on looking in certain directions leaves us unable to see what is right before our noses, may be the price of progress, an inevitable part of what happens when we try to make sense of the world's complexity." Krugman continues: "As an empirical proposition ... attempts to find alternatives to the economist's formula of self-interest plus interaction—or, to use the title of a marvelous book by Thomas Schelling, *Micromotives and Macrobehavior*—have been notably unsuccessful" (1995, 77).[3]

This chapter takes us down a different path into a world of dynamic, as well as static, increasing returns. The alternative, the production-centric approach, enables the characterization of the fundamental principles of production and organization, which have historically transformed the dynamics of global competition.[4] These include the principles of interchangeability, flow, multiproduct flow, product development flow, and system integration that distinguish, respectively, the American system of manufacturing, the synchronized mass production of Ford, the Toyota Production System, the Canon production system based on economies of time in new product development, and the Silicon Valley and Greater Boston regional innovation systems. Each represents a distinctive step in the evolution of production capabilities that determine structural advantage in the global competition of regional and national economies.

Business organization is the domain of the entrepreneurial firm and the "cumulative growth of collective knowledge" that drives value creation. Entrepreneurial firms are organized to achieve internal economies of expansion and are pivotal to interacting with external economies of expansion across groups of enterprises. Successful firms and regions strive to develop competitive advantage based on distinctive production capabilities and productive structures that cannot be purchased or easily imitated. But every firm also operates within, and its success depends upon, geographically bounded business development infrastructures and the strategic orientation of the associated economic governance system.

These ideas can be traced in the writings of the great thinkers reviewed below. Each can be seen as contributing important elements to

3. Krugman's argument is not that development theorists do not have insights; it is that only with the move from literary methods to a formal model are they properly understood and accepted by the profession: "Economists tended to regard the Big Push story as essentially nonsensical—if modern technology is better, then rational firms would simply adopt it! (They missed the interaction between economies of scale and market size)" (1995, 83). However, in the real world, technology adoption is not simple; if technology were simply a thing, it would be simple.

4. See box 8.1, in which any manufacturing enterprise can be precisely located along a production capability spectrum.

an alternative production-centric economics and, when combined, provide a new way of thinking about firms, regions, policymaking, and growth. Essentially the capability triad is read backward into the history of economic thought.

Adam Smith

Although Adam Smith did not advance a theory of the firm, he conceptualized the workshop and the market not as alternative means of coordinating economic activities but as complementary institutions in fostering "new divisions of labour and new improvements of arts" (Smith 1976 [1776], 748).

From a production perspective, Adam Smith's example of pin making illustrates the economic significance of *increases* in the division of labor, not because it was exceptional (in fact, it was widespread) but because it was a compelling example of the importance of organization in production and of the application of knowledge to advancing a nation's wealth-creating powers. In fact, the pin-making factory illustrated the application of product engineering before such knowledge was codified and widely practiced.

Going inside Smith's rhetorical pin factory reveals a five-stage organizational procedure for increasing labor productivity. First, a product's architecture is subject to decomposition into constituent parts. Second, each part is subject to methodical examination and decomposition into a sequence of the activities required to convert it from raw material to finished item. Next, each separate activity is examined and simplified to economize on time, to characterize the requisite skills, and to identify opportunities for introducing machines to improve performance. The fourth stage is to reorganize and lay out the workshop to achieve economies of speed or time (throughput efficiency, in modern parlance) in the conversion of raw material into finished product.[5] Finally, the workforce must be educated according to the requirements of the diverse, newly defined, and highly specialized activities. These stages outline a procedure for ap-

---

5. Strangely, Smith did not follow his French sources in using measures of time to illustrate the advances in each of the eighteen stages of pin manufacturing; he instead used weight. For a definitive account and a possible explanation, see Peaucelle (2006). It is worth noting that Alfred Chandler (1977) uses economies of speed and throughput, as distinct from economies of scale, to explain the organizational advantages of the Visible Hand in production, as did Henry Ford (Sorensen 1956) and Taichi Ohno (1988), organizational architect of the Toyota Production System.

Adam Smith, 1723–1790. *Source:* Vanderblue Collection,
Kress Collection of Business and Economics, Baker Library,
Harvard Business School (olvwork389444).

plying the logic of product engineering as a management practice to all
workshops. The division of labor is limited not only by the extent of the
market, as even casual Smith scholars know, but also by knowledge of the
principles of production.

Adam Smith's major contribution was to reveal how the division of
labor in the two spheres, inside the workshop and in the greater economy,
is part of a single interactive dynamic that underlies economic progress

(Best 2012). Smith's emphasis on the interplay involving the internal and societal divisions of labor resonates with that of Babbage, whose observations were of production processes half a century later. Both drew attention to the interconnectedness, interplay, and overlap of the divisions of labor within and outside the workplace to growth in a capitalist market economy. Both also foresaw dangers in the "application of the principle of the division of labor by the aid of machines" (Rolt 1970, 280). Smith demanded that the state intervene by providing universal education to prevent the working lives of "the laboring poor, that is the great body of people" from being reduced to a few simple, monotonous operations whereby people themselves could become "as stupid and ignorant as it is possible for a human creature to become" (Smith 1976 [1776], book 5, chap. 1, part 3).

Charles Babbage: Observational Principles and Production Systems

Production as the sphere of technological innovation became a subject of political economy with the publication in 1832 of Charles Babbage's *On the Economy of Machinery and Manufactures*. Unfortunately, as in the case of his drawings of the first computer, his contribution to political economy has long been neglected and rediscovered only in recent times.[6]

Born in 1791, one year after the death of Adam Smith and nearly seventy years after his birth, Charles Babbage grew up during the economic upheaval of the original industrial revolution. It would be hard to overstate the industrial changes taking place at this time. Machines were powering production, factories were being built, new engineering techniques and machine-shop practices were emerging, workforces were being organized, traditional industries were being disrupted and new industries created, and the urban landscape was expanding at a record pace. Simultaneously, new scientific disciplines were being organized and universal principles of change were being discovered as never before.

Babbage's purpose in life was not to write a book on political economy. Rather, it was to design and construct, first, a calculating machine to automate the creation of numerical tables and, second, an analytical ma-

6. The Babbage "new system of manufacturing" did not, however, disappear in the real world; instead the integration of technology development within production and scientific research reappeared in the form of real-world, vertically integrated industrial enterprises that drove the second industrial revolution in the United States (Chandler 1977; Lazonick 1991) and, as illustrated in chapter 2, the development policy framework to create America's Arsenal of Democracy.

Charles Babbage, 1791–1871. *Source:* J. Bedmar/lberfoto/Mary Evans.

chine to perform complex numerical operations. In both cases he made demands on British manufacturing's precision-machining capabilities on a scale that could not be met, but in the process he advanced the nation's engineering expertise.[7]

For the modern reader, Babbage's *On the Economy of Machinery and Manufactures*, published in 1832, can be read as an early version of Vannevar Bush's *Science: The Endless Frontier*, published in 1945. Both men were pioneers in designing complex machines that preceded the computer. Both combined deep practical and scientific knowledge surrounding the leading-edge engineering innovations and "mechanical principles" of their times. Both authored, although over a century apart, a visionary text

7. Babbage's influence on and links to James Nasmyth and Joseph Whitworth, two of Britain's most distinguished manufacturing engineers, can be found in Hyman (1982, 230–33). Nasmyth claimed that "manufacturers had benefited through the advance in machining equipment and techniques resulting from the first Difference Engine by many times the cost of the project" (Hyman 1982, 230).

in which productivity and national wealth could be continuously advanced by the iterative co-adaptation of science and production engineering.[8]

What makes Babbage's treatise unique is his opening of a world of technology development uncovered by his characterization of principles of production, in turn, discovered by observational investigations. He turned attention to the neglected study of technology as the holder of the Lucasian Chair of Mathematics at Cambridge University and as a prominent figure in a small group of natural philosophers, of which Charles Darwin is the most celebrated. This cluster of intellectuals revolutionized scientific methodology and scoped the scientific disciplines. The scientific endeavor was a task that combined keen observation with conceptual reasoning to discover principles of change. Babbage visited factories absorbing their production techniques with the refined powers of observation that Charles Darwin used to explore natural history on the voyage of the *Beagle*, William and John Herschel deployed when peering into the universe to characterize and classify distant galaxies, and Charles Lyell mobilized to examine and catalogue geological formations in order to interpret the earth's history (Snyder 2011).

Two other members of the group, William Whewell, a Cambridge University natural philosopher and mathematician who coined the term "scientist" in 1833,[9] and Richard Jones, author of *An Essay on the Distribution of Wealth* (1831), wrote critiques of Ricardo's deductive method as inappropriate to economics (Snyder 2011, 103ff.).[10] But it was Babbage who introduced the systematic observation of change as a methodology to political economy. He undertook, in his words, an "examination of the workshops ... which contain within them a rich mine of knowledge" (2005 [1832], 4) to understand the "processes of manufactures" and to apprehend their "general principles and mutual relations" (3–4). He distinguished "mechanical principles" from principles of political economy

---

8. Simon Kuznets and Babbage as well shared a common theme. Kuznets's empirical studies of long-run trends attributed the gains in productivity to the marriage of science and production and the creation of new industries. But while Vannevar Bush and Kuznets linked economic progress to scientific advance, Babbage articulated a political economy framework that brings technology out of the shadow of science.

9. The word first appeared in print in Whewell's anonymous 1834 review of Mary Somerville's "On the Connexion of the Physical Sciences," published in the *Quarterly Review* (Ross 1962, 71).

10. Whewell wrote, "[Ricardo's] starting axioms were so far from the truth that his conclusions bore almost no similarity to 'the actual state of things'" (1831, cited in Snyder 2011, 103). The disconnection between theoretical assumptions and real-world facts attributed to Ricardo resonates with Paul Romer's critique of macroeconomics nearly two centuries later (Romer forthcoming).

Charles Darwin, 1809–1892. *Source: Charles Darwin*
by Lock & Whitfield © National Portrait Gallery, London.

that "seemed to pervade many establishments." But at the same time he
found that the "interior economy of factories" and questions of political
economy were "so interwoven ... that it was deemed inadvisable to separate the two subjects" (7).

In the history of economic thought, no one has matched Babbage's
practical grasp of machinery and range of engineering expertise. Joseph
Henry's tribute to Babbage in the *Annual Report of the Smithsonian* in
1873 captures his prodigious knowledge of manufacturing:

Hundreds of mechanical applications in the factories and workshops
of Europe and America, scores of ingenious experiments in mining and

architecture, the construction of bridges and boring of tunnels, and a world of tools by which labor is benefited and the arts improved—all the overflowings of a mind so rich that its very waste became valuable to utilize—came from Charles Babbage. He more, perhaps, than any man who ever lived, narrowed the chasm [separating] science and practical mechanics. (Henry 1873, cited by Hyman 1982, 252)

Babbage's political economy focused attention on the "intimate connections" linking experiments with reasoning, manufacturing success with scientific progress, and workplace skills with technological advance. In his words:

> In reviewing the various processes offered as illustrations of those *general principles* which it has been the main object of the present volume to support and establish, it is impossible not to perceive that the arts and manufactures of the country are intimately connected with the progress of the severer sciences; and that, as we advance in the career of improvement, every step requires, for its success, that this *connection should be rendered more intimate.* The applied sciences derive their facts from experiment; but the reasonings, on which their chief utility depends, are the province of what is called abstract science ... it follows, that the efforts for the improvement of its manufactures which any country can make with the greatest probability of success, must arise from the combined exertions of all those most skilled in the theory, as well as the practice of the arts. (2005 [1832], 205)[11]

Babbage's major contribution to political economy was to pioneer a systemic-observation methodology in which historical experience serves as a laboratory to "discover new ways for thinking about" complex relationships.[12] As argued in chapter 1, the standard research paradigm is based on the presupposition that progress in the discipline of economics comes from theoretical advances in the tools that extend a conceptual

---

11. An important feature of a principle is to clarify for the purpose of a public conversation in matters of political economy with nonexperts. Babbage wrote: "I have not attempted to offer a complete enumeration of all the mechanical principles which regulate the application of machinery to arts and manufactures, but I have endeavored to present to the reader those which struck me as the most important, either for understanding the actions of machines, or for enabling the memory to classify and arrange the facts connected with their employment" (2005 [1832], 3).

12. "The important thing in science is not so much to obtain new facts as to discover new ways of thinking about them," wrote William Lawrence Bragg, quoted in Koestler and Smithies (1971 [1958], 115).

framework that starts and ends with ahistorical axioms captured by the "economist's formula" of self-interested individuals and the need for "things to add up" (Krugman 1995, 77). The real world of production, business organization, technological change, and innovation remains, as before, exogenous to the theoretical framework. If reality intervenes, it is as ad hoc nudges in policymaking relevance.

The role of "principles" is subtly but sharply different in the two methodological approaches to economics. In both cases, the idea of general principles is to simplify, characterize, and make sense of the otherwise baffling complexity of economic reality. The difference is the research process leading to the characterization of principles. For the deductive approach the scope for the discovery of principles is limited to a prior theoretical claim; a theoretical statement's relevance but not its logic can be rejected but not proven by empirical evidence. For the observation-based approach, the search for principles is not limited to logical deductions but includes, nay requires, principles discovered by investigations of the real world. For both the purpose of characterizing principles is to create tools for analyzing economic processes.

While Babbage's major focus was on "mechanical principles," he also called attention to organizational principles in a passage that goes beyond Adam Smith's sources of productivity growth in the workplace and foretells the principle of inclusion at the core of modern participatory management philosophies such as the TWI program of World War II America, total quality management, and *kaizen*. As Babbage wrote:

> I shall now present the outline of a system which appears to me to be pregnant with the most important results, both to the class of workmen and to the country at large; and which, if acted upon, would, in my opinion, permanently raise the working classes, and greatly extend the manufacturing system. The general principles are
>
> 1. That a considerable part of the wages received by each person employed should depend on the profits made by the establishment; and,
> 2. That every person connected with it should derive more advantage from applying any improvement he might discover, to the factory in which he is employed, than he could by any other course. (2005 [1832], 139)

Babbage's employee involvement principle, whereby the worker uses his mind as well as his body, is in the tradition of Adam Ferguson, a contemporary of Adam Smith, and what became known as the alienation critique of instrumental work in Marx's *Economic and Philosophical Manuscripts of 1844* (Fromm 1961) and *Grundrisse* (Kettler 1965; Hamowy 1968; Marx 1972, 124; McClellan 1972; Best and Connolly 1982 [1976], 126ff.).

The result of the application of these principles will increase productivity in the following ways:

1. Every person ... would have a direct interest in its [the company's] prosperity.
2. Every person ... would have an immediate interest in preventing any waste or mismanagement in all departments.
3. The talents of all ... would be strongly directed to its improvement in every department." (Babbage 2005 [1832], 141)

Babbage's influence on John Stuart Mill, and particularly on Marx's treatment of technology and factory size in *Capital*, are discussed by Hyman (1982).[13] While Hyman's main theme is that Babbage was a "pioneer of the computer," he emphasizes the uniqueness of Babbage's systematic approach to both computer design and political economy. In his words: "The combination [theory and practice] was remarkable: systematic development of industrial technology; operations research; rational cost accounting; profit sharing incentive schemes; economic theory using powerful mathematical techniques and grounded in extensive statistical information" (Hyman 1982, 120).

The importance Babbage attached to government leadership in advancing a "new system of manufacturing" resonates with accounts in this book of the US World War II production "miracle," the East Asian "miracle," the Massachusetts "miracle," and the success of Germany's "*Mittelstand*" as well as with the decline of British industrial leadership that he anxiously predicted. The successful experiences are not miracles but the outcomes of strategic development policy frameworks in which macroeconomic policymaking is calibrated to production capability development.

13. Lazonick's critique of Marx's political economy, inspired by Chandler's historical principles of business organization, is an application of Babbage's attention to empirical investigation in matters of political economy. To Marx's credit, he went inside the production process to discover the source of value creation in the capitalist system, but his exemplar was factually incorrect. Using historical evidence, Lazonick (1979) reveals that Marx's theme that the introduction of the self-acting mule replaced labor and thus was the source of capitalist success was in error. While Marx drew heavily on Babbage's pioneering analysis of technological change, he ignored the business organization principles that informed Babbage's political economy.

Karl Marx, 1818–1883. *Source: Karl Marx* by John Mayall
© National Portrait Gallery, London.

Babbage's political economy is also effectively the outline of a "capabilities-informed macroeconomics" policy framework (see chap. 5). Babbage contrasted the existing situation with a "new system of manufactures" in terms of institutional interrelations among workshops, the scientific community, and government policy, and he argued that British industrial leadership depended on political leadership in transitioning from the existing system to the embryonic "new system." The workshops were the sources of distinctive engineering practices, workforce skill development, and management practices, but they could not make the transition on their own to the "new system." Scientific research had to be integrated with advanced engineering practices within specialized workshops, management had to introduce profit-sharing business models in which workforce skills were continuously advanced, and the government had to fund basic research and pursue trade and education policies that maintained Great Britain's advantage in the technology of machine making.[14]

Babbage was motivated by his wish to shape government policymaking. He was not able to finish the construction of even the difference engine let alone start on the "analytical engine," stymied as already suggested by the lack of precision machining capability in the United Kingdom at the time. Consequently, Babbage called for an alternative political economy framework designed for the purpose of informing an industrial transformation to a "new system of manufacturing" in order to build and sustain national leadership in scientifically advanced machine building.

It is no criticism of Babbage to point out that he did not divert his extraordinary intellectual powers from laying the foundations of information technology to constructing an alternative economics paradigm on the basis of his systemic observations of mechanical inventions by engineering-intensive enterprises. His research methodology distinguished the alternative from what became the standard approach. But much remained and still remains to be done.

Alfred Marshall: Internal and External Increasing Returns

Marshall was a direct descendant of Babbage in relation to economic methodology. In his seminal text *Principles of Economics*, originally published in 1890, he linked the decline of the Swiss watchmaking industry to the rise of the "American system" of industrial organization based on the principle of interchangeability of parts (1920 [1890], 257). The following resonates with Babbage: "The importance of the principle of interchangeable parts has been but recently grasped; there are however many signs that it will do more than any other to extend the use of machine-made machinery to every branch of production" (257). In a footnote Marshall wrote that "the system owes its origin in great measure to Sir Joseph Whitworth's standard gauges; but it has been worked out with most en-

---

14. Principles, if understood, can be the basis of development policies. "Those who possess rank in a manufacturing country, can scarcely be excused if they are entirely ignorant of principles, whose development has produced greatness" (Babbage 1832, 4).

Alfred Marshall, 1842–1924. *Source: Alfred Marshall*
by Walter Stoneman © National Portrait Gallery, London.

terprise and thoroughness in America" (257). He refers to this new way of
operating as the "American System."[15]

Marshall went beyond his paradigmatic predecessors Smith, Babbage,
and Darwin to elaborate an economics of industrial organization based
on a novel extension of Babbage's concept of increasing returns explicitly linking these to changes in organization. In his words, "The *law of*

15. Babbage and Whitworth, Britain's leading engineer at the time, were allies in the
application of the scientific method to industry, and Whitworth worked on Babbage's difference engine and in the process led the way in using machine tools to make equipment
with interchangeable parts (Hyman 1982 2, 57, 231ff.). Whitworth visited, studied, and
wrote a book on the "American System of Manufacturing" (Wallis and Whitworth 1855).

increasing return may be worded thus:—An increase of labour and capital leads generally to improved organization, which increases the efficiency of the work of capital" (1920 [1890], 318, Marshall's emphasis).

Marshall distinguished "internal" from "external" increasing returns. The first, internal returns, were of the type previously explored by Babbage in the context of the enterprise. The second, external returns, "result from the growth of correlated branches of industry which mutually assist one another" (1920 [1890], 317). In both cases, the law of increasing returns derives from "improved organization," which "generally yields a return increased more than proportionally," which "tends to diminish or even override" diminishing returns to raw materials (318).

Marshall attributed internal economies to the "inventive and organizing power" of an "able man" who builds a particular "house" of business, which he explores at length (see 1920 [1890], 315–16, for a summary). The successful businessman is an organizer, not an optimizer. For Marshall, "Knowledge is our most powerful engine of production" and derives from organization, a "distinct agent of production" (138). In this he pioneered the "learning firm," later developed by Edith Penrose. Equally important, his concept of external economies extended the concept of knowledge creation from the individual firm to an aggregate of firms: "External economies," he wrote, "rise from collective organization as a whole" (preface to the first edition, xii). I argue below that Marshall laid the foundation for an integration of internal and external "economies of expansion."

In a paragraph that references both Smith and Darwin, Marshall calls attention to the many "profound analogies between industrial organization and biological worlds. While some [biological metaphors] have not survived ... there remains 'a fundamental unity of action ... set forth in the general rule ... that the development of the organism, whether social or physical, involves an increasing subdivision of functions between the separate parts on the one hand, and on the other a more intimate connection between them" (1920 [1890], 241). Both Babbage and Marshall use the term "intimate connection" to capture systemic economic relationships.

Marshall spends five chapters examining "those very important external economies which can often be secured by the concentration of many small businesses of a similar character in particular localities: or, as is commonly said, by the localization of industry" (1920 [1890], 266). Thus he was a founding father of both industrial organization and economic geography. He continued Babbage's mission to advance political economy in a new direction, away from the influence of Ricardian diminishing returns, a challenge that was taken up again in Krugman's new international trade theory a century later.[16]

Allyn Young: Dynamic Increasing Returns

Allyn Young's article "Increasing Returns and Economic Progress," published in 1928, outlines a cumulative innovation dynamic involving the interplay between the pursuit of distinctive capability by individual enterprises and a process of increasing differentiation among enterprises. Thorstein Veblen, the most prominent figure in the American institutional school of economics, had coined the term "cumulative causation" at the turn of the century (Hodgson 2004, 152).[17] But it was through Young's characterization of "increasing returns" that the concept took on the modern systems theory connotation of nonlinear positive feedback.[18]

Young wrote:

> Every important advance in the organization of production, regardless of whether it is based upon anything which, in a narrow or technical sense, would be called a new "invention," or involves a fresh application of the fruits of scientific progress to industry, alters the conditions of industrial activity and initiates responses elsewhere in the industrial structure which in turn have a further unsettling effect. Thus, change becomes progressive and propagates itself in a cumulative way. (1928, 533)

He enriched and extended Marshall's external economies into a systemic understanding of innovation processes: "The mechanism of increasing

16. Marshall wrote that "economic problems are imperfectly presented when they are treated as problems of statical equilibrium, and not of organic growth.... The Statical theory of equilibrium.... Its limitations are so constantly overlooked, especially by those who approach it from an abstract point of view, that there is a danger in throwing it into definite form at all" (1920 [1890], 461).

17. According to Veblen, "Any evolutionary science ... is a theory of a process, of an unfolding sequence ... of cumulative causation" (Veblen (1898: 375–8, cited in Hodgson 2004: 150). Gunnar Myrdal (1939, 1957), influenced by Knut Wicksell's "cumulative process" concept of positive feedback effects in monetary economics, independently advanced a concept of circular cumulative causation. The institutional school was prominent in American economics journals and research methods until the postwar emergence and triumph of general equilibrium theory and mathematical modeling. Geoffrey Hodgson's surveys of institutional economics are landmarks in the history of economic thought (1993, 2004).

18. Lauchlin Currie, Roosevelt's wartime personal economic advisor, had been a student of Young at Harvard.

Allyn Young, 1876–1929. *Source:* LSE Library.

returns is not to be discerned adequately by observing the effects of variations in the size of an individual firm or of a particular industry, for the
progressive division and specialisation of industries is an essential part
of the process by which increasing returns are realized" (1928, 539; emphasis Young's).[19] He adds: "With the extension of the division of labour
among industries, the representative firm, like the industry of which it is

19. Young (1928), as if foretelling but extending Kuznets's Victory Program bottleneck
analysis, describes indirect means in terms of an extension of the division of labor within a
firm to the firm's access to increasing specialized labor along a supply chain including the
provision of machines, tools, and equipment. He outlines a self-organizing process for an
increasing differentiation of skills and capabilities that generate dynamic increasing returns as follows: "An increasingly intricate nexus of specialised undertakings has inserted
itself between the producer of raw materials and the consumer of the final product."

a part, loses its identity. Its internal economies dissolve into the internal and external economies of the more highly specialised undertakings which are its successors, and are supplemented by new economies" (538).

Young explicitly, and with great respect, extends Smith's increasing division of labor into a dynamic and interactive process with the systemic capability to take full advantage of design changes in subsystems. It resonates with Marshall's "general rule," influenced by Darwin, of greater differentiation combined with more intimate connections in both the physical and the social worlds. This is, in brief, the principle of system integration that captures the distinctive characteristic of open-system business models in regional innovation systems.

Edith Penrose and Internal Economies of Expansion

As noted earlier, Paul Krugman famously distilled the essence of the standard paradigm down to two observations: "Mainstream economic theory rests on two observations: obvious opportunities for gain are rarely left unexploited and things add up" (Krugman 1995, 74). Edith Penrose's *Theory of the Growth of the Firm* (1959) also rests on two observations: Everything cannot be done alone or at once.[20] Opportunities figure in both the standard paradigm and Penrose's theory. In the standard paradigm, opportunities are seized instantly, but how they are created and recognized is ignored, indeed invisible.[21] For Penrose, "productive" opportunities are emergent and integral to a dynamic process by which innovative enterprises create new productive resources and drive capitalist growth.

Seizure of the opportunities whereby growth is realized, however, is an entrepreneurial challenge. In an uncertain world, management must recognize and successfully pursue "productive opportunities," and their

20. Penrose's methodological approach to theoretical advance can be found in Best and Humphries (2003).

21. Ronald Coase's seminal article, "The Nature of the Firm" (1937), asked the question Why do firms exist given that "production could be carried on without any organization at all" and that "the price mechanism should give the most efficient result." He introduced the concept of transaction costs to explain both why firms exist and their size, for which he received the Nobel Prize in 1991. Ironically, his Nobel Prize lecture, "The Institutional Structure of Production," is a sharp critique of the economics profession for treating the "institutional structure of economics" like the postman in G. K. Chesterton's Father Brown tale *The Invisible Man*. As a logical theory of how perfect markets can produce an optimal allocation of resources, the standard paradigm has been successful. But at a price: It required assumptions, such as given technology and universal markets, which reduce production to a theory of exchange: "What happens between the purchase of factors of production and the sale of goods that are produced by these factors is largely ignored" (Coase 1991).

Edith Penrose, 1914–1996. *Source:* Courtesy of the Penrose family.

pursuit links the firm to the customer in an interactive relationship in which new products are developed. The advances in productive services can extend the firm's "productive opportunities" by enlarging the members' capacity to recognize and respond to new product concept possibilities in the environment: "Experience ... develops an increasing knowledge of the possibilities for action and the ways in which action can be taken by ... the firm. This increase in knowledge ... causes the productive opportunities of a firm to change" (Penrose 1995 [1959], 52).

From the perspective of Penrose, the firm shapes the market as much as the market shapes the firm, but within a moving, historically contingent environment. As firms develop and respond to productive opportunities, they alter and further differentiate and, in the process, recharacterize the parameters (technological, product, organizational) of the "market."

Penrose's innovative enterprise growth dynamic resonates with Young's extension of Smith's principle of increasing specialization into a concept of self-sustaining growth. But her enterprise growth dynamic derives from an extension of the principle of increasing specialization from skills to the "productive services" (think capabilities) of enterprises.[22] Penrose draws a distinction between resources, which are homogeneous, and productive services, which are heterogeneous: "It is never *resources* themselves that are the 'inputs' in the production process, but only the *services* that the resources can render" (1995 [1959], 25; emphasis in original).

The services of resources derive from the unique experience, teamwork, and purposes of each enterprise. Consequently, every enterprise is unique: "The services yielded by resources are a function of the way in which they are used—exactly the same resource when used for different purposes or in different ways and in combination with different types or amounts of other resources provides a different service or set of services" (Penrose 1995 [1959], 25). While new technical people can be hired in the market, company-specific experience and teamwork cannot be. Consequently, the "productive opportunity ... is unique for each firm" (Penrose 1960, 3).

Productive services are potentially dynamic: "The process by which experience is gained is properly treated as a process of creating new productive services available to the firm" (Penrose 1995 [1959], 48). And the generation of new productive services is a knowledge-creating process: "The very process of operation and of expansion are intimately associated with the process by which knowledge is increased" (56). Production involves both the making of products or services and the creation of new production-related knowledge.

In the standard paradigm, technology is exogenous to the resource coordination treatment of the market and the firm. The production challenge is to squeeze the maximum amount of output from a fixed pool of resources; the challenge can be met by satisfying a set of optimality rules involving inputs, outputs, and prices for a *given* technology. Unlike in Penrose, unused resources have no role to play as part of a dynamic process of increasing a firm's productive services (1995 [1959], 67–68).

22. Penrose's term for capability was "productive service." Richardson (1972) suggested the change in terminology.

For Penrose, the new production-related knowledge has a by-product in the form of an unused productive service that, in turn, creates both an imbalance and an opportunity.[23] The source of the imbalance is inherent in the execution of business plans: "The execution of any plan for expansion will tend to cause a firm to acquire resources which cannot be fully used ... and such unused services will remain available to the firm after the expansion is complete" (1955, 533). Thus, while unused productive services are a source of inefficiency in the standard theory of the firm, Penrose sees them as driving an internal innovation dynamic:

> At all times there exist, within every firm, pools of unused productive services and these, together with the changing knowledge of management, create a productive opportunity which is unique for each firm. Unused productive services are, for the enterprising firm, at the same time a challenge to innovate, an incentive to expand, and a source of competitive advantage. It is largely because such unused services are related to existing resources and partly because of the pressures of competition that firms tend to specialize in broad technological or marketing areas, which I have called technological or market "bases." (Penrose 1960, 2–3)

The reference to "bases" is to the "basic position" that a firm must establish and protect (as distinct from merely achieving efficiency in production):

> In the long run the profitability, survival, and growth of a firm does not depend so much on the efficiency with which it is able to organize the production of even a widely diversified range of products as it does on the ability of the firm to establish one or more wide and relatively impregnable "bases" from which it can adapt and extend its operations in an uncertain, changing and competitive world. It is not the scale of production nor even, within limits, the size of the firm, that are the important considerations, but rather the nature of the basic position that it is able to establish for itself. (Penrose 1995 [1959], 137)

The drive to establish a basic position, or what can be called a distinctive technological capability, limits the productive opportunities that any

23. The process of creating new productive services, a by-product of goods production, engenders a balancing or coordination problem: "Only by chance [will] the firm ... be able so to organize its resources that all of them will be fully used" (Penrose 1995, 32). The coordination problem, however, is partly the outcome of planning limitations: "In general there will always be services capable of being used in the same or in different lines of production which are not so used because the firm could not plan extensively enough to use them."

single firm can pursue. But in an open system of firms (see below), such opportunities are not lost but instead are shifted into market "interstices" and become opportunities for other firms, existing and new. In this way, Penrose's iterative technology capability and market opportunity growth dynamic are propagated to the larger population of firms. The interstices represent new opportunities for expansion that develop out of industrial change and innovation but cannot be pursued by the originating enterprise: they are inconsistent with reinforcing the basic position, or unique productive services, of the firm in which they emerged but not lost to the productive system as a whole (Best 2001, chap. 3).

George Richardson: Networking and Competing Business Systems

Whereas Penrose introduced a distinction between resources and productive services to propose a theory of the growth of the firm, George Richardson introduced a distinction between activities and capabilities to propose an alternative theory of the "organization of industry" (1972).[24] The standard theory presupposes only two forms of coordination of economic activities, either market or plan. Richardson introduced a third form and reconceptualized the market or plan dichotomy into an empirical interrelationship:

> It is convenient to think of industry as carrying out an indefinitely large number of *activities*, activities related to the discovery and estimation of future wants, to research, development and design, to the execution and co-ordination of processes of physical transformation, the marketing of goods and so on. And we have to recognize that these activities have to be carried out by organizations with appropriate *capabilities*, or, in other words, with appropriate knowledge, experience and skills. (1972, 888; emphasis in original)

As an academic turned business executive, Richardson observed that firms internalize similar activities and externalize complementary activities. To benefit mutually from specializing in complementary activities, the firms must develop collaborative relationships with producers with complementary capabilities. Collaboration creates channels for consultation on investment plans and the shaping of designs, new products, and

24. This section draws from but extends Richardson's contribution in Best (1990, 131–32).

George Richardson, 1924–. *Source:* Courtesy of George Richardson.

processes across functional specialties without a corporate hierarchy. The choice for firms is not only whether to make or buy but also whether to make, buy, or collaborate.

Thus Richardson extends Penrose's learning firm to include an interfirm differentiation dynamic. Each firm within an emerging interfirm relationship takes on a distinctive but complementary resource-creation strategy that can enhance the collective resource-creation activities of a group of collaborating enterprises. Networking emerges as a means of coordination in contrast to the standard dichotomy of either market (external) or vertical (internal) integration coordination. The firm and the market are no longer simply substitute means of resource coordination with nothing in between.

Richardson's distinction between similar and complementary activities substantiates an image of a sector as a networked association of producers of complementary products. Sectors in which firms specialize by activity will have a different competitive advantage and development dynamic from sectors composed of identical firms engaging in the same activities. The first requires collaboration and information flows across firms; the second fits the formal plan-market dichotomy of economic theory, in which firms are linked by "spot" relations in markets.

A sector in a region in which firms have not specialized by activity can persist if insulated from interregional competition. But once the barriers to trade are relaxed, market-coordinated enterprises will come under competitive pressure from coordinated systems of specialized and networked enterprises. It follows that a sector of homogenous enterprises can be outcompeted in interregional or international competition if they have organized themselves according to the free-market ideal of perfect competition.

Combining the insights of Penrose with those of Young and Richardson, we can speak of internal and external economies of expansion. The external economies of expansion do not require large scale or even large firms, but they do require interfirm relationships and business strategies in which enterprises *focus* on core capabilities and *network* for complementary capabilities.

The focus on the advantages of networked firms has implications for the standard economic theory of perfect competition and economic governance. Competition within a sector does not ensure that specialized firms with networked complementarities will emerge or be maintained, and, in fact, market competition can thwart the emergence of cumulative and collective benefits of capability specialization. The reason is that a single firm that specializes by activity is dependent on firms specializing in complementary activities. If complementary products and services are not available or are available only from firms that seek to exploit short-run market advantages, the firm will likely struggle in the market.[25] Government

25. Richardson's "Organization of Industry" article (1972) is an empirical elaboration of the theoretical role of cooperation in his masterpiece, *Information and Investment* (1960). Written while Richardson was a student of John Hicks, his book proposes an internal critique of the perfect competition model even as a hypothetical system. In the words of Paul Duguid (n.d.), "With perfect competition between autonomous, interchangeable agents and with perfect information, entrepreneurs would in fact not know what to do" and the market would collapse.

policy that focuses only on market failure without awareness of business system failure will risk contributing to sectoral collapse and regional economic decline. On the other hand, government policies that do account for interfirm capability development dynamics can have a powerful growth effect.

These ideas make clear rapid growth experiences, such as that seen in the United States during World War II. The example of the wartime development of the US aircraft industry illustrates the concept of cumulative increasing returns. The building of Ford's B-24 production system is an example of the creation of new market opportunities for yet greater specialization in the division of labor along the supply chain and with it dynamic increasing returns. The transition from car to aircraft assembly forced a sharp increase in precision engineering standards on the production units along a supply chain that yielded a new bomber every hour (Overy 1995, 240). The cumulative effects continued beyond increasing returns to technical advance from specialization as machine shops, for example, spread the technological advances to other industries.

This brings systems integration into the transformational framework as a fundamental principle of production engineering and business organization. The principle of systems integration is manifest in the organizational capability of firms, individually and networked, to foster rapid technological change. Entrepreneurial firms drive innovation and sectoral transitions. However, they do so not alone, but rather as members of networked groups of collectively innovating enterprises that foster regional innovation dynamics.

Application of the principle of systems integration to business organization means integrating an ongoing technology-management capability into a production system. The effect can be a network or a cluster of entrepreneurial firms in which design is decentralized and diffused. It is a business system model suited to product-led strategies and technological innovation.

The combination of entrepreneurial firms and interfirm networks/cluster-dynamic processes was a factor underlying the growth dynamics of Silicon Valley and the unexpected resurgence of Boston's Route 128. Chapter 3 describes open-system dynamics or mutual adjustment processes that, in turn, fostered new rounds of capability specialization, decentralization and diffusion of design, and technological experimentation. The consequent increase in regional differentiation of enterprises and technologies increased the opportunity for local innovation based on novel combinations of existing technologies or "externalities" (of the kind associated with the work of Jane Jacobs, discussed below).

The implications for the theory of industrial organization and economic policymaking are deep and profound. They mean that government policies can target production and business capability developmental infrastructures to foster external economies of expansion across networked groups of firms. Policies that promote "focus-and-network" business strategies can be successful in part because they enable small specialist suppliers to achieve economies of scale by supplying a regional system of enterprises. Such a system of networked enterprises has a structural competitive advantage over either vertical integration or market modes of coordination. In contrast, a department within a vertically integrated enterprise supplies only a single firm. Elsewhere I have called this the principle of increasing specialization (see Best 2001, 61ff.).

Real-world successful regional economies constituted by populations of SMEs, as in the case of Greater Boston and the *Mittelstand* (see next chapter), co-evolve with a unified set of developmental infrastructures. Some are self-organizing, and others are policy-driven. In the case of Greater Boston, we found a vibrant machine-tool industry and a legacy of precision and system engineering, a financial ecosystem with a capability in linking early-stage technology development with business development growth, and a science and technology infrastructure.

Even big firms depend on developmental infrastructures, particularly those related to science and technology, as well as material infrastructures. In Chandler's historical accounts of the rise of the vertically integrated and multidivisional modern corporation, similar developmental infrastructures were internalized. But vertical integration is not the only way. Policymakers have an opportunity to craft development infrastructures that enable a population of firms collectively to evolve new product development and technology management capabilities that might otherwise be the exclusive preserve of corporate giants. The firms that produce success stories develop a structural advantage in resilience and the flexibility required to respond to technological and market changes and, in the case of Greater Boston, sectoral transition.

Jane Jacobs and City Growth Dynamics

In his path-breaking article on "endogenous growth theory," Robert Lucas paid the following tribute: "I will be following very closely the lead of Jane Jacobs, whose remarkable book *The Economy of Cities* seems to me mainly

Jane Jacobs, 1916–2006. *Source:* Library of Congress
Prints & Photographs Online Catalog.

and convincingly concerned ... with the external effects of human capital" (1988, 37).[26]

Jacobs extends the ecological concept of "reciprocating systems" from
nature to "man-made contrivances" to explain the economy of growing
and successful cities. Her examination of the puzzle of why some cities
grow and others decline led her to characterize a process in which a city's
exports and the local suppliers to the export sectors "act together to create an economic reciprocating system" (1969, 126).[27]

26. As a major contributor to macroeconomics over the past few decades, Lucas does
not pursue his admiration for Jacobs to examine the links between policymaking and economic performance. In the words of Paul Romer: "Macroeconomists got comfortable with
the idea that fluctuations in macroeconomic aggregates are caused by imaginary shocks,
instead of actions that people take" (forthcoming, 4). The "real business cycle" model attributes changes in macro performance to exogenous changes in the growth accounting residual defined as the difference between growth in output and growth of an index of inputs
in production. The residual, which Abramovitz (1956) famously referred to as "the measure
of our ignorance," has remained unmeasured but has not deterred macroeconomic theorists from strongly held policy viewpoints that depend upon it (Romer forthcoming). This
is the terrain of the Capability Triad.

27. According to Jacobs, "This is an economic reciprocating system analogous to a
natural one in which the animal eats, has strength to find food, hence finds more food, is

The idea is that a requirement for sustainable growth is that some among the local suppliers take up exporting products of their own and create new exporting industries to replace the original exporting industry. In her words: "The system with which we are now concerned is simple, being built wholly of exported goods and services and the local industries that supply things to the exporting industries. But unless some among the local industries take to exporting products of their own, the system halts. And if new local industries do not arise as older ones take to exporting their work, the system likewise halts" (Jacobs 1969, 126).

"This simple reciprocating system," Jacobs writes, "functions in cities not only when they are first forming and growing, but as long as their economies grow and diversify, no matter how complex the cities themselves become" (1969, 126). A city, like an embryo, grows not through a process of enlarging what is already there but through a process of gradual diversification and differentiation from an initially undifferentiated entity. It starts from little more than its initial export work and the suppliers to that work. "Cities radically differ in their growth processes from "inert" towns and from villages *even when they are still as small as towns and villages*" (129, emphasis in original).

Jacobs's reciprocating systems provide a growth dynamic of new sectors that complements Penrose's new product dynamic internal to the firm. Whereas Penrose's emphasis is on distinctive capability development and growth via value creation processes and the creation of new products within a single company, Jacobs's focus is on increasing product differentiation and the creation of new sectors that drive city growth dynamics. In her words: "Existing divisions of labor multiply into more divisions of labor by grace of intervening added activities that yield up more sums of work to be divided" (1969, 58). The "intervening added activities" are described in terms of new "work" combined with multiple trials and errors linking the old to the new divisions of labor.

In a parallel to Penrose's learning theory of the firm, Steven Johnson describes Jacobs's masterwork, *The Death and Life of Great American Cities* (1961) as a learning theory of cities: "They get their order from below; they are learning machines" (Johnson 2001, 52). In Jacobs's words, "Vital cities have marvelous innate abilities for understanding, communicating, contriving and inventing what is required to combat their difficulties" (1961, 447–48). For Johnson, cities, by the sharing of ideas and information across networks, generate a group intelligence instead of an atomized

---

strong again to seek more food, on and on. The body has hundreds of such reciprocating systems which are what growth is about" (1969, 126).

group of smart people. This social-network variant of organized complexity may be a key to understanding the competitive advantage of open-system over hierarchical business models observed in differentiated industrial districts such as Greater Boston and the Third Italy (discussed in chap. 5)

Jacobs, however, did not lose sight of leadership in policy design or the crafting of institutions of economic governance in understanding city development. She independently celebrated the role of Ralph Flanders in the emergence of Greater Boston's high-tech industry. Flanders, she writes, first became aware that the region's trouble was not the loss of old industries but the lack of new ones; second, identified the bottleneck to the growth of new high-tech firms as finance; and third, established a new financial organization, unencumbered by tradition and focused specifically on financing new firms but without usurping proprietorial control (see Jacobs 1969, chap. 7, "Capital for City Economic Development"). Others, including George Doriot and Karl Compton, as described in chapter 3, were part of the triangular banking, university, and enterprise interinstitutional system that emerged. Together these men successfully convinced the trustees of the investment funds of the area's rich universities to invest in what became the region's venture capital industry.[28]

Jacobs warns against economists' practice of concentrating on nation-states, because it causes them misleadingly to group together rich regions and poor ones in the same nation. However, the officially published economic data tend to be most comprehensive for the nation-state, less comprehensive for regions, and almost nonexistent for cities. This has undoubtedly deflected attention away from what Jacobs regards as the true engines of regional growth: namely, dynamic and vibrant cities.

Moses Abramovitz: The Productivity Puzzle

Moses Abramovitz published a seminal work on national income growth accounting in 1956. He asked two questions with respect to the economic growth of the United States from 1870 to 1951: how much had net output per capita grown and "to what extent [had the] increase been obtained as a result of greater labor or capital input on the one hand and of a rise in productivity on the other[?]" (1956, 5). Others before him had addressed the first question. His distinctive contribution was to ascribe the apparent changes in output growth to increases in inputs or to productivity.

---

28. Jacobs also appreciated the role of a vibrant machine tool industry in city growth dynamics (1969).

Abramovitz's methodology was to construct an index of inputs of labor and capital resources on the one hand and an index of net output on the other. The residual or difference between the estimated value of resource inputs and the net value of output was a measure of productivity defined as the increase in output per unit of resources used and can be traced over time. Measurement issues abounded for both inputs and output, but Abramovitz creatively used and expanded on the broad concepts and data collection methods pioneered earlier by Simon Kuznets in the construction of the national income and product accounts.

Abramovitz estimated an average rate of growth of US net national product of 3.5 percent per annum and 1.9 percent per capita per annum over the preceding eight decades. From a historical perspective, these were very big numbers but were in line with earlier and forthcoming studies conducted by Kuznets and others at the National Bureau of Economic Research.

What made the work of Abramovitz important additionally was the divergence between the expectations of conventional economic theory and his own growth accounting estimates of the relative contributions of inputs and productivity to the growth of output over the period. Since the time of Adam Smith, capital accumulation had been the perceived engine of growth, almost amounting to a "law" of economics. However, the input index of labor and capital accounted for only between 10 and 20 percent of output growth. Abramovitz wrote: "This seems to imply that almost the entire increase in net product per capita is associated with the rise in productivity" (1956, 11). He identified the residual in his innovative growth accounting as a "measure of our ignorance about the causes of economic growth in the United States and some sort of indication of where we need to concentrate our attention" (11). His results were confirmed a year later by Robert Solow (1957).

Despite a small army of researchers trying to account for growth over the years, the anomaly has persisted. Decades later Abramovitz critically reviewed the empirical growth literature in an article titled "The Search for the Sources of Growth: Areas of Ignorance, Old and New" (1993). He argued that research conducted over the intervening decades has not advanced economic knowledge: "We know all too little about the interactions among our infamous 'proximate causes.' They constitute an area of ignorance even larger than the old primitive Residual" (1993, 237). Nevertheless, the standard growth model has "fixed itself in the minds of most economists who study growth in the contemporary world" (220).

Abramovitz wrote that the standard model persists: "Many economic historians, like most economists, depend on standard growth accounts to provide some quantitative description of the proximate sources of growth, but this is misleading" (1993, 217). He continued: "Remember Mr. Dooley: 'It ain't what we don't know that bothers me so much; it's all the things we do know that ain't so.' That is really the nub of the matter" (219).[29]

With respect to the issue of explaining growth, what is it that we know that ain't so? First, we "know" that the proximate sources of economic growth are independent and can be added up. In the words of Abramovitz: "Standard growth accounting is based on the notion that the several proximate sources of growth that it identifies operate independently of one another. The implication of this assumption is that the contributions attributable to each can be added up.... We should have seen the contradiction between ... interactive connections and the standard growth accounts at once" (1993, 221).

Second, we "know" from a series of studies that the contribution of technological progress to economic growth can be explained and measured by the residual in growth accounting. "By astute measurement of a range of factors, the residual was progressively reduced. But all came to a final unmeasurable residual attributed to technological progress," Abramovitz wrote (1993, 220).

More recently, Paul Romer has declared that economics has yet to address the "measure of ignorance" charge levied by Abramovitz. This oversight has been at a cost both to the advance of economic theory and the effectiveness of policymaking. In the real business-cycle models that have dominated macroeconomic research in recent decades, the residual plays a central role. Macroeconomic theorists explain recessions as "negative technology shocks"; Prescott calculated that 84 percent of output variability is due to technology shocks (1986, cited in Romer forthcoming, 17). The problem is that instead of explaining "technology shocks," macro models deduce them from the residual, which remains, in Romer's words, a "disturbing blind spot."

The blind spot has not deterred macroeconomic theorists from strongly held policy viewpoints that depend on it.[30] Romer asserts that over re-

29. Mr. Dooley was a fictional Irish immigrant bartender created by American journalist Finley Peter Dunne. The quote is often attributed to Mark Twain; otherwise its origins are somewhat obscure. A similar theme of Daniel Kahneman (2013), a Nobel Prize winner, is that we can be blind to the obvious and also blind to our blindness.

30. As Lucas wrote (and is quoted in Romer forthcoming, 19): "My thesis ... is that macroeconomics in this original sense has succeeded: its central problem of depression prevention has been solved, for all practical purposes, and has in fact been solved for many decades" (Lucas 2003, 1).

cent decades macroeconomic theorists became lazy and created the facts mathematically to feed into the macro models without demanding that the deduced facts be linked to empirical evidence that can be independently examined. Mathematically deduced facts cannot establish the "truth value" of a fact (forthcoming, 12). But for Romer, "an indifferent tolerance of obvious error is even more corrosive to science than commited advocacy of error" (22).

Abramovitz's colleague economic historian Gavin Wright pointed to a disjuncture between economics and economic historians: "The discipline as a whole has not yet come to grips with the distinctive features of technological research and knowledge accumulation." Importantly, Wright surveys a "small and specialized ... [group of] ... successful empirical studies ... that have stayed close enough to the industry and firm levels to use measures that reflect true changes in technological practice or achievement, in contrast to the now-entrenched tradition of inferring technology from productivity" (1997, 1562). Examples from this small but distinguished group include studies by Landes (1969), Abramovitz and David (1973), Floud (1974), Berg (1980), Rosenberg (1982), Allen (1983), Devine (1983), Hughes (1989), Mokyr (1990), von Tunzelmann (1995), David and Wright (1999), Freeman and Louçã (2001), and Mindell (2002).[31]

Abramowitz himself suggested a way to shine light into the blind spot in growth theory and accounting, a way that is consistent with a production and organization capabilities perspective. He explains rapid growth experiences of technology late-comers in terms of a dynamic between "social capabilities" and technological progress. Social capabilities include "organization and management of large-scale enterprise and with financial institutions" and "well-established connections of [a nation's] science, technology and industry" (1986, 388, 405). Drawing again on Kuznets, Abramovitz went on to argue that the stock of "capital" is made up of two asset classes, tangible and intangible. Forms of intangible capital include the "infrastructure of the economies of scale and scope," such as "corporate managerial structure" and "business capability" (Abramowitz 1993, 229–30; see Kuznets 1971, 2).[32]

31. Chapter 6 contains many other examples in the context of British economic history.

32. In the same year, 1956, that Abramovitz published his famous article on macroeconomic growth accounting, Kuznets was president of the American Economic Association and personally invited Edith Penrose to present her findings on the theory of the growth of the firm three years before her book was published. As reported by Angela Penrose, Edith and Kuznets had known each other well as colleagues at Johns Hopkins in the mid-1950s

Although we cannot turn to Abramovitz for further development of these concepts, his focus on "interactive connections" provides a lasting contribution. To illustrate we turn to Schumpeter, who, like Keynes, put interactive connections between finance capital and productive capital at the center of economics.

Joseph Schumpeter: Entrepreneurial Activity and Industrial Finance

Abramovitz, like Penrose, paid homage to Joseph Schumpeter as the patron saint of the entrepreneurial function in economic theory. In Schumpeter's words: "The mechanisms of economic change in capitalist society pivot on entrepreneurial activity." But, he added, the "bursting" influence of entrepreneurial activity must be understood in the context of an interactive dynamic with the "shaping" influence of institutional forms. This dynamic remains a major topic for further inquiry. Why? As Schumpeter wrote: "Detailed investigation of this process (industrial dynamics) which may take many forms might teach us much about the actual working of capitalism that we are but dimly perceiving as yet" (1947, 153, 156).

As a former minister of finance, Schumpeter had real-world experience in finance and developed a unique but underappreciated perspective between the two key functions of the investment banker and the entrepreneur. The wealth-creating potential of innovation and technological progress cannot be realized without financial investments. The challenge for capitalism is that entrepreneurial activity and financial activity operate according to different motives and time scales, but capitalist progress depends on constructive interactive connections.

For Schumpeter, the entrepreneur and the financier are interdependent drivers of capitalist innovation (Schumpeter 1939, vol. 2, 109–18). The entrepreneurial function is to generate new wealth by investment in productive activities and innovation. Productive capital, unlike financial capital, is locked into distinctive products, processes, technologies, and organization. Productive investments demand financial commitment; the financial function demands liquidity. While the financier's motive is to make money with money, the financier's capitalist function is to reallocate preexisting wealth toward projects with "future values."

(Penrose forthcoming). Unfortunately, the two men did not seize the opportunity to integrate a theory of the firm into the transformative development perspective that they otherwise pioneered.

Joseph Schumpeter, 1883–1950. *Source:* Harvard University Archives.
HUD 343.04, p. 43 (olvwork369538).

Investment bankers are the intermediaries between agents who have wealth in the form of money and other paper assets and entrepreneurs who undertake financial investments in production activities without which new wealth would not be created. According to Schumpeter, "The money market is ... the headquarters of the capitalist system" (1934, 126). It is in the money market that economic projects are compared, development is financed, and the "system of future values first appears" (125). As "the monetary complement of innovation" (Schumpeter 1939, 111), credit creation and its allocation shape not only the level of output but "future values."

Drawing on the Schumpeterian distinction between financial capital and production capital, Carlota Perez (2002) has extended her earlier work on "techno-economic paradigms" into the complex but historically repetitive relationships linking technological revolutions, golden ages, and financial bubbles.[33]

In *The General Theory of Employment, Interest and Money* Keynes famously warned of the risks to the fabric of the real economy of financial "bubbles": "Speculators may do no harm as the bubbles on a steady stream of enterprise. But the situation is serious when enterprise becomes a bubble on the whirlpool of speculation." He called attention to the dependence of wealth creation on financial stability: "When the capital development of a country becomes a by-product of the activities of a casino, the job is likely to be ill-done" (1936, 159). In the *General Theory*, Keynes was concerned with the short run, defined as a period in which the stock of capital is fixed. Consequently, in that book he did not address matters of growth related to an economics of production, technological progress, and industrial organization, the topics that constitute a capability-informed macroeconomics and policymaking framework.[34]

The Schumpeterian dynamic between bursting and shaping operates at two levels: within the firm and between the firm and the "shaping influence of institutional forms." In the historical case studies described in this book we extend the former to a Penrosian dynamic between technological capability and market opportunity and extend the latter to the "shaping influences" of interfirm linkages, extrafirm infrastructures, and economic governance.

For example, chapter 2 revealed how the government-financed DPC was created to fund the production capability development needs of American industry during World War II, and chapter 3 revealed how early-stage technology development and business growth were financially enabled by a financial ecosystem shaped in major part by the Bank of Boston and the pioneering creation of a venture capital industry.[35] In both of these success stories, as well as in the other historical cases in the chapters that follow, financial capital is institutionally aligned with production and with technology capability development in business enterprises. This takes us beyond the realms of monetary and fiscal policy to institutions of economic governance.

---

33. William Janeway (2012), a venture capital investor, advances a Schumpeter-inspired thesis of the enabling roles of the state and speculative funding of asset bubbles, including financial crises, in innovation.

34. He did elaborate on the production side elsewhere. See chapter 6.

35. Jacobs, too, argued that the creative introduction of a venture capital industry was pivotal to the creation and growth of Greater Boston's high-tech business model and the ensuing process of increasing diversity that drives growth (1984, 228–30).

Drawing from these and other success stories, we find evidence of a common enabling feature of industrial finance that can be interpreted in the following terms. The due diligence required of the funding agency, whether private or public, is based on a strategy and structure assessment of an enterprise's future value proposition. Implicit are a Schumpeterian concept of competitive strategy and a concept of productive structures informed by the insights of Babbage and Penrose, anchored by fundamental principles of production and organization. The critical importance of the distinction is not to make a moral judgement. The purpose is to understand better the relationship between financial and production capital in economic development as well as macroeconomic stability.

Any economic theory that collapses finance capital and production capital into a single kind of homogeneous capital does not tell us much about capitalist growth, and treating it in this way can lead to policymaking failure. Whereas the focus of Nobel Prize–winning macroeconomic theory in recent decades has been on questioning whether monetary policy impacts the real economy, the deeper issues are the real-economy consequences of the deregulation of financial markets, innovation in debt instruments, the stability of the banking system, the government's role as lender of last resort, and economic austerity.

This takes us beyond the neoclassical textbook search for a synthesis of micromotives and macrobehavior to a postclassical synthesis of micro- and macroeconomics that is not anchored by the micromotives of the individual in the market but rather is embedded in a theory of the enterprise as an institution of production capability development shaped by localized institutions of economic governance and subject to global competitive forces. It calls for economic policymaking informed by an economics of the real economy in which the interdependent domains of production, enterprise, and governance are not opaque.

The Capability Triad as Dynamic Increasing Returns

Standard economics uses constant returns as its starting point even though, in brief, (1) this assumption is obviously wrong, contradicted by much of what we see in economic development, growth, spatial patterns of economic activity, and the growth of firms; (2) standard economics has therefore now incorporated increasing returns via "new" growth theory and trade theory, but in both models and empirical work tends to collapse dynamics into a single proxy variable, like "human capital," while in fact the types and sources of increasing returns are multitudinous and complex;

and (3) the tension between items 1 and 2 is not new. The impossibility of ignoring increasing returns has been known since Adam Smith's times, and the difficultly of incorporating them into formal models has been known since Ricardo's.[36]

The economic theorists whose ideas are discussed in this chapter examine the innovation dynamics that underlie productivity growth. They share an alternative economics framework to the competitive market ideal for understanding how economies function and for informing and conducting policymaking. Each thinker focuses on a different interactive connection in the economy to characterize an innovation dynamic within a multidimensional and complex economy. But taken together the innovation processes have common features and can interact with one another. Strategically organized, they can produce dynamic increasing returns.

For example, Jacobs's theory of city growth can be read as a city-level analogue to Penrose's theory of the growth of the firm. Jacobs's ideas about an innovation dynamic that brings new sectors into existence is analogous to Penrose's about the new product dynamic internal to a firm. For both, success at organizing a new technical process or innovating to produce a new product to meet a new market opportunity is a learning- and capability enhancing process. Enhanced skills, fresh technical expertise, and additional organizational capabilities are created that are, in effect, new and differentiated productive resources available to trigger a search for new market applications where they can be effectively used.

However, whereas Penrose's emphasis is on the creation of new productive resources within a single company, Jacobs focuses on the increased innovation opportunities for new combinations of skills, expertise, and techniques created by firms' increasing differentiation. Collectively, existing and new firms engage in mutual adjustment dynamics that foster import substitution, import replacement, and exports and, in the process, drive sector transitions.

Furthermore, Jacobs's city growth framework can accommodate and is enriched by the spatial interactions of Marshall's industrial districts, Young's dynamic increasing returns, and Richardson's focus-and-network business model. All operate in the intermediary domain of a region's industrial organization and link the internal capability development of enterprises with cluster-dynamic processes (see Best 2001, chap. 3).

Babbage, like Jacobs, focuses on the innovation dynamics of aggregates: manufacturing systems for Babbage, the diversifying city for Jacobs.

36. I am indebted to Frederick Guy for this formulation.

Babbage's observation-based principles linking engineering innovations in Victorian workshops and the emergence of yet newer areas of technical expertise and scientific domains go beyond both Penrose and Jacobs in ways that open the door to a political economy framework in which technology is endogenous and technology management is both an enterprise capability and a government policymaking target.

These great scholars lived and wrote about the real world, which their descriptions suggest is not amenable to the magic bullets dreamed up by policymakers based on economic theory. But there is no throwing up of hands in despair and depicting episodes of rapid growth as unexplained and inexplicable. Each contribution does offer, at the minimum, an analytical framework in lieu of a "growth miracle." These models can protect policymakers from unreflective failures. Together they offer more. Economic policymaking is always informed and defended by models, but no single model can mimic modern complex economies or fit all contexts. The capability triad is a better way to understand how crises can be overcome and robust growth achieved. Policymaking must start with a clear statement of objectives and craft plans and instruments into a development policy that accounts for each analytical framework and exposes systemic interactions. Failure to do so can have permanent and long-term damaging consequences for regional and national economic performance.

The Capability Triad as Strategic Development Policy Framework

The economics advanced by a review of the historical experiences of growth and decline in this book do not advance a policy framework with the clarity or certainty of the market fundamentalist or even Keynesian perspectives. Together they tell us that economies are inherently complex and not reducible to mechanical relationships. The methodological argument is that an alternative paradigm, beginning with case studies and empirical research rather than formal models grounded in a priori principles, is a more fruitful approach to understanding real-world economies and guiding policy. This is the position taken by all the thinkers in the production-centric paradigm.

Perhaps the most daunting aspect of the capability triad is that it requires public policy to be articulated with the detailed mechanics of change that occur within private firms. In this framework, public policy and private entrepreneurial actions do not operate in isolation from each other but become mutually reinforcing. There is some scope for a separable public policy, such as in skill formation, to ensure that the right mix of education and skills is produced to accommodate the changing demands of the economy as it develops. But even here, the links between public and private activity are crucial.

Why do we need such frameworks? The historical experiences described in this book tell us that a development policy framework is important for success. The case studies reveal extraordinary leaders responding to daunting challenges by crafting appropriate strategic policy frameworks at both enterprise and government levels. At the same time, luck plays a large part in successful outcomes. The expected external conditions needed to support success do not always arrive conveniently, and their absence may frustrate otherwise admirable policy initiatives. Nor is the true significance of the internal elements of a strategy always fully understood even by its own designers. But luck and chance, however random, can be handled best within well-thought-out and coherent frameworks that take full account of the nature of the external environment (opportunities and threats), as well as realistic views of domestic capabilities (strengths and weaknesses). What we can add, as well, is that the resulting SWOT (strengths, weaknesses, opportunities, and threats) analysis can be much richer if it is guided by the alternative economic baseline of the capabilities and innovation perspective and of the dynamic growth processes that it illuminates.

There is an old Gaelic proverb that says: "An té nach bhfuil láidir, ní foláir dó bheith glic," or "If you are not strong, you had better be smart." In the quest to break free from narrow, dependent, and reactive policy mindsets, the capability triad framework proposed here does not provide all the answers. But it helps those who hope to fashion transformative policies to be smart when time is pressing and when financial and human resources are limited. Such policies are essential if we wish to bring focus and synergy to the disparate policies that make up a broad enterprise-development strategy in a national, provincial, or local economy.

Conceptual frameworks and policy design, implementation, and renewal usually evolve in parallel with each other. Frameworks are rather like maps that tell you where you are, where you need to go, and the direction that you must take to get there. Policy design and implementation deal with the messy business of gathering resources, making pragmatic choices, overcoming obstacles, and bringing the team along to a collective goal. To confuse these separate but interrelated elements of strategy, or to emphasize one at the expense of the other, will almost certainly lead to failure. Having a wonderful map, but of a route that would take you over impassable terrain, is useless. Wandering aimlessly in the wilderness bereft of any maps is equally futile.

An obvious question to ask is: How can the capability triad, if indeed it is a universal process, be used to explain both the phenomenal growth that occurs in some regions as well as development failure in others? On the one hand, how much of the difference in performance is explained by domestic policy initiatives, in which there may be some degrees of freedom and scope for action? On the other hand, how much is the result of autonomous localized systems that operate within the private sector (operations systems, entrepreneurial skills, social capital) and are less amenable to direct policy influence? An initial reason for hesitation might be that the capability triad acts as a closed system that describes success or failure but—rather like meteorology and the weather—does not permit one to have much influence over the outcome.

Fortunately, the capability triad is not like the weatherman! It can offer diagnoses, and even contingent predictions, and it can also suggest ways forward. The country case studies examined in this book suggest that the logic of the capability triad, based as it is on a distillation of actual experience, provides both structure and content to strategy design. To neglect its lessons, and to focus on price competition and stabilization processes as advocated in standard economics, has condemned national and regional economies to stagnation and decline and to all the social problems that such failures propagate.

CHAPTER FIVE

Germany's Capability Triad and Economic Governance

WHEN ASKED THE SECRET to Germany's success by then Prime Minister Tony Blair, Angela Merkel famously replied, "We still make things." In this chapter we explore the productive structures that underpin Germany's manufacturing capability.

Chancellor Gerhard Schröder's 2003–5 package of structural reforms, known as Agenda 2010, is widely acknowledged to have contributed to the resurgence of the German economy powered by manufacturing exports. The structural reforms centered on increasing the flexibility of labor markets and welfare state cutbacks. Consequently, Agenda 2010 is commonly described as the adoption of Anglo-American neoliberal policies by the German government. However, this is a serious misreading of Germany's economic policy regime and of how the German economic system works. Unfortunately, it has contributed to the imposition of austerity agendas as a misguided means to increase the competitiveness of the peripheral economies of the EU.

The Schröder reforms came about because of the relative stagnation of the German economy around the turn of the century. But when the financial crisis was followed by the Great Recession beginning in 2008, the German economy proved to be remarkably resilient. This was also the case when in 1993–94 the German machine-tool industry suffered losses in export markets to China, as did the United States with the post–Cold War contraction of the defense and aerospace industries.

Agenda 2010 differed from neoliberal economic reforms and austerity agendas in two ways. The first is that Germany was committed to the consensus model, a defining feature of a *social* market economy. Increasing labor-market flexibility involved negotiating a three-way short-week agreement to share the burdens of structural reforms: employers and unions agreed to reduce people's hours of work instead of laying them off, and the government funded a portion of the reduced wages. The program is estimated to have cost the government €4.6 billion at its peak in 2009 and saved approximately 500,000 jobs (Rattner 2011). It illustrates a different approach to how business, labor, and the state can triangulate.

The second is that Agenda 2010 did not depart from the highly successful German postwar development strategy or seek to erode any of the core assemblage of institutions that underlie the nation's historic organizational advantages in industrial production. The goal was not to extend the sphere of market relations; rather it was to reform German *productive structures* to meet the challenges of increased globalization, an ageing population, the costs of reunification, and global warming.

Germany's Postwar Economic Development Strategy

The dismantling of the German state by the Allied powers following the war and the sharp curtailment of the German federal government's powers over the economy were widely thought to mean the end of German industrial might. But within a short period, the German economy started to grow again at as rapid a rate as it had done during the last quarter of the nineteenth century, when it had become a leading industrial power. This was unexpected, and it was not based on an ex ante systematic development strategy framework. So why was it so successful? We can rule out two explanations. First, it did not slavishly follow any existing theoretical model. And second, it did not imitate US historical experience. The unmatched economic performance of the American mass production system and multidivisional business model was not widely appreciated in Germany during the 1930s. It was thereafter, but the postwar German government development strategy was not to imitate the production system of the United States. Nor did it parallel the emerging Japanese industrial system and governance institutions. The business systems that drove the growth experiences of all three countries were and remain organizationally very different.

In the early postwar days, policymakers did not rely on any existing development strategy. But in time one emerged that combined a reshaped legacy production system, an emphasis on SMEs as the backbone of German industry, with a multilayered economic governance structure.

The decentralization of policymaking imposed by the Allied powers was critical to the crafting of Germany's development policy framework through trial and error. It played to the historic competitive advantage of German engineering-intensive manufacturing sectors in which the cost advantages of mass production mattered less and flexible production mattered more. This was particularly so in sectors such as machining, tooling, equipment making, instrument making, and otherwise technically advanced products and services. The *"Mittelstand"* business system (discussed below), the municipal banking system, and the technically oriented educational system had long combined synergistically.

At the same time, the postwar institutions of economic governance changed in two ways. First, industrial policymaking power was decentralized to cities and regions. Second, Germany's science and technology infrastructure incorporated a bottom-up demand pull from the *Mittelstand* business system to combine with the nation's historic top-down supply push from the federal government. These two decentralizing reforms caused Germany's traditional engineering business strengths to be reinforced with and complemented by centrally funded but locally administered R&D institutions. The reshaped production system did not self-organize; the constituent research agendas and institutions were overseen, focused, organized, and aligned by regional government industrial policies. Germany's *Mittelstand* business system and the strategic organizing capability of local and regional governments were structurally linked, but this was empirically obscured by economic theories and political ideologies that idealize perfectly competitive markets and laissez-faire government.

The architect of the emergent "social market economy" was Ludwig Erhard, the German economics minister from 1949 to 1963 and chancellor from 1963 to 1966. He is known as the father of West Germany's *Wirtschaftswunder*, or economic miracle. Erhard was a champion of the potential for markets to foster growth and the limits of government intervention to control business cycles given the inherent complexity of the economy. At the same time, a guiding principle of his concept of statecraft was that unguided capitalism undermined itself as monopolies cornered markets and captured the state.

The concept of the market, for Erhard, was less about an economic theory of exchange and more about the critical importance of business organization and skill formation to the production foundations for globally competitive economic performance and long-term economic stability. To these ends he stressed the social foundations of the market economy and the importance of individual responsibility to the continued development of a nation's regulatory framework (Erhard 1963; Kohl 1989).

Ludwig Erhard, 1897–1977. *Source:* Harvard University Archives.
Photo: Eric Koch/Anefo © Nationaal Archief.

Mittelstand

As explained above, the German business system does not fit either conventional theoretical models or historical experience of other large industrialized countries. Its evolution and structural characteristics can be understood only by historical and empirical examination.

The *Mittelstand*, a population of small- and medium-sized, largely family-owned business enterprises, is a business model that predates German national unification in the nineteenth century and has persisted through the political revolutions of twentieth-century Germany up to the present. In 2010, more than three million small and mid-sized enterprises, companies with fewer than 500 employees and annual sales of less than €50 million, together employed over 70 percent of German workers and contributed roughly half of the country's GDP (Randow and Kirchfeld 2010).[1] International comparisons are problematic, but US census data imply that the United States, with approximately four times the population of

1. Enterprise sizes are defined by employment: micro enterprises (up to 9 employees), small enterprises (10–99), medium enterprises (100–499), and large enterprises (500 or more). In 1992, 1 in 500 was large in Germany, one in 140 in the United States, and the contribution of medium-sized enterprises to turnover was 24.4 percent in Germany and only 13.9 percent in the United States (Frenkel and Fendel 1999).

Germany (315 million versus 82 million), has only two times, or six million, the number of employer firms with fewer than 500 employees of Germany (for data on US small businesses, see http://www.census.gov/econ /smallbus.html).

However, the number of SMEs is not the issue; it is what they do. Specifically, it is their production capabilities, particularly for new-product development, technology management, and innovation. These are the entrepreneurial firms with the organizational capabilities to engage in Schumpeterian competition, to pursue strategies of superior products, processes, technology, and/or organization. They are the firms that create value, increase productivity, and sustain high-paying jobs and upon which regional and national competitive advantage depends.

We have no direct estimates of entrepreneurial firms as a proportion of SMEs anywhere. But indirect measures such as the ratio of R&D expenditures to GDP indicate a huge gap between the entrepreneurial activity of enterprises in the social market economies at the core of the EU (Germany, Austria, Denmark, Finland, the Netherlands, and Sweden) and activity in the nations peripheral to the EU (Ireland, Greece, Portugal, Italy, Spain, plus the new EU member states of central and southern Europe). The superior innovation performance of the German and Nordic economies can be seen in the Eurostat map of patent application data by NUTS 3 regions.[2] As shown in figure 5.1, in 2006 the ratio of R&D to GDP in Germany, Denmark, and Finland was between 2.5 and 3.5 compared to 0.5–1.0 in Greece, Spain, and Ireland. As shown in table 5.1, the R&D EU Scoreboard of the nationalities of the thousand leading companies reveals the dearth of representatives from Europe's periphery. The small Nordic countries of Finland and Denmark, as well as Sweden, have dozens of such companies; at the other end, Greece has four and Ireland twelve.

The economies with high ratios of R&D to GDP also have larger manufacturing sectors. Germany's manufacturing share is estimated to be 20 percent, but if industry-related services are added, manufacturing's share is estimated to be more like 30 percent (*Economist* 2012b). Within manufacturing, Germany has particularly large capital goods and toolmaking

2. See Eurostat 2012, map 4: "Patent Applications to the EPO [European Patent Office], by NUTS 3 Regions, 2006 (per million inhabitants)," available at http://epp.eurostat .ec.europa.eu/statistics_explained/index.php/Science_and_technology_at_regional _level. NUTS stands for Nomenclature des Unités Territoriales Statistiques, or Nomenclature of Territorial Units for Statistics, "a geographical nomenclature subdividing the economic territory of the EU into regions at three different levels (NUTS 1, 2, and 3, respectively, moving from larger to smaller territorial units). Above NUTS 1, there is the "national" level of the Member States" (Eurostat 2016).

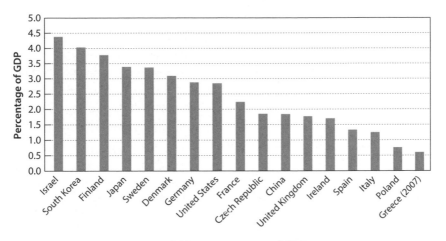

FIGURE 5.1. R&D as a percentage of GDP, 2011.
Sources: OECD (2013), table 4; UNESCO.

subsectors. Nearly one-third of the German *Mittelstand* companies are in machine equipment, and half are in machine equipment, electrical engineering, and industrial products.

The large size of the capital goods sector is itself an indirect measure of the extent of new-product development capabilities of the *Mittelstand*. The capital goods sector performs as a system-level resource or infrastructure that can be leveraged by individual firms to develop new products and processes. Interfirm connections of this type enable product differentiation strategies, heretofore an organizational advantage of the M-form or multidivisional enterprise.

The combination of a vibrant capital goods sector and an open-system business model lowers the barriers to the transition of mid-sized, nonspecialized firms to product-differentiating entrepreneurial firms. A small- or mid-sized firm can pursue a strategy of flexible specialization because of the large number of partners available with which to coordinate jointly not only along a product chain but for the development of new products. These are extrafirm, collective organizational capabilities that enhance participant firms' new-product and technology management capabilities.

Schumpeterian Competition and Dynamic Increasing Returns

The internal organization of a firm is structurally linked to the prevailing mode of competition in the market. Product-led and price-led modes of competition have different industrial organization consequences. To

Table 5.1. R&D EU Scoreboard Top 1,000 Companies and Employment Impact, 2008

	Companies	Population (millions)	R&D investment (€ millions)	Employees	% of LF[a]
EU[b]					
Germany	208	82.1	45,097	5,885,277	18.00
Finland	58	5.3	6,787	534,814	25.00
Sweden	70	9.2	6,952	834,151	23.00
Netherlands	53	16.4	9,703	1,003,566	15.00
Denmark	47	5.5	3,418	310,776	14.00
Belgium	30	10.7	2,558	570,200	13.00
Spain	21	45.3	1,471	485,379	2.80
Ireland	12	4.4	532	60,602	3.40
Greece	4	11.2	53	6,281	0.13
Non EU[c]					
Switz.	38	7.6	17,468	950,875	32.00

[a] Percentage of labor force derived by assuming a labor force equal to 40 percent of a country's population.
[b] The EU Industrial R&D Investment Scoreboard is a compilation of the top 1,000 European headquartered companies by R&D investment.
[c] The EU Industrial R&D Investment Scoreboard has a separate scorecard for the top 1,000 non-EU companies.

paraphrase a famous philosopher: anarchy in the market begets despotism behind the factory gate.[3] Put differently, intense price competition among producers of an identical or nearly identical product is a market that rewards cost-cutting, routinized methods of work organization that divide managers and workers, planning and execution, thinking and doing. These shop-floor practices are not consistent with new product development and innovation capabilities, which depend on inclusive and flexible models of work organization.

Thus product-led competition creates a different set of pressures on internal organization than does price-led competition. Efficient new-product development is about the integration of design and manufacturing on the shop floor and entails ceaseless improvement via experimentation to establish best practice. As Babbage noted more than a century earlier, the introduction of new technologies requires cross-disciplinary teamwork, and companies that are organized to tap the creative input of a committed workforce are better placed to succeed.

3. Marx (1961 [1867], 243): "If, in a society with capitalist production, anarchy in the social division of labour and despotism in that of the workshop are mutual conditions . . . ."

Product-led competition fosters business strategies of focus and net-working. Firms focus on core capabilities and network for complementary capabilities. But just as focus begets interfirm networks, networks beget intrafirm focus. The growth of networks creates opportunities for further specialization and new specialist enterprises that focus on niches in the evolving market system. The consequence is a group of firms that collectively share the benefits of increasing internal specialization and differentiation of capabilities. Innovations in one company feed through to innovations in a second company and induce dynamic, cumulative, increasing returns. The spread of focus and network strategies can generate iterative cluster-dynamic processes. Price-led competition among firms, in contrast, does not generate the systemic interfirm feedback effects on capability development at the individual-enterprise and group levels.

Germany's Intangible Infrastructures

The transfer of political authority and budgetary controls to German cities and regions created opportunities for local leadership and civic action to shape industrial and community development. While tax revenues were limited, city policymakers drew on, reformed, and extended the resources of the consensus model in order to make the most of limited monetary resources. The creation of jobs and economic development were immediate priorities. They drew on the organized participation and expertise of business, labor, education, bankers, and others to develop reflexive, evidence-based industrial policies.[4] In the process, they negotiated an informal strategic development framework that built on and modernized Germany's unique family-based business system. It became integral to Germany's production system.

City governments did not use their new powers to undermine the long-established apprenticeship, social banking, and SME family-based business system. In the social market economy, civic action in the form of local alliances to tackle issues such as education, market regulation, and economic development substituted for policymaking by market-correcting economic incentives. Active civic engagement facilitated the access to qualitative local knowledge that was critical to create and operationalize effective strategic industrial policymaking. At its best, it provided a common

4. Reflexivity here implies a developmental "learning" policy framework in which policymakers analyze the outcomes of enacted policies both to formulate subsequent policy and to identify and adjust institutional relationships that have an impact on regional economic performance.

ground for democratically and transparently negotiating competing values and goals that needed to be reconciled for a community to establish and implement strategies to grow and sustain successful enterprises.

THE DUAL VOCATIONAL EDUCATION SYSTEM

The story of Germany's rise as an industrial power cannot be told without reference to its dual vocational education system. The dual system linked apprenticeship and vocational schools to create a national "continuation" education system for the nation's 16- to 18-year-olds. It led to direct employment in companies that were simultaneously investing in the establishment of a national labor force with practical production experience and technical education in government-funded vocational schools.

The national scale and government investment in a national system of vocational training institutes solved the "free-rider" challenge to investment in human resources of economic theory. But it operated at the level of regional governments which matched the demand and supply of skills to the regions' distinctive technical capabilities. Moreover, it created a public and private partnership that facilitated increasing a region's pool of vocationally educated labor to meet the needs of growing firms and whole sectors.

The consequence was that the German dual system provided the otherwise missing link in the industrial innovation process chain by which basic research, development research, applied research, design for manufacturing, production engineering, and new-product development could be seamlessly linked. With these enabling institutions, German SMEs can pursue product-led competitive strategies and cumulatively advance their distinctive technological capability.

The vocational educational training system and the family firm of the *Mittelstand* business system are complementary institutions. Because of the high quality of the training system and the access to specialized applied research institutes, owners of family firms commonly send a son or daughter through the "continuation" track, after which they move into management or specialist engineering jobs within the family firms.

The postwar German education system continued to excel at educating the technically skilled workforce required to implement business strategies in advanced manufacturing. The technical education curriculum integrates school-based and experiential learning within enterprises and is co-shaped by educators, unions, and employer federations. While not universally popular, it would not work if enterprises were not engineering-oriented and did not provide career opportunities. It is estimated that around half of German high school students are educated in the vocational system. The willingness of enterprises to participate is built into the nation's distinctive business model: one study estimates that half of the successful *Mittelstand* companies have been established for over seventy years. These must be mutually reinforcing characteristics.

R&D SYSTEM AND INNOVATION
PROCESS INTEGRATION

Sustaining high-wage regional economies depends on technological innovation and business enterprises with technology management capabilities. The interesting feature of the German economy is the combination of the *Mittelstand* business system with high levels of public and private R&D. A high level of private R&D signifies investment in innovation, for which SMEs need interorganizational relationships.

The German national science and technology infrastructure is funded at the federal level but is administered by a range of regionally decentralized specialist agencies such as the Fraunhofer Institutes, the Helmholtz Research Establishments, and the Max Planck Institutes. These agencies are incentivized to push R&D resources into business enterprises. Success, however, depends on the pull of R&D resources into the technology-management and product-development activities of business enterprises. Matching demand-pull with the supply-push of technological and scientific research expertise is coordinated not by prices in a market but by networking connection channels and consultative relationships. Local-level industrial policymakers can be well situated to play the broker role not only in fostering networks but in mobilizing local communities to attract federal R&D institutes and agencies to their regions. This can foster a self-reinforcing dynamic by which regions establish distinctive technological capabilities that become magnets that draw firms to the regions, making them yet more attractive to those allocating further federal government S&T resources.

Technology management policy in Germany is a multi-layered governance process. Mission-driven initiatives at the federal level are informed by a political consensus on national priorities, but the administration and execution are decentralized. The challenge is to organize chains of innovation that link basic research, development research, and applied research with the new-product development and technology management capabilities of firms.

Processes of opportunity creation can be found at both ends of the chain of innovation: mission-driven research is the prerogative of government and funded by it at one end, and at the other end is a population of entrepreneurial firms in the form of niche-seeking SMEs with the capacity to detect opportunities, organize innovation networks and nurture customers, and create a market. Matching demand with supply for S&T services involves establishing interrelationships involving industry, R&D institutions, and local along with national levels of government. Prices adjust as part of the process of creating and responding to capability-development opportunities.

DEVELOPMENT CAPITAL

In contrast to that of the United States or the United Kingdom, the German banking system is highly localized, long-term-oriented, and socially owned and governed. By one estimate, 431 savings banks operate a network of more than 15,600 branches and offices and employ more than 250,000 people.[5] Each savings bank is independent, owned by a single municipality or several, and focuses on local activities.[6] Some 1,116 cooperative banks are owned by members, each of whom has a vote independent of capital share (Hufner 2010, 9). It is estimated that the savings banks and 1,116 cooperative banks provide about two-thirds of all lending to *Mittelstand* companies and 43 percent of lending to all companies and households (*Economist* 2012b). While private banks reduced their medium- and long-term lending to companies and households between 2007 and 2012 in favor of short-term loans, the savings and cooperative banks increased theirs and, to quote the *Economist*, had "come through the crisis with barely a scratch so far."[7]

Another class of public banks is owned by the federal or state governments and can operate on a national strategic development scale. KfW (Kreditanstalt für Wiederaubau), which is 80 percent owned by the German state, is an example. It was formed as part of the Marshall Plan in 1948 and has continued to plow back returns from business-development investments. Today it has half a trillion euros of assets, making it roughly

5. German Public Bank, https://en.wikipedia.org/wiki/German_public_bank#cite_note-20, accessed November 12, 2017.

6. According to Magarete Wagner-Braun: "Between 1850 and 1903 the idea of the municipal savings banks spread and the number of savings banks in Germany increased from 630 to 2,834"(n.d., 16–17).

7. *Economist* 2012a

twice the size of the World Bank. In a recent examination, Damian Carrington estimated that it lent €70 billion in 2011, raised from international markets at low interest rates. About a third of this went to energy and climate-change investments, including €24 billion from 2009 to 2011 on energy efficiency in homes, which leveraged a much greater total investment (Carrington 2012).

The key to the success of local financial institutions is effective due diligence capability informed by technical and business expertise. Having supervisory boards with representatives from business, labor, and academia enhances the flow of information and the discovery processes for evaluating and funding long-term loans. Banks rely heavily on specialist engineering consultancies, for which Germany is renowned in the business world.[8]

The German and Italian Miracles Compared

To better understand the distinctive features of the German model we contrast Germany with Italy, which was also transformed by a postwar "miracle." The Italian economy experienced an average rate of growth of GDP of 5.8 percent per year between 1951 and 1963 and 5.0 percent per year between 1964 and 1973 (Rossi and Toniolo 1996, 441). Only Japan did better. In 1963 President Kennedy described Italy's change of fortunes as follows: "A nation once literally in ruins, beset by heavy unemployment and inflation, has expanded its output and assets, stabilized its costs and currency, and created new jobs and new industries at a rate unmatched in the Western world."[9]

The Italian postwar economic miracle transformed the country from a poor, mainly rural nation into a global industrial power. As in Germany, Italian industrial districts constituted by networked groups of specialized SMEs displayed a remarkable economic dynamism in terms of sales, exports, and employment and were the central players in the Italian manufacturing system (Becattini and Coltorti 2006). Firms cumulatively and collectively developed distinctive regional capabilities, which in turn created a knowledge resource base in deep craft skills for the next generation of innovative activities. Sebastiano Brusco (1982) and Giacomo Becattini (1978) independently characterized the stewardship governance

8. Ibid.; Carrington 2012.
9. Kennedy 1963, cited in "Italian Economic Miracle," https://en.wikipedia.org/wiki/Italian_economic_miracle, accessed November 14, 2017.

function in terms of social identity and community institutions that give voice to the collective will and the common good. Extra-firm infrastructures were created primarily at the local level. For links between industrial districts and culture, see Bellandi and Santini 2016; for historic examples of infrastructures in Emilia Romagna, see Brusco 1982 and Best 1990, chaps. 7 and 8).

During the miracle years, Italian success in international competitiveness was concentrated in light industry. Referred to as "made in Italy" products, the output of this industry included textiles and clothing, leather goods and footwear, furniture, jewelry, household goods, and things created through light mechanical engineering (Becattini and Coltorti 2006, 1116). Italian industrial districts thrived at the expense of sectors located elsewhere, such as in the United Kingdom, as we will see in the next chapter, in which business enterprises were organized to compete on price alone and located in regions without the extra-firm capability-development infrastructures of their Italian competitors.

However, at the turn of the century the economic performance paths of Germany and Italy diverged as the Italian economy experienced a marked slowdown. The decline has been striking in the light-industry sectors that drove the miracle. Unlike Italy, Germany successfully transitioned into new sectors, and *Mittelstand* enterprises enjoyed the benefits of a multilayered governance structure that focused on advancing the nation's technology-management capabilities. Italy, in contrast, illustrates the limits of the industrial-district model, in which local governance operates largely without the intermediate and national technology capability-development institutions of Germany.[10]

German economic policymaking illustrates how productive infrastructures can play a triple developmental role: they are accessed by firms pursuing product-led strategies; they are the means of delivering centralized industrial policy measures designed to enhance the new-product development and technology management capabilities of a region's or a nation's enterprises; and they are major components of the central government's countercyclical macroeconomic policymaking armory. It is an illustration of macroeconomic policymaking that combines Keynesian demand-side expenditure with supply-side capability development measures. Policy attention to capability development and renewal increases

10. Italian GERD (gross expenditure on R&D) was 1.3 percent in 2015, and that of Germany was 2.9 percent. See "Gross Domestic Spending on R&D," OECD data, 2017, https://data.oecd.org/rd/gross-domestic-spending-on-r-d.htm.

the resilience of enterprises and regions to competitive turbulence in the world economy.

The German model is not unique to Germany. It is representative of the economic governance frameworks and competitiveness structures of the much smaller social market economies of the Nordic countries. But it does not exist, except perhaps in limited cases, in the peripheral economies of the EU. The contrast in institutions of economic governance is stark.[11]

Germany and the Nordic economies have proven resilient to the emergence of China as a global economic power. This is not the case in Italy (Bellani 2008; Dei Ottati 2009; Rabellotti, Carabelli, and Hirsch 2009). Although there have recently been debates between proponents of Marshallian specialization and Jacobs-type diversity theories of geographical advantage, the success of Germany's regional economies suggests the emergence of a model of economic governance that combines the advantages of both. We return to these matters in the following chapters, which explore multiple dimensions of economic governance and real-world economic performance that tend to be obscured by the conventional separation of microeconomics from macroeconomics in the market competitiveness paradigm.[12]

Most commentary on the divergence in economic performance between the successful center and the peripheral countries of the EU is offered in terms of barriers in the periphery to national "competitiveness," the lack of labor-market flexibility, and excessive government regulation. Missing in the commentary is an economic analysis of the productive structures and the infrastructural functions of the successful regions and nations. A better understanding of structural competitiveness is critical to characterizing the challenges to government policymaking and constructing long-term development strategies to improve economic performance in the periphery of the EU.

11. See the second section of chapter 7 for a case study of a peripheral subeconomy within the EU.

12. In contrast to the German and the Nordic social market economies, the Italian economy has not been successful in moving up the production capability spectrum (box 8.1) or transitioning to new sectors (figure 8.1). Germany, in contrast, created dynamic new sectors at the west and north poles of figure 8.1.

CHAPTER SIX

Capability Triad Failure

THE UNITED KINGDOM

The Historic Decline of British Industry

The United Kingdom was the first economy to undergo an industrial revolution. Many northern cities grew rapidly as labor was pulled from the countryside into the factories and as workshops were erected to create and grow new sectors and the nation became known as the workshop of the world. But industrial leadership was short lived. Historical research suggests that in 1840 labor productivity in US manufacturing was twice that in British manufacturing, a gap that persisted until the end of the century (Broadberry and Irwin 2004, 11, 24). In the twentieth century, the United Kingdom's manufacturing productivity gap relative to Germany, the United States, and France persisted, and manufacturing output declined steadily in absolute terms (Jones 2016).

Behind the productivity gap lies a stark reality captured in a review by Robert Skidelsky (2013) of Nicholas Comfort's *The Slow Death of British Industry: A 60-Year Suicide* (2012):

> In the early 1950s, Britain was an industrial giant. Today, it is an industrial pygmy. Manufacturing was industry's bedrock. In 1952, it produced a third of the national output, employed 40 per cent of the workforce and made up a quarter of world manufacturing exports. Today, manufacturing in this country accounts for just 11 per cent of GDP, employs only 8 per cent of the workforce and sells 2 per cent of the world's manufacturing exports. The iconic names of industrial Britain

[144]

are history; in their place are the service economy and supermarkets selling mainly imported goods. (Skidelsky 2013)

Was the decline of UK manufacturing inevitable? Could different economic policies have made a difference? The standard paradigm asserts that the economic rationale for government intervention is to correct for market failure. The conventional narrative of the causes of British industrial decline cites the failure of government to restrict the market power of trade unions added to stagnant and inefficient government ownership and excessive market interference/regulation. The policy implication is that structural reforms defined in terms of government enforcement of flexible markets could have stopped the decline, improved competitiveness, and closed the productivity gap.

An industry case study informed by comparative capability triads is a research methodology that may be used to examine a region's or a nation's structural advantage in terms of respective mutual adjustment processes linking production, business, and governance. Although every industry is different, the fundamental principles of production and organization cut across industries.[1] But while a nation's system of economic governance is national in scope, its infrastructural configuration may vary to address the circumstances of specific sectors and regions that operate within it.

The capability triad as a development policy framework focuses attention on three economic governance roles. The first role is that of an extended "scope" of macroeconomic policymaking in which stabilization plays a supportive rather than a dominant role. The second is that of shaping and unifying extrafirm development infrastructures in ways that blend government policies with innovation within and across independently managed firms. The third role is that of providing leadership to react strategically to internal and external threats to a region's or a nation's economic livelihood (see chap. 9).

In the chapters on successful rapid-growth experiences we find policymakers who have responded to internal and external crises by crafting industrial strategies to implement major shifts in economic structures and successfully galvanized innovation and growth dynamics. The term "strategic" is used in the business-school sense of starting with a SWOT analysis of an individual company's strengths, weaknesses, opportunities, and

1. See Best (1990, 227–40) for an application of comparative production systems methodology to the furniture industry contrasting industrial districts in the United Kingdom and the "third Italy."

threats. The difference is that here each of the terms is characterized in terms of the production-centric paradigm and the unit of analysis is not a single firm but populations of firms in a regional or national economy.

The production-centric perspective takes us inside a business enterprise to examine where it fits on the global production-capability spectrum (see box 8.1). While the firm drives innovation, it does not do so alone. Firms are embedded in networked groups of competing and cooperating enterprises. These interfirm relationships may or may not foster a range of cluster-dynamic processes and innovation dynamics that include Marshallian external economies, Jacobs's differentiation and new combination dynamics, Young's diffusion dynamics, Myrdal's cumulative causation, Richardson's network economies, and Babbage's machine-shop expertise backed by scientific research. Economic governance in the form of the design and crafting of infrastructures, physical and developmental, can influence enterprise innovation directly and indirectly through fostering cluster-dynamic processes. This is the terrain of strategic development policy and complementary institutions of economic governance.

In chapter 2 we saw the opportunity for a nation to make a step-change in productivity by the successful design and implementation of a strategic policy framework that focused on the production system. In chapter 3 we saw the elements of a regional financial ecosystem combined with access to a national S&T infrastructure and a legacy of local technical expertise combined to nurture the emergence of a diverse population of entrepreneurial SMEs that have collectively created and grown new industrial sectors. In 1949 the West German minister for economics deliberately demolished the apparatus of government controls and industry cartels and formulated the social market theory of economic governance.

This chapter has six sections. We start with production systems and examine the British indigenous road-car industry from a comparative manufacturing systems perspective. This allows us to characterize the causes of low "total factor productivity" directly rather than as a residual in growth accounting exercises. In the second section we find that the British volume car industry never committed to the fundamental production principles of interchangeability and flow pioneered in the United States and extended in Japan and lost out to global competitors that did. Locked into a low-productivity system, the British volume car industry collapsed in bankruptcies in the 1970s despite an increasingly desperate series of industrial polices including organized mergers, bailouts, and state ownership.

The third section reports on a regional success story: Motor Sports Valley, which occupies a portion of the West Midlands and Oxfordshire, is home to most of the world's Formula 1 race-car teams and production sites. It is an innovative "Marshallian" industrial district that has a global structural competitive advantage that we examine closely. It illustrates both the continuing excellence of British innovation engineering but also the limited scale of its wider economic impact. While it presents a fascinating tale of cluster dynamics within a single sector, it is the exception in UK experience that proves the rule: an articulated set of extra-firm infrastructures is required to foster regional intersector growth processes.

The fourth section examines a second success story, the rebirth of volume car production with the establishment of branch plants of Japanese and German companies beginning in the 1980s. These plants introduced world-class manufacturing practices to the United Kingdom but are largely independent of the UK industrial ecosystem.

The fifth section characterizes two extrafirm infrastructures that have historically distinguished the United Kingdom's industrial ecosystem from those of Germany and the United States. Both made a major impact on industrial performance through feedback effects on enterprise innovation and production-capability dynamics. The first is an advanced engineering machine-tool industry that has historically served to diffuse technological innovations across new sectors and enabled emergent downstream sectors to ramp up while building partnerships with volume producers to facilitate rapid new-product development and technology-management capabilities. The second is a set of institutions that deliver comprehensive technical skill formation. The links between technical education and new-product development and technology management capabilities created a structural competitive advantage in translating engineering innovations into economically engineered products and enterprise growth.[2]

The productivity "puzzle" of British excellence in innovation and design engineering alongside low productivity and a lack of successful industrial enterprises is in major part a consequence of policy failure. While often the United Kingdom and the United States are categorized together

2. Peter Hall and David Soskice's account of "institutional complementarities" is a complementary concept to the "infrastructural complementarities" that feature in this book (2001). However, they do not address transformative experiences and group together the United Kingdom and the United States as two prime examples of "liberal market economies" in contrast to "coordinated market economies" such as Germany and the social-market Scandinavian economies.

as liberal market economies, once the shared free-market ideology is stripped away we identify three major structural changes in the US economy undertaken by government leadership that advanced the nation's skill formation system. The United Kingdom is the single outlier in pursuing independent industrial and education policies. Instead of creating the regional-level social partnerships and investing in the technical skills of an industrial workforce required to grow entrepreneurial firms, the government inadvertently created a class of educational orphans. It is here that we find the missing link in the nation's ability to translate S&T into growing firms, sectors, and regional cities.

The final section describes three examples of unintentionally counterproductive policymaking that by commission or omission failed to arrest industrial decline. UK government policymaking has never been informed by a production-centric perspective in which a unified set of mediating infrastructures has been crafted to advance mutual adjustment processes linking production, business, and skill formation, as in Germany (see chap. 5). This claim is illustrated with examples of industrial policy that at best had little positive effect and at worst were counterproductive.

Production System Failures

It would be hard to overstate the transformative effects on the manufacturing industry of the rise of the automobile industry in 1920s America. By 1929 the car industry employed 447,000, fractionally less than the leading employer, foundry and machine-shop products (454,000) and above the third-ranked cotton-goods industry (425,000) (Fearon 1987, 55). The automobile industry fit the description of a "development block" in Eric Dahmén's theory of industrial transformation (1970). The steel, glass, tire, and petrol industries were pulled along, as was the machine-tool industry. John Kendrick's index of manufacturing productivity as measured by output per manhour increased from 61.5 to 100 between 1920 and 1929 (1961, table D-11, cited in Fearon 1987).

The conventional narrative was that the sources of superior productivity of the Ford mass-production system were vertical integration, economies of size, and the organization of work according to Frederick Taylor's scientific management, including his piece-rate pay system. All were false presuppositions that were immediately evident to any observer with knowledge of the production-engineering principles of interchangeability and flow as widely practiced in many US industries.

THE PRINCIPLE OF INTERCHANGEABILITY

Awareness of the significance of interchangeability of parts in the emergence of the "American system of manufacturing" was not lost on leading British engineers in the mid-nineteenth century. In 1854 a visiting English delegation of engineers and military men conducted a famous test on interchangeability at the armory in Springfield, Massachusetts, in which they haphazardly reassembled parts from ten disassembled Springfield muskets, each produced in a different year between 1844 and 1853, and found that performance was unaffected (Wallis and Whitworth 1969 [1855]). The English team set about purchasing the full range of machines and gauges needed to set up the new Enfield Armory in North London (Smiles 1883, 362–63, cited in Roe, 1937; Best 1990, 31–33); Thomas Jefferson's leadership role is described in chapter 9.

However, in the formative years of the car industry the principle of interchangeability was not widely established in British industry. For British writers George Maxcy and Aubrey Silberston, the source of American competitive advantage from the beginning was that in the United States the "engineering industry had developed a system of standardized interchangeable parts and of extensive sub-contracting that had no equivalent in this country." They continued: "William Morris ... had to turn to the United States in 1914 when he could find no British firm which could produce large enough quantities of standardized parts" (1959, 12, 13).

Consequently, the British car industry suffered from low levels of productivity. No British firm managed to exceed the production level of one car per man per year as late as 1914; in contrast, Ford's three hundred workers were producing 1,700 cars per year in 1903/4, demonstrating nearly six times greater productivity (Saul 1962, 43–44). Saul explains why: "The interchangeable idea caught on only very slowly.... A considerable amount of hand finishing was still to be noted at the Austin works in 1914" (1962, 38). Machines were being introduced to reduce hand work, "but still there was far too much touching up by hand during general assembly as a result of errors in jigs or machinery and this made it all the more difficult to supply accurate spare parts" (*Automobile Engineering*, July 1912, 212–17, cited by Saul 1962, 39)[3]

3. According to Saul, instead of embracing the step-change increase in performance standards achievable by transitioning to the new principles of production and organization, "the average attitude to new ideas was one of disbelief or sheer ignorance.... The pity was that influential journals such as *Autocar* sought to belittle Ford's achievement" (1962,

The government became painfully aware of the failure of British industry to internalize interchangeability during World War II. The need to mass produce Rolls-Royce Merlin engines to power the Avro Lancaster bomber and other aircraft led the British government to build a new £6.6 million factory in Trafford Park, Manchester, to be run by Ford. "This factory made built [*sic*] 30,428 engines between June 1941 and March 1946. 10,116 men and 7,200 women worked there. Ford had to produce new drawings for the Merlin that were more precise than those used by Rolls Royce. This allowed interchangeable parts to be produced by lower-skilled workers and made mass production possible" (Manchester Museum of Science and Industry, March 2016; the engine on display was on loan from the Ford Motor Company).

Five decades later the lessons for government procurement had not been learned or at least standardized. According to Comfort, "Britain's plane makers continued with the same handcraft approach.... Engineers noted that no two of the Nimrod aircraft, flown by the RAF until 2011, had exactly the same dimensions" (2012).[4]

Interchangeability and standardization went hand in glove to advance productivity across the production system. Ford was famous for offering any color of Model T, so long as it was black. Decades later, in 1947, Oliver Lucas of the electrical components firm Lucas Industries invited a group of journalists to press the case for standardization on the British car manufacturers. He laid out 68 models of distributors, 133 headlamp types, and 98 windshield-wiper variations (Adeney 1988, 200). Had the final assemblers followed Ford and driven the principle of interchangeability combined with flow through the supplier network, an opportunity could have been seized to increase productivity and build a high-performance supply base for multiple industrial sectors. Instead they ignored Lucas's plea as well as Ford's principles. It was not too late, given the lack of global competition in the industry, but the opportunity was missed.

In line with conventional theories of optimum inventory and worker motivation, British car manufacturers continued to organize their plants on batch-production principles and individual piece-rate incentive sys-

---

41): "It is highly to the credit of our English makers that they choose rather to maintain their reputation for high grade work than cheapen that reputation by the use of the inferior material and workmanship they would be obliged to employ to compete with American manufacturers of cheap cars" *Autocar*, September 21, 1912.

4. A Nimrod generation upgrade was abandoned by the UK government in 2010, with billions of pounds spent, years behind schedule, and with it Britain's capacity to manufacture a large airframe (see Comfort 2012).

tems. In 1971 Austin-Morris's Cowley plant had eighty rates of pay for inspectors (Adeney 1988, 261). This was a half-century after Ford had scrapped piece-rate pay to apply the principle of flow and concurrent with the emerging Toyota Production System, which applied the principle of multiproduct flow on the same production line without sacrificing throughput efficiency, and the widespread adoption of participatory work practices to design quality into the process. These changes in the productive structure sharply reduced the need for inspectors, drove down the indirect-to-direct labor ratio, cut waste, and increased inventory turns from single- to triple-digit levels (Best 1990).

THE PRINCIPLE OF FLOW

Interchangeability was a prerequisite to the Ford mass-production system. But interchangeability alone is not the secret to understanding the Ford system and how it revolutionized manufacturing.[5] The secret to mass production is not interchangeability, the moving assembly line, or economies of size but synchronization in the form of equalizing cycle times. It is captured in the words of Charles Sorensen, Ford's chief engineer: "It was ... complete *synchronization* that accounted for the difference between an ordinary assembly line and a mass production one" (1956, emphasis mine).[6]

Synchronization was "first tested in 1908" at the Piquette Avenue plant with the Model T but "first installed" where all the links in the chain were first connected, at the Highland Park plant with the Model A in August 1913:

> Each part was attached to the moving chassis in order, from axles at the beginning to bodies at the end of the line. Some parts took longer to attach than others; so, to keep an even pull on the towrope, there must be differently spaced intervals between the delivery of the parts along the line. This called for patient *timing* and rearrangement until

5. The Ford and Toyota production systems are contrasted in chapter 8.
6. My account of the Ford production system is indebted to Hounshell, who also references the sentence by Sorensen in which the term "synchronization" appears. But Hounshell does not elaborate a principle of flow based on the equalization of cycle times. Consequently, he suggests that the Ford system spread rapidly in America, albeit as "flexible mass production" (1984, 261). In fact, what followed Ford was mass batch production: flexible mass production based on the principle of flow, in which the synchronization deployed for multiple products was diffused in the form of just-in-time production only decades later by Japanese volume manufacturers (Best 2001, chap. 2).

the flow of parts and the speed and intervals along the assembly line meshed into a perfectly *synchronized* operation throughout all stages of production. (Sorensen 1956, 125, 130–31; emphasis mine)

Sorensen finishes the paragraph with this: "A new era in industrial history had begun." Few would deny this conclusion. But, ironically, most explanations do not capture the fundamental achievement that ushered in the new vision of production and thereby the real difference between the old and the new approach to production as articulated by Sorensen. Mass production involved the successful application of the principle of flow and revolutionized process engineering.

Ford misled the world when he famously stated: "Mass production is production without fitters" (1926, 40). In fact, interchangeability, not mass production, was production without fitters. Interchangeability, then as now, meant organizing a production system to eliminate the need for hand fitting to assemble parts into a product. Tasks such as the sanding of wood or filing of metal and the associated job categories, skills, and labor costs were all designed out of production. This is the domain of product engineering.

For Henry Ford, the new production methods required the driving down of critical size dimensions. To achieve this, he incorporated precision engineering into organizational capability and opened a new era in the history of manufacturing. In his words: "Advance in manufacturing skill permitted the new car to be made with tolerances approaching five ten-thousands of an inch, whereas in the old Model T, a thousandth of an inch had to be the practical limit of accuracy in quantity production" (Ford 1926, 492).

Henry Ford's famous promise in 1914 of a wage of $5 a day for line workers presented a challenge to the nation's employers and production engineers. The challenge was to increase productivity by making a transition to production methods and organizational practices that would support a doubling in wage rates. However, Ford proved that it could be done. It involved sharing productivity gains from advancing production capabilities with the workforce: "We put into operation in January 1914, a kind of profit-sharing plan in which the minimum wage for any class of work and under certain conditions was five dollars a day. At the same time we reduced the working day to eight hours ... and the week to forty-eight hours" (Ford 2008 [1920], 87).

No one could have foreseen the ensuing production/technological trajectory of ever-greater machining precision, which, in turn, fostered applications at ever-smaller device sizes and in ever-wider product domains.

Along the way, institutionalizing an industrial precision machining capability created, sustained, and deepened a series of technological transitions that began in the mechanical age before ushering in the later electrical, electronic, and nanotechnology periods (see figure 3.1 in this book and Best 2001, 133–40).

As important as interchangeability has been to this historical process and to Ford Motor Company's success, it preceded mass production. Ford Motor Company's distinctive capability at the time was that of combining the principles of interchangeability and single-piece flow. The implementation of both principles drove down the costs of production and organized a step-change in productivity. It created a new organizational basis for competitive advantage and introduced a new manufacturing system.

THE MACHINE-TOOL INDUSTRY
AND INNOVATIVE ENTERPRISES

Ford's mass-production system required organizing a supply chain of machine-tool, component, and equipment-making companies that also applied the principle of interchangeability and the closely related principle of standardization upon which mass production depended. Success at the thorough-going implementation of the principle of interchangeability was a prerequisite to mass production. Fortunately for Ford, interchangeability had become widely diffused in US industry from its beginnings nearly a century earlier. Ford was able to tap into a population of component and parts manufacturers that could supply his assembly lines to the tolerances of "five-ten thousands" of an inch.

To keep his assembly lines moving without interruption Ford forced suppliers to enter a dynamic learning process and establish production capabilities and productive structures to produce to ever-tighter tolerances. Just as the American system, based on the principle of interchangeability, enabled the era of mass production, the application of the principle of flow entailed scaling up the nation's component and machine tool supply base and embedding the precision engineering pursuit of ever-smaller size dimensions into the nation's production system. Unfortunately, this was not the case in British industry.

In the United States, the interactive connections that networked and grew a region's or the nation's machine-tool industry and the production of complex products and emergent downstream consumer goods created a structural competitive advantage relative to the United Kingdom. The emergence and diffusion of a growing population of entrepreneurial enterprises defined as those with new-product development and technology-management capabilities grew in sync with an innovative machine-tool industry and transformed the American business system. The US machine-tool industry was in effect a capability-development infrastructure that enabled the nation's business enterprises to shift from price-led to product-led competition.

Enterprises with new-product development capabilities have superior resilience to changes in markets and technologies; they have the capability to reposition from declining to growing market segments. Chapters 2, 3, and 5 give accounts of regions and nations with the capacity to create and grow new entrepreneurial firms and of existing enterprises with such capabilities to reposition from declining into growing markets. The consequence is sectoral transition dynamics as entrepreneurial enterprises iteratively develop new expertise, skills, and capabilities in the process of early identification of emerging market opportunities. An ancillary lesson is the underlying importance of the size and innovativeness of the machine-tool industry.

The lesson from this application of the comparative capability triad methodology is that the growth in the population of a nation's entrepreneurial enterprises is limited by the size and innovativeness of the nation's machine-tool sector. The small size of the UK machine-tool industry was linked to the backward production capabilities of its car industry. The UK car industry was not organized around the principles of interchangeability and flow and consequently did not organize a precision-engineering supply base on a scale sufficient to assist in development and advance on the scale required of an innovative car industry or to diffuse new-product development and technology-management capabilities across multiple smaller-scale sectors. Small, highly innovative machine shops have always existed in the United Kingdom, as has world-leading design engineering expertise, but they were not infused into a national "manufacturing system" that could generate high levels of productivity or grow the new sectors necessary to compete with regions and nations that had built such systems to great success.

Production System Success: Motor Sports Valley

The future of the British motor-sports industry looked bleak in the 1950s. Aston and Williams (1996, 2) cite an article in *Motor Racing* from May 1954 that stated:

[Britain has] designers of outstanding ability and we are not behind in original thought, nor backward in studying designs and improving upon them. We have good mechanics but what chance have they of gaining real racing experience in the big class? We have not been in the top flight of Grand Prix racing for thirty years, and that has left us without a comparable number of specialists upon which to draw.

Unexpectedly the tables turned. Within years the United Kingdom replaced Italy as the global center for all single-seat racing cars, Grand Prix included. Not only Formula 1 teams but most of the major car companies of the world have at various times descended on Motor Sports Valley for the purpose of accessing the region's world-leading capabilities in engine design and development and the co-located complementary production capabilities and expertise in motor racing. No other country has a similarly successful motor-sports industry, neither Germany nor the United States, France, Italy, or Japan. In fact, the dominance of Motor Sports Valley (MSV) is such that no serious rival exists.

The region's success in motor-sports racing has long been recognized:

The UK really is the Silicon Valley of world motor sport. It is the only place with such a large technology base in one relatively small area. If you want any kind of specialist, high tech components designed and made and within a time scale which any mainstream commercial engineering company would regard as lunatic, you virtually have to come here. (Jonathan Ashman of the Motor Sports Association, quoted in Griffiths 1990)

The Motorsport Industry Association (MIA), representing 4,500 companies involved in the industry, locates the industry as follows: "Most of the British motorsport industry is based in the so-called Motorsport Valley ... in Northamptonshire and Oxfordshire, around the Silverstone Circuit."[7] MIA's website provides a snapshot of the industry. It states that "around 75 per cent of motorsport research and development takes place in the UK," that 30 percent of turnover is spent on R&D, and that around 25,000 qualified engineers are in the industry).[8]

Ironically, MSV vanquished its greatest rival, located in the heartland of the Third Italy, at the same time that a range of design-intensive Italian

7. "Motorsport Industry Association," https://en.wikipedia.org/wiki/Motorsport_Industry_Association, accessed January 2, 2016.
8. Ibid., accessed October 10, 2013.

industries were decimating their British competition (Best 1990). While motor-sports racing is not a large sector, the question remains: why is it so successful? A 1990 *Financial Times* industry survey made the point: "If the UK motor industry overall were as successful as that part of it devoted specifically to motor sport, it would be running a huge balance of trade surplus instead of a £7bn deficit" (Griffiths 1990).

My intention is to use the industry's success as a real-world laboratory to draw lessons for an economics of business and industrial innovation and for the capability triad methodology. The claim is that the success of the UK motor sports industry can be understood in terms of the emergence and development of a world-class production system with many of the same innovative engineering and collective entrepreneurial open-system business-model properties as that of America's postwar regional innovation systems. Elsewhere I have described the more general model in the following terms:

> A more fully entrepreneurial industrial district is one in which associations of firms along the production chain can collectively and simultaneously redesign products. This requires close consultation along the production chain. A fully developed industrial district would behave like a collective entrepreneur: it would possess the capacity to redesign process and organisation as well as product. (Best 1990, 206)

MSV, like Boston's Route 128, connotes a localized industrial experimental laboratory for technological innovation. Like Greater Boston, MSV has distinctive regional technology capabilities, regionally specialized engineering skills, and collective system-integration properties. Whereas Greater Boston does early-stage technology development that fosters the emergence and growth of new sectors, every enterprise in MSV is focused on establishing a specialist niche within a highly differentiated performance-driven industry unified by collaboration ties to win races.

The origins of MSV involved complementary interrelationships between the emerging local production system and leaders of the global car industry. Later the unique innovation capabilities of a group of localized specialist engineering-led companies were like a magnet for the mass producers; they could not afford to miss a beat in detecting opportunities that could be "productionized" to advantage in the struggle over global market share in the road-car industry. Thus we find an international focus-and-network dynamic building local capabilities to drive innovation by linking two dissimilar but complementary production systems. The mass producers that tried could not match the technological innovation performance of the decentralized MSV production system driven by an internal focus-and-network, open-system business model. The partnerships across production systems meant that the innovation capabilities of MSV generated technological externalities internalized by the mass producers.

MSV is an SME variant of an open-system business model of a mutually adjusting population of highly differentiated but collaborating enterprises with collective entrepreneurial capabilities. The personal computer industry model of Silicon Valley evolved at the same time to capture the superior innovation dynamics of a regional open-system business model over its competitor, which is vertically integrated or top-down supply-chain business models and linked productive structures. The open-system business model of focusing on core capability and networking for complementary capabilities fosters Adam Smith–type productivity gains from increasing differentiation of labor extended to the specialized capabilities of business enterprises. It is the "Smithian" externality of an individual firm that is internalized within a regional system of enterprises by the propagation of improvements in the "arts" from one to the next trading partner.[9]

In the case of Greater Boston, a distinctive industrial ecosystem emerged that acts as a "manufactory of species" (see chap. 3). In MSV a similar but different industrial ecosystem evolved. While the functions were the same, they involved different forms. In Greater Boston a triple-helix Department of Defense–funded S&T infrastructure combined with a local development-finance banking system. In MSV we find a functional equivalent in the form of technology and marketing sponsorships by global road-car companies and commercial advertisers. Global car companies are attracted to the region not to acquire companies or establish supply chain links but to pursue partnerships for and early identification of strategic technology transfer opportunities from racing to road cars.

The engineering expertise and technology legacy dimension is critical to the origins of regional industrial ecosystems. They can be characterized in terms of the evolutionary principles of increasing differentiation, descent with adaptation, and mutual adjustments across a population of technologically differentiated enterprises. In the process, a region's distinctive engineering expertise, knowledge base, and skill formation/education

9. Allyn Young (1928) added a reverse feedback effect to Adam Smith's division-of-labor concept, which forms the basis for the concept of dynamic increasing returns (see chap. 4 of this book).

practices are cumulatively and collectively advanced and foster distinctive regional technological capabilities.

Once a technological capability becomes regionally consolidated, its knowledge base and skills become a global magnet for R&D. Just as today virtually all biopharmaceutical companies have an R&D presence in Greater Boston, virtually all road-car companies view MSV as the site for cutting-edge technological experimentation that may have a big pay-off in the future.

The comparatively hidden engineering history of Greater Boston underscored technical legacies in, for example, precision engineering, optics, chemical engineering, and turbine technology that can be found in today's successful companies and the region's distinctive technological capabilities. These represent intertemporal linkages or networks. A second type is innovation networks that integrate or interlace activities that link R&D, technology development, and new-product development. The focus of the latter on innovation distinguishes them from the supply-chain networks by which large system integrators create global supply chains or production networks.

A similar story of an engineering legacy and innovation network linkages can be told through the business histories of key entrepreneurial firms that fostered the emergence and development of MSV. Although it did not begin with the Cosworth group, that is a good place to start. *Cosworth: The Search for Power* by Graham Robson (1990) sets the business-history standard for the design and precision engineering of high-performance racing and road cars that Alfred Chandler's *Strategy and Structure* did for the organization of the multidivisional business enterprise. I draw heavily from Robson but also from others in this industry that are notable for the exceptional quality of their business and innovation reporting.

ENGINE-DESIGN ENGINEERING EXPERTISE

In the words of Ford Motor Company executive Walter Hayes: "[Cosworth] dominated Formula 1 for sixteen years, won 155 Grands Prix and became the dependable power behind the throne for a dozen or so world champions.... In a different form, it was also victorious at the Indianapolis 500 for the best part of a decade" (Hayes, quoted in Robson 1990, 11). For well over a decade Cosworth's DFV [double four valve] engine was equivalent to the Intel semiconductor, whose "Intel Inside" slogan signaled the semiconductor's presence inside the personal computers built around it, much as the DVF engine was inside high-performance cars of a dozen-plus world Formula 1 and Indianapolis 500 champions. Cosworth, like Intel, established the interface rules for an emerging open-system business model.

Cosworth's engine was developed in a process that involved three companies with very different but complementary capabilities: Ford, Colin Chapman's Lotus, and Cosworth. Lotus was an innovator in chassis design, Ford understood its limits in high-performance engineering and engine development, and Cosworth's distinctive capability and engineering expertise were in the design and development of the highest-performance racing engines.

Ford did not seek to acquire Cosworth's unique capability or to run its own racing teams. Lotus did not build engines, but it designed a chassis in which the engine became a part of the structure and formed a partnership with Cosworth to design, develop, and build its engine using Ford engine blocks. Cosworth made prototypes not for testing but as the final product and did so with the intention that the engine not be improved upon. Rather than engage in serial production, Cosworth certified other companies to tune and modify the DVF engine; several of these companies also became successful engine-design and -development companies.[10] Ford did not use the race-car engines made by Cosworth in its own cars; instead it made them available to all competitors in motor sports, including Formula 1 teams, to foster experiments and innovation in engine design. Thus Cosworth supplied the same engine to all. It was a critical contribution to the establishment of an open-system business model that came to outcompete the vertically integrated enterprises that had dominated the industry. Within a few years, all of the Italian race-car companies except Ferrari had succumbed and dropped out of Formula 1.

The Ford, Lotus, and Cosworth alliance in the early success of MSV led to a deepened and lengthy relationship between Ford and Cosworth, but it also attracted other car manufacturers to develop partnerships for the purpose of direct involvement in technological innovation at the frontiers of engine-performance engineering. For example, General Motors, Chrysler, Honda, Nissan, and Mercedes-Benz all established a presence in the emerging MSV by establishing engine development partnerships. None of

10. Cosworth was pivotal and fostered imitators such as Ilmor, Judd Power, and Mugen and collaborators such as Hart. Ilmor, near Cosworth's Northamptonshire plant, was acquired by Mercedes, where its Formula 1 engines are designed and constructed; Mercedes Formula I cars are designed and built in nearby Brackley, Oxfordshire.

the car-manufacturing enterprises established mass-production facilities in MSV, and none of the indigenous MSV companies engaged in series production. The two distinctive production systems were complementary.

THE CONSTRUCTORS

By 1990 the motor-sports car columnist John Griffiths, who wrote for the *Financial Times*, described the region's cutting-edge advantage not in terms of engine design and development but in terms of race-car constructors:

> At least three-quarters of the purpose-built, single-seater racing cars used anywhere in the world come from a cluster of perhaps two dozen small factories, most of them in the south of England or the Midlands. Almost every car taking part, and certainly all the winning ones, in North America's most famous motor race, the Indianapolis 500, throughout the 1980s, has been designed and built at premises deep in the British countryside.... [He adds:] Some of Ferrari's core design and development Grand Prix activity was directed from premises in Surrey. (Griffiths 1990)

Thus a third set of major players was integral to the emergence and development of MSV. They were the single-seat constructors such as Lotus, McLaren, and Williams (see Aston and Williams 1996, 31). These companies focused on designing and building racing cars; they did not design or develop engines, transmissions, and power trains but partnered with companies that did. This meant the interfacing of engine and chassis development and innovations in both.

The revolution in car design started with the Cooper Climax, a car combining an engine built by Coventry Climax and Charles Cooper's racing car. To get the best out of both, Charles Cooper introduced the mid- or rear-engine vehicle. Founded in 1946, through the 1950s and 1960s the Cooper Car Company's rear-engine, single-seat cars "altered the face of Formula 1 and the Indianapolis 500 and their Mini Cooper dominated Rally racing."[11] The Cooper name lives on in the version of a BMW-owned Mini line produced today in Cowley, Oxford.

In partnership with Cooper, Colin Chapman of Lotus Motors replaced the internal-frame with the monocoque body structure to reduce weight

---

11. "Cooper Car Company," https://en.wikipedia.org/wiki/Cooper_Car_Company, accessed November 16, 2017.

and increase safety. Monocoque body structure originated as a feature of aircraft construction.[12] The aero-engineering innovations in structure and materials did not end here. Equally innovative was the application of fluid flow principles to the design of the racing car. The racing car became, in effect, an inverted airplane with the "ground-effect" revolution in 1978–82 (Jenkins and Floyd 2001, 995–98). In the words of Jenkins and Floyd (955), "The ground-effect concept uses the underbody of the car, rather than upper body or wings, to create a low pressure area, thereby holding the car to the ground and allowing it to travel at far greater speeds when cornering."

Thus, after engine design and the rear-engine car, a third defining feature of MSV's growing dominance was the successful integration of aero engineering with race-car engineering. The United Kingdom's wartime aircraft and aeronautic engineering legacies were leveraged by constructors (Henry and Pinch 2001, Aston and Williams 1996, Foxall and Johnston 1991) to apply aerodynamics to the design of racing cars. Lotus was the first to realize the downdraft consequences of applying skirts to the sides of race cars, which the company rapidly followed by the introduction of the ground-effect car in 1977. As a consequence of these cumulative and radical innovations in chassis design, race cars became, in effect, inverted airplanes. The updraft forces of an airplane were reversed to create downward forces to stabilize the racing car at high speeds. The 1978 Lotus won the constructors' Formula 1 championship using Cosworth's DFV engine.[13] The Cosworth engine, unlike the twelve-cylinder engine of Ferrari, could be attached to an independently designed chassis. This opened a juncture in approaches by the constructors between those who sought increased engine power and designed their cars around bigger engines and those who focused on improved aerodynamics. Ferrari built a new flat twelve-cylinder engine that was more powerful but structurally locked into a Ferrari chassis that could not be engineered to take advantage of ground-effect aerodynamics and could not compete.

Lotus also began a trajectory of innovation in transitioning from aluminum to carbon-fiber materials both to reduce weight and to improve aerodynamics. In 1981 McLaren, in a partnership with an aircraft manufacturer,

12. This is an example of a Jacobian externality, in which innovations are precipitated by new combinations of diverse technologies.

13. Jenkins and Floyd quote a former technical director of Lotus: "Colin wouldn't consider departing from the Cosworth engine because ... Cosworth founders Keith Duckworth and Mike Costin had both worked for Lotus in the early '60s)" (Jenkins and Floyd 2001, 956).

introduced a carbon-fiber body. This trajectory has continued, and today most of the parts of the modern race car are made of a range of carbon-fiber materials in production processes within MSV. All have to go through mechanical or computer-simulated wind tunnels to test for aerodynamics and also through a layering process of building up the material before putting it into autoclaves.

The racing car of today is a laboratory for integrating electronics and information technology with vehicle performance. Some 5,000 sensors transmit information on performance linking driver and engineer both for testing purposes and in real time during races. More broadly, the industry has led the way in computational fluid dynamics (CFD), a tool to test, for example, wing settings. Although a wind tunnel enables research into aerodynamic forces by blowing wind over a real object in a controlled environment, CFD allows the same experiment to be conducted in the form of a computer simulation of virtual objects. In related technology developments, Formula 1 teams have developed lap simulators based on computer simulations followed by driver-in-the loop simulators in which a real driver replaces the mathematical driver.[14]

OTHER SPECIALIST SUPPLIERS:
A REGIONALLY SPECIALIZED SYSTEM

Aston and Williams (1996) created a data set of firms in the UK motor-sports business based on *The Complete Autosport Directory 1995* and Company House research.[15] They combined the audit of companies broken down by specialist categories with a survey questionnaire courtesy of *Racecar Engineering* to shed further light on the industry. More recently the UK Department of Trade and Investment published *MotorSport in the UK* (2007), which offers a range of company case studies including leading service firms and educational resources. Together these two sources

---

14. See "The Importance of Simulation in F 1," www.grandprix.com/ns/ns21101.html.

15. There were at least 633 UK firms in the motor-sports business in 1995. There were eight Formula 1 constructors, thirty brand-name constructors, and seventy-two other constructors, as well as fourteen manufacturers of component/kit cars, twenty-one of Karts, four of brand engines, forty-nine of other engines, and fifty-nine of engine components. Seventy-six firms offered engineering services; twenty-eight data acquisition and telemetry; nineteen specialty glass and carbon fibre, composites, plastics, moulds, and mouldings; six body shells; twenty-nine fabrications; thirteen body styling; and seventeen electrical systems (Aston and Williams 1996, 32–33).

provide a profile of the population of specialist suppliers in the United Kingdom as well as the support and infrastructural services that fill in otherwise missing components of MSV's unique industrial ecosystem.

The company data set makes it clear that MSV is an industrial sector that has high levels of R&D but does not have an oligopolistic market structure. It is an industry with a large population of SMEs and without any large companies.[16] This makes the economics of coordination interesting. Industry activities are coordinated neither by managerial hierarchy in a multidivisional enterprise nor by price changes and spontaneous exchange in the market. Moreover, the relationships and networks by which the companies in MSV are integrated into the global car industry are not captured by the corporate administration of global production chains.

Nevertheless, in the case of Formula 1 some 6,500 parts plus services supplied by many hundreds of specialized companies are integrated into a new car within a five-month time frame every year in an industry in which performance is measured in thousandths of a second and in which safety and reliability are essential. Annual changes in rules, materials, and technologies feed through to design changes in most components and parts. Further, each part must be individually tested by the Federation Internationale de l'Automobile (FIA).[17] Coordination is not about purchasing pre-designed, off-the-shelf parts but about design consultation involving hundreds of companies in an environment in which the failure of any single part can have catastrophic effects on safety and performance.

A LESSON IN CLUSTER DYNAMICS

MSV's distinctive R&D capability integrates design-engineering expertise from many disciplines and legacy experiential knowledge from car engineering, aircraft engineering, and electrical engineering enterprises

16. Along the way, specialist engineering companies like CP Engineering, Pi, and Production Engineering Services spun out of engine designers and constructors to become global leaders in testing equipment and engineering services in automobile and technically related sectors ("Additive Layer Manufacturing in Formula One," www.pes-performance .com/news/additive-layer-manufacturing). Pi, for example, was created by former employees of Cosworth and grew to supply motor sports and other industries with digital controls. Operating at the cutting edge of digital controls, Pi provides services to companies in other high-performance engineering sectors and, in the process, enhances its technological expertise, which feeds back to Motor Sports Valley.

17. The FIA is the industry's governing body. It has effectively lobbied to be exempt from competition policy.

into a complex mix that has undergone successive rounds of system-integration dynamics. Firms constituted by multidisciplinary teams stay small for the same reason as those in Greater Boston's industrial ecosystem. Together they have created a networked system of flexibly specialized enterprises with superior innovation capability and collective resilience. Experiments are incessant, but so, too, is the termination of failed experiments followed by system reshuffling in pursuit of emerging design advantages within each company. This has culminated in a structural competitive advantage that cannot be matched by enterprises located outside the region. In fact, the MSV has a sustained performance record in technological innovation that rivals any single Boston industrial sector and has an even greater global dominance. But here the similarities end.

The firms of MSV are virtually a stand-alone cluster tightly organized by a private government. Successful as MSV is in global competition, it is not embedded in a regional industrial ecosystem that includes a complementary range of intangible infrastructures including a business and technology–development financial ecosystem and thick networks of enterprises that cut across sector boundaries and foster dynamic increasing returns, all of which work together to drive new-sector creation as in Greater Boston (Best and Humphries 1986). The difference in scale is huge: MSV employs approximately 50,000, while Greater Boston has many similarly sized sectors.

The UK's Foreign-Owned Car Industry

In the 1980s the Conservative government led by Prime Minister Margaret Thatcher pursued an industrial policy designed to establish a car industry constituted by affiliates of foreign car companies. This policy initiative proved very successful. In 1985 Nissan became the first Japanese car company to establish a facility in the United Kingdom. It was soon followed by Toyota and Honda and later by Germany's BMW. Together these companies established a new high-volume car industry in the country by introducing the Toyota Production System or lean production system. The foreign-based affiliates all practice *kaizen*, or continuous-improvement, self-directed work-team organization practices.

Within twenty-five years an entirely new car industry had emerged in the United Kingdom to produce over a million cars per year. The Nissan plant is regarded as the most efficient mass producer in Europe in a plant that manufactures the Leaf, an electric car that is an industry leader. The legacies from the previous car industry include some enduring designs and brand names such as the Mini, MG, Jaguar, Land Rover, Rolls-Royce, and Aston Martin, but they are produced in the United Kingdom by foreign-headquartered multinational enterprises with the exception of Aston Martin, which is owned by a consortium of international investment houses. The Mini is produced by BMW at the same Cowley site where the original Mini was designed by Alec Issigonis decades before, but now at the rate of one car every 68 seconds or 1,000 per day, each of which is configured to final customer specifications.

BMW and Nissan built plants that are replicas of those established at their home bases and quickly achieved world-class manufacturing facilities and productivity levels. In this way, the United Kingdom has benefited from the capability triads and economic governance systems long established in Japan and Germany. What does not come with foreign direct investment, however, are the economic governance systems by which they were shaped along with other industries and intersector learning processes in both countries. Unlike production facilities, capability triads and economic governance systems cannot be transplanted. For these, the affiliates of MNEs depend largely on their home bases.

For this reason, the foreign car companies have not induced the emergence of a large UK supply base. By some estimates, roughly two-thirds of the foreign-sector car company components are imported. In fact, Nissan strategically entered the UK market to access the European continent's supply base, not only that of the German car companies but also those of the aircraft and space industries, in which the standards for precision and quality manufacturing are an order of magnitude higher than in their own supply base in Japan (Best 1990, 15–16).

Nissan's entry into the United Kingdom was intended to establish a "first mover" competitive advantage over Toyota by establishing an open-system supply base that encompassed design expertise from component suppliers of aircraft (such as Airbus) and space (such as Ariane), as well as cars. Nissan's engineers, unlike Toyota's, would not prepare specifications for the manufacture of components. Instead they would describe the function of the component and ask a specialist supplier to design a prototype as a basis for dialogue, alterations, and development.[18]

18. Personal interview with Ian Gibson, managing director of Nissan UK, July 1985. For a related discussion on the distinction between open- and closed-system supplier networks in new product development, see Best (1990, 15–16, and 2001, 40ff.).

Neither MSV nor the creation of the foreign-sector car industry in the United Kingdom has been a component of a strategic development policy framework crafted to transform the low productivity and innovation performance of British industry. Missing is an economic governance system in the form of a unified set of intangible infrastructures (S&T, a development finance ecosystem, and skill formation institutions) in which an indigenous industrial innovation system could take hold and in which technologically driven business enterprises could grow and contribute to the growth of new sectors.

The Capability Triad: Enabling Infrastructures

It is generally agreed that investments in human capital and technical progress are two primary sources of long-term growth. But the organizational processes by which they do so and how they are interrelated is opaque in the market-centric paradigm. In each of the previous chapters we examined their interrelationships in terms of the capability triad and institutions of economic governance. For example, in chapter 5, four features of the German economic governance model were identified: the multilevel balance between central and regional governments, the dual education system, a decentralized financial ecosystem, and the subservience of macroeconomic stabilization policymaking to production capability development.

More generally, three key infrastructures are common in rapid-growth, transformative, and high-productivity economies: a unified skill formation system, a technologically informed financial ecosystem, and a precision-engineering machine-tool sector that diffuses technological change across multiple sectors. While there are exceptions in terms of either direct or indirect access to the services of all three infrastructures, they form the basis for crafting strategic development policy frameworks in all cases.

In chapter 9, we describe three historical experiences in which the US national government crafted and pursued strategic development policy frameworks that combined investments in human resources and technological progress. In this section we underscore the role that Germany's investment in a comprehensive skill formation system played in creating a structural advantage in new-sector development relative to the United Kingdom. But we start by introducing the role of the machine-tool industry in a nation's innovation system; it is a sector that continues to serve as an extrafirm infrastructure to innovation in Germany and the United States.

THE MACHINE-TOOL INDUSTRY
AS EXTRAFIRM INFRASTRUCTURE

The World War II experience in the United States demonstrated another link between manufacturing capability and technological innovation, this time with complex product systems. President Roosevelt's industrial war strategy was to marry mass production with technological innovation to create an Arsenal of Democracy. It involved designing and building technologically advanced weapons systems. The nation could do so in part because design engineers of complex product systems could leverage a supply base of instrument-making, machine-tooling, and equipment-making companies.

Charles Babbage's pursuit of his complex product systems in the form of his emergent computer machines was blocked by the lack of precision-engineering manufacturing capacity on the requisite scale in the United Kingdom a century before. The same story is described in chapter 2 with respect to radar technology, which, while designed in the United Kingdom, has fostered the development of Greater Boston's distinctive regional capability in microwave technology, a core component in a successive range of new sectors to the present day. But there are other examples of path-breaking design engineering done and initially developed in Britain that failed to foster related sector growth, including the Whittle jet engine.

Henry Ford had turned down a UK-US government request during World War II to build Rolls-Royce engines in Detroit because of Ford's antipathy to Roosevelt and the United States' entering the war. The contract went across town to Packard, who, in the words of Charles Sorensen, Ford's chief engineer, "built a fine engine" (1956, 275). The point here is that not only Ford but other manufacturers could leverage the region's tooling and machine-making engineering expertise and capabilities to convert design drawings of complex products requiring a deep supply chain into high-volume production facilities, even in labor-intensive industries, in a matter of months.

In these examples the machine-tool sector not only forms the supply chain for mass producers but is a pivotal regional and national productive link in the industrial-innovation process chain connecting basic research, developmental research, applied research, design for manufacturability, pilot projects, and the scaling of final production processes. Consequently, these feats of design engineering migrated to foreign nations and regions where they fostered the emergence and growth of entrepreneurial enterprises and new sectors.

SKILL FORMATION: GERMANY VERSUS
THE UNITED KINGDOM

Awareness of Germany's superior technical education system was not lost in nineteenth-century reports. Over the decades, various reports have compared the German and British education systems and their effects on productivity. A Royal Commission report in 1868 stated: "Our evidence appears to show that our industrial classes have not even the basis of a sound general education on which alone technical education can rest.... We shall gradually but surely find that our undeniable superiority in wealth and perhaps in energy will not save us from decline" (quoted by Barnett 1986, 205).

According to Correlli Barnett, the Samuelson Royal Commission on Technical Education (reporting in 1882–84) warned that technical secondary schools like those on the continent were "singularly lacking in our own country" and was particularly impressed by the advanced education offered in the German polytechnics:

> To the multiplication of these polytechnics ... may be ascribed the general diffusion of a high scientific knowledge in Germany, its appreciation by all classes of persons, and the adequate supply of men competent, so far as theory is concerned, to take the place of managers and superintendents of industrial works.... In England, there is still a great want of this last class of person. (Barnett 1986, 207)

Barnett also reported that the Carnegie Trust Report *Disinherited Youth* compared education opportunities for German and British youth in 1937–39 as the country prepared for war. Germany was found to have 3,199 *Berufsschulen* (vocational training schools). The United Kingdom had a single compulsory day continuation school and forty voluntary day-continuation schools.[19] In the evocative words of Barnett: "Thus while most young Germans were learning a trade as well as continuing their education, most young Britons had been dumped out of school to look for work in obsolete, failing industries situated in decrepit 'depressed areas'— the educational orphans of the Carnegie Trust Report" (1986, 202).[20]

---

19. A continuation school provides education beyond the elementary level, enabling young people in trade or industry to continue their educations in their spare time for a certain number of hours per day.

20. Orphaned children worked in staple industries of the first industrial revolution (Humphries 2011); "education orphans" lacked the education and skills required for employment to meet the New Competition in the industries of the second industrial revolution.

To the present day, the failure of the UK governments to embark on a development policy framework that turns this segment of the population into an educated labor resource, has fragmented the nation's regional capability triads and production capability, and enterprise growth has been artificially limited. A UK vocational education training system would have provided the missing link in the UK industrial innovation process chain, a large class of technically trained graduates from "continuation" schools, as they were originally described and still are in many countries. Instead the United Kingdom remains a nation with a vast class of educational orphans, which has limited the number and growth of entrepreneurial firms. Lacking access to a pool of the technically educated employees required to support new-product development capabilities, British industrial enterprises have historically narrowed their business strategies to price competition and thereby spread what Schumpeter aptly described as "the bacilli of depression" (2008 [1942], 106).

Consequently, Germany, not the United Kingdom, seized leadership in the new chemical and electrical industries of the second industrial revolution and a permanent productivity gap opened between the two nations' production systems. Julia Wrigley quoted from an account by Ivan Levinstein in the *Times* (March 3, 1906) of the "puzzle" of Britain's world-renowned scientists and poor record of industrial research: "In the land where the dynamo and the arc lamp originated, the land which witnessed the birth of the electro-magnet, of the Swan lamp, and of the induction-coil, it is, indeed pitiable to see—that electric pioneering has largely ceased" (Wrigley 1986, 184).

Conclusion: Economic Governance Failure

The low productivity and loss of competitiveness of UK industry has been an economic issue for at least a century and a half but never been successfully reversed. It is not for want of trying. UK governments have undertaken numerous industrial strategies, but they have all failed to arrest the decline.

The policymaking spectrum has been wide. Proponents of government ownership of production and central planning, laissez-faire, Keynesian demand management, monetarism, supply-side tax reform, and light-touch regulation have all been at the policymaking helm in at least one government over the decades. But beyond the strongly held disagreements on the efficacy of specific policy instruments, the competing perspectives share an explicit or implicit theoretical conception of the economy in which the production system, business organization, and economic governance are exogenous. It is a theoretical conception in which systemic linkages and mutual adjustment processes are invisible and one that ignores the lessons of successful policymaking experiences at considerable cost to economic performance.

Neither UK business nor government policymakers properly characterized the challenges of, first, the American system of production based on the principle of interchangeable parts; second, the multidivisional managerial enterprise that created in-house infrastructures to build and diffuse production and organizational capabilities to pursue product-led strategies; and third, the German system in which federal and subnational governments coordinated and organized extrafirm infrastructures to foster enterprise capability development in sync with skill-formation institutions.

As we have found, in real-world successful transformation experiences, enterprise development and production capabilities are bound up together and mediated by infrastructural institutions. The production-centric policymaking spectrum extends to linking developmental infrastructures in ways that advance change within and across networked enterprises. Economic governance in the form of the design and crafting of infrastructures, physical and capability-developmental, can influence enterprise innovation both directly and indirectly through, for example, fostering cluster dynamics. This is the terrain of strategic development policy and calls attention to the ways in which financial, S&T, and educational infrastructures can be strategically unified to foster enterprise innovation and cluster dynamics at both regional and national levels.

UK government policymaking has never been informed by a production-centric perspective linking production, business, and skill formation. The claim is illustrated with examples of industrial policy that had at best little positive effect and at worst reduced the performance of the nation's economy.

First, much of postwar industrial policy has been about managing declining sectors or depressed regions by relocating existing enterprises to new places rather than restructuring them to meet global competition and about building infrastructures that enable enterprise capability development. In the aftermath of World War II, the UK government used wartime building controls as a powerful regional policy instrument. Location approval, building licenses, and allocation of materials were used to steer private firms (Heim 1987, 374). These building controls, which were highly effective in concentrating factory-building into areas that had suffered high rates of unemployment during the interwar years (1919–39), were designated as Development Areas and had been dominated by traditional industries. But in ignoring implications for business organization, the implementation of the policy created unintended consequences that worked against the revitalization of the same regions.

Carol Heim examined the R&D location plans of industrial firms and governments in the late 1940s using data from applications for location approval between 1944 and 1948. She found that firms could expand their R&D facilities and pilot production in Greater London or Greater Birmingham "if they agreed to disperse standardized production, simultaneously or in the future" (1987, 375). Acting with something resembling a spatial product life cycle in mind, the Board of Trade took virtually no steps to disperse R&D activity. The board passed applications for virtually all new R&D activities in London and Birmingham. The applications cited needs for skilled labor and scientific staff.

The thinking of the Board of Trade and firms was understandable within the standard policymaking framework. The Barlow Report of 1946 on "Scientific Man-Power" argued that unless the annual output of scientific graduates was doubled, there would be a shortfall of at least 26,000 against an estimated demand of 90,000 in 1955 (Heim 1987, 373). But this only underscores a narrow interpretation of policymaking that does not simultaneously address all three elements of the capability triad. In fact, the policy ignored the critical importance of skill formation for the success of both R&D and production, which were separated by policy.

The policy of locating factories in depressed areas had little chance of success. It was a missed opportunity at the time. It promised jobs but ignored the challenges of the lack of production capabilities and the need for change in business organization in British factories, as well as the lack of vocational education and the absence of decentralized city governance and banking institutions.

Unfortunately, the lessons were not learned by the next generation of policymakers, who repeated the policy. With good intentions but bad economics, "industrial development certificates" were introduced by the British government in the Local Employment Act of 1960 to disperse factories to depressed areas. Rootes, the United Kingdom's giant holding company long owned by the Rootes family, was forced to move its new factory for the Hillman Imp, an innovative rear-mounted, all-aluminum-engine car, away from its other plants located near Coventry in the English Midlands to Linwood near Glasgow in Scotland. Linwood was over 300 miles from Ryton, Coventry, where engines had to be machined and assembled. "The supply chain required a complex schedule of trains shifting completed cars and raw castings south, and trains loaded with engine-gearbox assemblies and many other Ryton-sourced goods running north." By the mid-1960s, Rootes was progressively taken over by Chrysler "following huge losses amid commercial failure of the troubled Imp."[21]

The second example is the subsidization of firms based on the false proposition that the productivity gap was based on insufficient enterprise size and physical economies of scale. For example, in 1968 the government organized a merger of British Motor Holdings, already a massive conglomerate, and British Leyland, a small but efficient truck-making company, to form BL. Continued loss of sales led to partial nationalization in 1975, a year in which British Leyland was producing "just over four cars per employee per annum, against seven for Ford's UK plants, and almost 23 for Honda in Japan and 36 for Toyota" (Comfort 2012, 64). In 1986 BL was renamed the Rover Group, and it went into administration in 2005, "bringing mass car production by British-owned manufacturers to an end."[22]

Nicholas Kaldor, an important postwar economic advisor with awareness of the Babbage, Marshall, and Young increasing returns legacies, likely came closest to a production-centric approach (1970). Nevertheless, he maintained that central government policies to foster internal returns to scale were the means to industrial productivity improvement and regional development success. The government of Harold Wilson followed Kaldor's advice and introduced a "selective employment tax" on services to subsidize employment in manufacturing in order to induce business leaders to build large firms and thereby benefit from economies of scale.[23]

21. "Rootes Group," https://en.wikipedia.org/wiki/Rootes_Group, accessed October 20, 2016.

22. "British Leyland," https://en.wikipedia.org/wiki/British_Leyland, accessed November 16, 2017. The origins of the British Motor Industry Heritage Trust Archive Collections go back to the creation of British Leyland Motor Corporation in 1968 in a merger that brought together most of the surviving British motor manufacturers, who were themselves results of earlier mergers and therefore encompassed a large variety of firms. These included not just car, bus, and truck manufacturers but also manufacturers of some very obscure products indeed—bridges, construction equipment, refrigerators, milk floats, castings, asphalt and tarmacadam plants, scaffolding, and concrete mixers. As a result, the records in the archives encompass a total of ninety-seven different companies! BL was "effectively" nationalized in 1974 (Adeney 1988, 277).

23. Unfortunately, given Kaldor's links to both Allyn Young and Gunnar Myrdal, it is surprising that he did not go beyond the conventional economic policy framework's con-

Together management and government policies created large enterprises in the mistaken belief that economies of size would improve performance. Some became huge, such as British Leyland, GEC, ICI, and Schreiber, but none survived. In this UK industry never solved the challenge of scaling production to effectively commercialize the nation's historic and extraordinary capability in technological innovation.

Third was the failure to take strategic advantage by productive investment from the windfall gains from the discovery of huge North Sea oil and gas resources off the UK continental shelf in 1959. By the time UK policymakers acted, the opportunity to build a domestic drilling and platform industry was lost. In 1973 the government set up the Offshore Supplies Office, with the remit of increasing local content to 70 percent, with Norman Smith as director. According to Smith:

> The first published figures on the UK content in UKCS [UK Continental Shelf] expenditure for a specific year related to 1974 (Department of Energy 1975) and showed it as only about 40%, illustrating how heavily UK industry must have "lost-out" during the first great North Sea "boom." For it to have been otherwise would have required a government policy aimed at expanding the scope and capacity of the small export-oriented British oilfield supply industry several years earlier than was actually the case. (Smith 2011, 21)

The opportunity was seized in the meantime by foreign-owned companies. According to Smith it was too late to instigate the rapid expansion of domestic capacity necessary to prevent the huge surge of new orders then already being placed without a heavy reliance on imports and inward investment by foreign suppliers. Ironically, states Smith, "The enormous opportunity of North Sea oil and gas industry illustrated the backward state of industry to take advantage" (2011, 21).

Worse, the export sales revenues increased the demand for sterling, drove up the exchange rate, and fostered a consumption boom that grew the retail sector. Known as the "Dutch disease," the overvalued exchange

---

cept of economies of scale, in which production, technology, and business organization are exogenous. As discussed in chapter 4, increasing returns to scale is a static concept in contrast to dynamic increasing returns that account for internal and external economies of expansion and is anchored by the technology capability and market opportunity dynamic of the entrepreneurial firm. Such is the power and the danger of the standard paradigm in both academic economics and exclusively national policymaking narratives.

rate reduced manufacturing exports and contributed to the hollowing-out of British industry.[24]

It did not have to be this way. Ironically, John Maynard Keynes was a major contributor to *Britain's Industrial Future* (1928) and co-author with H. D. Henderson of the follow-up pamphlet *Can Lloyd George Do It?* (1929), which focused attention on the production-side challenges facing the British economy and called for a comprehensive Programme of National Development. For example, in reference to a fourfold increase in real wages over the nineteenth century we find: "The technical foundations of this progress were the utilization of power derived from coal, the development of railways and steamships, and the revolutionizing of one branch after another by the application of engineering methods" (*Britain's Industrial Future* 1928, 6). Links between organization, productive structures, economic policies, and national prosperity are emphasized: "Efficient business organization and management and the effective cooperation of partners in industry are the foundations of economic prosperity, and the solution of these twin problems is the main theme of this report" (43).

Ironically, the policy framework recommended in *Britain's Industrial Future* may have inspired Franklin Roosevelt. Lady Asquith is reported to have seen "a well-thumbed copy which had belonged to President Roosevelt which still had his copious penciled comments in the margin" (1977, second impression back cover).[25] If this is true, it suggests that Keynes may have had a greater impact on US industrial-development policymaking during World War II than the Keynesian demand-management revolution ever had on American stabilization policies. In the United Kingdom the short-term demand-management aspect of Keynes's economics was incorporated into the standard paradigm and the long-term industrial-development supply side has been ignored.

David Sainsbury, while minister of science and innovation from 1998 to 2006, produced a report titled "The Race to the Top" recommending political leadership by the prime minister for a major commitment to a UK national innovation system. Sainsbury wrote: "There is no other way

24. In economics, the Dutch disease is the apparent causal relationship between the increase in the economic development of a specific sector (for example, natural resources) and a decline in other sectors (such as the manufacturing sector or agriculture).

25. Jeremy Thorpe, once the leader of the Liberal Party, claims that a copy of the "Yellow Book," as the book became known in politics, is in Roosevelt's private library at Hyde Park, "with annotations in the margin as to how the proposals contained in the report could be applied to America" (1999, chap. 4).

that Whitehall could deliver such a change" (2013, 205). The report describes the national innovation systems of global innovation leaders such as the United States, Japan, Germany, Sweden, and China. Unfortunately, it produced no policy response, perhaps in part because of the absence of academic support from mainstream economics. Little has changed since Babbage's call for a "new system of manufacturing" fell on deaf ears in the mid-nineteenth century.

CHAPTER SEVEN

Ireland's Divided Economy

GROWTH WITHOUT INDIGENOUS INNOVATION

Co-authored with John Bradley

Successive Policy Frameworks

Ireland provides an interesting historical case study for examining development-policy shifts and economic performance through the comparative capability triad lens.[1] The partition of the island in 1922 split off the one heavily industrialized region that was centered on Belfast, leaving the new Free State with the modest remainder.[2] From 1922 to 1932 the governments continued with pre-independence policies: a fixed link with sterling and free trade with the United Kingdom. After 1932, the liberal economic agenda was abandoned and tariff protection was put in place that continued into the late 1950s. The comprehensive economic and trade integration of Ireland with political incorporation into the United Kingdom in 1801 persisted through both free-trade and protectionist policy regimes. The proportion of Irish exports going to the United Kingdom declined only slightly, from 99 percent in 1924 to 93 percent in 1950. Balance-of-payments crises in the 1950s were handled in the conven-

1. The history of policy regimes in the following paragraphs is from John Bradley's "Changing the Rules: How the Failures of the 1950s Forced a Transition in Economic Policy-Making" (2004).

2. The only area of the island of Ireland that participated fully in the second industrial revolution of the mid- to late nineteenth century was Northern Ireland, which remained part of the United Kingdom when the island was partitioned in 1922 (Bradley and Best 2012b). The constitution of 1937 changed the name of the state to Ireland.

tional way, by higher taxes and cuts in public expenditures to reduce demand. Modest growth in the early postwar period was not sufficient to create jobs, and emigration continued at very high levels.

A bold strategic policy shift in the late 1950s was precisely what was needed to ride the future wave of American FDI, in contrast to the declared policy aim of growing on the back of an expanding indigenous agri-industrial base. The policy thrust was uniquely appropriate to Ireland's development challenge, but the outcome eventually produced by these policies turned out to be very different from that originally envisaged by the policymakers in the late 1950s.

Against a backdrop of economic stagnation, inflation, and emigration, the secretary of the Department of Finance, Kenneth Whitaker, authored *Economic Development* (Department of Finance 1958) calling for a strategic policy shift from isolation and protectionism to free trade and "productive" capital expenditure. Accepted by the government, it was codified into the *First Programme for Economic Expansion* (Bradley 1989). The Industrial Development Authority (IDA), established by the Irish government in 1949, seized the opportunity and designed and implemented what became the world's first development strategy based on attracting multinational corporations (MNCs) to set up affiliate plants with world-class manufacturing practices. Supported by other agencies of the government, the entirely new framework combined a policy mix of commitment to trade liberalization, enthusiastically joining the then European Economic Community (EEC) in 1973 with eventual adoption of the euro, a range of direct and indirect grant aid to private firms, and the singular incentive of a zero corporation profits tax on exports of manufactured goods. Enabling educational, financial, fiscal, and transportation infrastructural institutions were organized and unified to implement the strategy.

As an export diversification strategy, all this was strikingly successful. Between the 1950s and the mid-1990s, export volumes increased massively and the share of Irish exports going to the United Kingdom diminished from about 90 percent to about 20 percent. Since 1973, when Ireland had joined the EEC, the Irish economic policymaking environment can be characterized as having shifted from one appropriate to a dependent state on the periphery of the United Kingdom to that of a region more fully integrated into an encompassing European economy. FDI created an export platform with productive capacity, and the European Single Market provided the primary source of demand. What remained was a big push on improvement in physical infrastructure, education, and training, and this arrived in the form of a dramatic innovation in regional

T. K. Whitaker, 1916–2017. *Source:* The Whitaker Family
and author Anne Chambers.

policy at the EU level with the advent of Structural Fund aid from the late
1980s.

The export platform strategy to attract FDI worked. Mass-production
capabilities were, in a sense, imported rather than homegrown. The
MNCs set up remotely managed branch plants in Ireland, many of which
operated according to world-class manufacturing practices. The output
of the foreign-owned mass-production business units propelled export-
led growth of GNP as well as employment from under 1.4 million in the
1980s to over 2.0 million in the early 2000s. Exports grew twentyfold in
the thirty years between 1970 and 2000 and imports eightfold. It is estimated that the MNE export platform generated 45 percent of Irish growth
in the first half of the 1990s and 85 percent in the second half (Foster
2007, 11). This was and remains an extraordinary success story in terms of
creating an export growth strategy for an economy virtually without any
significant industrial legacy.

Economic conditions and employment opportunities were transformed. As recently as the 1980s, one million Irish people in a nation of slightly over three million lived below the poverty line. Astonishingly, by the turn of the century the Bank of Ireland could claim that Ireland had become the second-richest country in the world, measured in terms of GDP per head (Lewis 2011, 87). It is an extraordinary economic-growth success story. However, it is well known that FDI introduces a wedge between GDP (what is produced) and GNP (a more accurate measure of income retained within the host country). The GDP per capita measure exaggerates the benefits of growth in the presence of foreign firms.

But suddenly, as if out of the blue, Ireland's economic conditions dramatically reversed in the mid-2000s with the advent of the global financial crisis and the subsequent recession. The property bubble burst, the Irish banks were declared insolvent, and the stock market crashed. The Irish Stock Exchange general index, which reached a peak of 10,000 points in April 2007, fell to 1,987 points by February 2009.

Unemployment and emigration returned with a vengeance. Among those aged 15–24, the percentage with jobs nearly halved, dropping from 47.8 percent in 2005 to 27.9 percent in 2012. More than 228,000 people left the country between 2009 and 2013, roughly 10 percent of the nation's labor force. Sixty-two percent of the emigrants in the age group 25–34 had a university qualification. A study carried out by University College Cork found that at least one household in four in rural areas of Ireland had been affected by the emigration of at least one person since 2006.[3]

What went so wrong, so fast? What does it tell us about the Irish economy, how it is organized, how it functions, and why, despite the success of the government's MNE export-platform strategy, did it offer insufficient opportunities to deter the emigration of such a large wave of young, educated citizens? The depth and extent of the Irish recession was more than a failure in macroeconomic policymaking. It calls for attention to deeper structural challenges masked by the high-growth period.

To find answers we examine the Irish economy from the emergent structural competitiveness framework that is described using the capability triad. We go inside both the foreign and domestic business systems in search of entrepreneurial firms and cluster dynamics and to assess the state of the nation's industrial ecosystem. The existence of cluster-dynamic

---

3. The data in this paragraph are from an OECD study reported in *Financial Times*: "Special Report, Ireland and the World," October 22, 2014, 2.

processes is the engine of industrial renewal and an indicator of a production capability–enabling industrial ecosystem that, from a structural competitiveness perspective, is the determinant of a regional/national economy's adaptability to change. The industrial ecosystem is made up of entrepreneurial firms and the extrafirm enabling infrastructures to which they have access. Governmental responsibility for the effectiveness and extent of their articulation for purposes of industrial renewal takes us into the realm of economic governance and the target of development-policy frameworks.

The driver of innovation is the entrepreneurial firm. While this is not a category for which comparative data are collected, the available data on enterprises are informative. Two structural features of the Irish economy can be inferred and inform our investigations. First, Ireland has become a nation of two business systems that function differently and independently of one another. Ireland's foreign-owned business system has performed in line with the core economies of the EU. Both have proven reasonably resilient to the global financial collapse and the ensuing austerity policies. While some of Ireland's foreign enterprises and sectors have declined, others have been attracted to replace them. The absence of a comparable base of foreign enterprises resilient to the crash made the policymaking in response to the post-2007 global market forces much more difficult for Portugal and almost impossible for Greece.

In contrast, the indigenous Irish economy has suffered a decline in activity similar to those of the peripheral economies of Europe. The contraction in the number of enterprises in the periphery of the EU contrasted sharply compared with that in the core economies, as shown in table 7.1.[4] While the Eurostat business demographic statistics do not separate foreign from domestic enterprises, the total population of nonagricultural active enterprises in Ireland declined from 203,083 to 185,530 between 2008 and 2012, or nearly 9 percent of the total population.

Second, despite targeted development agencies, fiscal incentives, and generous grant supports, international comparisons suggest that Ireland remained a nation with an innovation deficit. Even with a large population of MNEs, Ireland's R&D as a percentage of GDP of between 1 and 1.2 remained well below those of the core economies of the EU at 2.5, led by Finland at 3.5 (see fig. 5.1).

4. See "Eurostat: Business Demography Main Variables," http://ec.europa.eu/eurostat /tgm/table.do?tab=table&init=1&language=en&pcode=tin00170&plugin=1.

Table 7.1. EU Business Demography Changes, 2008–2012

Country	Percentage change
Ireland	↓ 9
Portugal	↓ 16
Spain	↓ 8
Italy	↓ 2
United Kingdom	↓ 5
Germany	No change
Netherlands	↑ 14
France	↑ 14
Sweden	↑ 16

Source: Business demography main variables—NACE Rev. 2 (B-N excluding K64.2), http://ec.europa.eu/eurostat/tgm/table.do?tab =table&init=1&language=en&pcode=tin00170&plugin=1.
Note: NACE is the Statistical Classification of Economic Activities in the European Community, whose abbreviation comes from the French term "nomenclature statistique des activités économiques dans la Communauté européenne." It is the industry standard classification system used in the EU.

High R&D ratios indicate new-product development and technology-management capabilities in a region or nation's business enterprises.[5] They are a measure of R&D production absorptive capacity. Table 5.1 compares the number of companies by country that were listed in the top 1,000 EU companies ranked by R&D investment in 2008. Greece, with a population of 11 million, had four such companies, while Finland and Denmark, with less than half that population, had 58 and 47, respectively. Ireland had twelve. Table 7.2 reveals that one was a bank that was supported after 2008 by large amounts of state assistance; another had only nine employees; three were food producers.

The two-way division of Ireland's economy is reflected in the policy-making division between the IDA's responsibility for the foreign-owned sector and Enterprise Ireland's responsibility for domestically owned enterprises. Enterprise Ireland is the government's agency responsible for supporting Irish businesses in the manufacturing and internationally

---

5. A pattern similar to that of the patent statistics emerges. See "Research and Innovation Statistics at Regional Level" for Eurostat maps illustrating the regional concentration of R&D-related data, including patent applications and high-tech employment, at http://epp.eurostat.ec.europa.eu/statistics_explained/index.php/Science_and_technology_at _regional_level. For data on productivity see "Real Labour Productivity per Person Employed—Annual Data," http://ec.europa.eu/eurostat/tgm/table.do?tab=table&init=1& plugin=1&pcode=tipsna70&language=en.

Table 7.2. Irish Companies in Top 1,000 EU R&D Investment Scorecard, 2008

No	Company	Rank	ICB Sector NACE Sector	R&D Investment 2008 €m	Employees 2008 #	Market Capitalisation		Change 08/07 %
						2008 €m		
Ireland				531.72	60,602	10,725		-41.0
1	Elan	80	Pharmaceuticals (4577)	227.92	1,683	2,574		-30.1
2	Kerry	118	Food producers (357)	147.46	22,312	3,184		-10.6
3	Bank of Ireland	247	Banks (835)	56.00	15,868	2,248		-66.1
4	SkillSoft	322	Software (9537)	35.86	1,124	588		
5	Trinity Biotech	638	Health care equipment & services (453)	11.49	757			
6	AGI Therapeutics	640	Pharmaceuticals (4577)	11.47	9	7		-89.4
7	Glanbia	688	Food producers (357)	10.13	3,400	742		-46.3
8	Norkom	773	Software (9537)	7.78	304	99		-22.6
9	Kingspan	799	Construction & materials (235)	7.10	6,692	958		-23.6
10	Greencore	823	Food producers (357)	6.74	8,066	282		-34.7
11	Datalex	903	Computer services (9533)	5.40	164	19		-33.3
12	Trintech	997	Software (9537)	4.37	223	25		12.9

Source: The 2009 EU Industrial R&D Investment Scorecard, European Commission.
Note: The location of EU R&D investment for the top 1,000 companies is particularly problematic for small countries that have large amounts of foreign direct investment.

traded services sectors. Although we will critique this split, we first examine each separately.

In the second section of this chapter a peripheral Irish region made up of domestically owned business enterprises is examined. We report on an investigation that found many examples of entrepreneurial firms but a lack of cluster-dynamic processes and a nonexistent industrial ecosystem.

We then turn to the foreign-owned, high-tech business system, which, we argue, has clusters of similar enterprises but without cluster-dynamic processes. It is an autarchic business system consisting of stand-alone affiliates of MNEs that benefit individually from the industrial ecosystems in the regions of their parent companies.

Finally we summarize and integrate our findings, where the bottom line is that Ireland lacks, and does not create or grow, mid-sized entrepreneurial firms. The resulting lack of indigenous innovation limits the economy's adaptive capability to develop new productive structures to seize emerging market opportunities and respond to market and technological shocks. The nation's development-finance, S&T, and material infrastructures are not interconnected to form a joined-up industrial ecosystem that fosters production-capability development across a population of enterprises.

The Peripheral Economy: Entrepreneurial
Firms without Clusters

RESEARCH METHODOLOGY

The structural competitiveness framework that emerges from the capability triad characterizes the drivers and the enablers of successful economic development experiences at both national and regional levels. It holds that production, enterprise, and governance are not separable entities but interconnected and that governments have a stewardship role in fostering entrepreneurial business systems and production-capability development.

The challenge for economic policymaking in low-productivity regions is to design bottom-up policy frameworks to advance a region's production capabilities. For this task, entrepreneurial firms are the drivers. But the key message from a structural competitiveness perspective, as illustrated in earlier case studies, is that firms do not develop capabilities in isolation or compete alone in the global marketplace; the individual and collective capability development of a region's enterprises depends on enabling linkages. The latter include interfirm cluster-dynamic relationships, extrafirm business- and technology-development infrastructures, and regional economic stewardship to integrate the otherwise fragmented agencies.

The starting point for a successful development policy framework is to examine the population of enterprises within a region in search of entrepreneurial firms and barriers to the emergence, growth, and increase in the numbers of entrepreneurial firms. Existing entrepreneurial firms tell us much about production capabilities, skill formation, intangible infrastructures, and institutions of economic governance within the regions in which they operate.

The opportunity to carry out just such an investigation arose during a research project that was designed to find out more about the regional economies and development strategies of the Republic of Ireland and Northern Ireland (Bradley and Best 2012b).[6] The project was limited to the thirteen border counties, but along the way we conducted experiments with the aggregate economies on both sides of the border.

We used a research methodology that combined official macrosector data with FAME (Forecasting Analysis and Modeling Environment), a commercial database of companies, augmented by personal visits to enterprises in the border counties of Ireland and Northern Ireland (Bradley and Best 2011, 2012a, 2012b). We were forced to use FAME because official and commercial data on companies are very limited in the cases of both the Republic of Ireland and Northern Ireland.

We started with the fundamental proposition that entrepreneurial firms are the drivers of successful regional growth policies. The second proposition is that SMEs do not compete individually in the global marketplace but as members of networked groups that foster cluster-dynamic processes. The third is that successful industrial policy needs to focus attention on fostering extrafirm infrastructures and not on grants and subsidies to individual enterprises.[7]

6. The research project was carried out for the Centre for Cross Border Studies and supported by the Special EU Programmes Body under the INTERREG IVA program.

7. The research built on an application of the capabilities and innovation perspective to Northern Ireland (Best 2000; 2001, 191–215). An examination of the results concluded that the poor performance of the Northern Ireland economy in terms of low wages and low productivity was not due to the lack of government funding of industry. In fact, regional assistance to Northern Ireland manufacturing enterprises regularly funded between one-third and one-half of net capital spending. But the large subsidies turned out not to be catalysts for innovation, capability development, skill formation, or regional growth dy-

Together these three propositions underlie the difference between cluster-dynamic processes and mere clusters of enterprises, between collectively entrepreneurial industrial districts and industrial districts, and between unified and fragmented industrial ecosystems. In each case it is the former that points to the economics of successful regional growth; the latter points to business systems that are lacking in production-capability development and are, consequently, highly vulnerable to competition from the former.

HETEROGENEOUS SUBREGIONS

In contrast with the foreign sector, regions play a much bigger role in the indigenous sector. The Irish regions (see map 7.1) retain distinctive characteristics. Our research suggests that even an area as small as the Irish border region (some 150 miles wide) is internally very heterogeneous and that there are at least three broad subdivisions of the border economy with rather different production characteristics.

The northeast subregion

Here one finds many examples of advanced manufacturing, foreign and indigenous, in specialties such as engineering, pharmaceuticals, and food processing, as well as evidence of specialized producer services in finance, accounting, and other areas. Our interpretation of these findings was that this segment of the border economy benefited from spillovers from the Dublin and Belfast metropolitan poles at either end of the so-called east coast corridor. This issue had been explored during the 1990s, and what we see today is the realization of the benefits of a massively improved transport and communications infrastructure in a region of the island that has about one-third of the whole population.[8]

The mid-border subregion

This is a heterogeneous subregion containing many examples of more traditional manufacturing (food processing, furniture, etc.) but also retaining traces of pre-partition engineering specialties from an era when the Belfast growth pole of the late nineteenth and early twentieth centuries

---

namics. Worse, UK industrial policy as applied to Northern Ireland contributed to a subsidy-seeking business culture.

8. For information on the Belfast-Dublin Corridor, see Bradley (1995).

MAP 7.1. Map of Border Regions: Island of Ireland.

was the main (indeed, the only) industrial driving force on the island (Bardon 1992). The situation here is complex, and it is only when we moved to a more detailed insider perspective that we began to understand the history and likely future potential of this region.

The northwest subregion

Looking at earlier data from the 1950s to the 1990s, we saw that it was clear that the Donegal manufacturing specialties either reflected those of the adjoining Derry City region (e.g., clothing and textiles) or were specific to resources available in the county itself (e.g., seafood processing). The decline of the clothing and textiles sector in Derry since the 1960s probably dragged down these sectors in Donegal as they became progressively uncompetitive.[9] An added negative factor was that the city of Derry has never played the role in its Donegal hinterland that it might have played in the absence of any border. Take away Derry City and Donegal becomes an economic island, peripheral to any large or even medium-sized urban center.

ENTREPRENEURIAL FIRMS: THE LONE-FIRM STRATEGY

We found and visited many successful entrepreneurial firms that transcended their environments, including that of the border. A full account is available online (Center for Cross Border Studies 2012) and is summarized by Bradley and Best (2011, 2012a, 2012b). Most pursued a strategy of developing a distinctive product/service and constructed the production capability to deliver it.

A variety of firm strategies existed. We found foreign-sector examples of high-volume production within single production units. Seagate (based in Derry City) produces on a scale that matches those of East Asian mass producers. Bose, though on a much smaller scale, has a one-piece flow, high-throughput, efficient plant in a niche market. Scale economies in segments of the dairy and poultry industries are also important but are rarely the sources of competitive advantage.

When we visited locally owned firms it was usually very clear that their success was traceable to gifted individuals who had founded and developed dynamic business ventures and developed distinctive capabilities in response to niche opportunities. They are distinguished by new-product development and technology-management capabilities. All had developed production systems consistent with the fundamental principles of production and organization but in ways that leveraged local resources to gain competitive advantage.

A number can be characterized as mid-sized, indigenous, multinational companies. From them we drew an important lesson: these companies have radically reinvented themselves at least once, as if they became

9. From the 1830s until the 1960s, shirt making was one of Derry's main industries, making it, at its peak, the shirt-making capital of the world. It even gained an explicit mention in Karl Marx's *Das Kapital* (1961 [1867]: 301).

new firms. In fact, we might say that new firms were created out of previous incarnations of the same firms. Other times we found succeeding generations of the same firm in the form of the establishment of new production systems out of old. Walter Watson, for example, moved from steel fabrication of agricultural implements to structural steel fabrication to the construction of fabric mesh and pile cages to the building of overhead cranes—all the while deepening the company's core capability in steel fabrication. The transition to a range of reinforced steel products involved erecting a new, state-of-the-art production facility.

We found examples of system-integration strategies to drive a process of enterprise reinvention. In these cases the new management leveraged legacy skills and capabilities but within the context of reengineering the core production system in order to take full advantage of new technologies and market opportunities. Often this was precipitated by a transition to the second or third generation of family leadership. Simon Hunter, for example, established his management-service agent business model by seizing the opportunity provided by the Internet and the web to redesign the system by which service uniforms are designed, manufactured, and delivered. This transition required an alliance with an information technology (IT) company to develop a web-portal system. But it also meant the construction of a new production process at Hunter Apparel and new service offerings that could become resources for companies in other sectors. This process of increasing differentiation of capabilities by a focus-and-partner business model to target innovation led to the creation of a new business system as envisioned by Simon Hunter. It also hints at how network alliances can be incipient clustering processes. The success of Hunter Apparel to network with an IT company to develop a new product or service has created a new opportunity to form an R&D technology-development alliance to create a material with built-in functionality that could revolutionize medical-services apparel.

Castlecool is another notable exception. Specializing in logistics and warehousing, Castlecool enables its food-processing partners to focus on what they do best and, at the same time, enjoy the benefits of efficient complementary business services. It is an example of the dynamic between internal organization and interfirm relations that fosters distinctive capability development. To reduce refrigeration energy costs, Castlecool established an R&D partnership with engineers at Queen's University Belfast to create and introduce renewable-energy innovations.

At the same time, this focus-and-network, network-and-focus dynamic was exceptional. Even the most successful firms developed a lone-firm strategy; they were not members of networked groups of firms or adaptable dynamic clusters. Nothing was wrong with these companies. In fact, they were quite extraordinary, but the economic development challenge is that there are far too few.

BUSINESS SYSTEM FAILURE:
THE MONAGHAN FURNITURE CLUSTER

Wooden furniture has been manufactured in Monaghan at least since the statistical survey conducted by Sir Charles Coote and published in 1801.[10] A study of the period from 1973 to 2006 found that Counties Monaghan and Meath have the largest concentration of furniture-making firms in Ireland by a considerable margin (Heanue 2008).[11] Unfortunately, 2006 was the last good year for Monaghan furniture makers, as few have survived. Exiting from the industry were not only the weaker companies but the county's anchor furniture manufacturer, John E. Coyle Ltd.[12]

What went wrong? In this case, it was not a lack of private investment or government funding. John E. Coyle Ltd., the focal firm, was established in County Monaghan in 1936.[13] Between 1995 and 2003, Coyle invested €8 million in new equipment to meet the increasing competition from "low-cost producers of Eastern Europe" (Enterprise Ireland 2003, *30–31*). In 2003, with 130 people and €12.5 turnover, Coyle set the regional if not the national standard for the industry in investment, training, design, and quality.

Coyle suddenly stopped manufacturing in 2007, catching its investors, including Enterprise Ireland, by surprise. They should not have been. The

10. Coote reported that "near Glennon is a thickly inhabited neighborhood where about a hundred carpenters reside, who are constantly employed in furnishing the neighboring fairs and markets with the several articles of country work and furniture; the adjoining wood supplies them with timber on very cheap terms" (Coote 1801, 154, cited in Mottiar and Jacobson 2000, 8).

11. In 2006, the furniture industry location quotient was roughly 5 for County Monaghan and slightly under 4 for County Meath; Leitrim was next at 3, followed by Longford at 2.5 (Heanue, 2008, appendix A).

12. The following have exited the industry in the past few years: S. F. Quinn Ltd., Glenmore Beds, Newcraft Furniture, Huenna Kitchens, and Turnwood Accessories. We estimate the remaining employment in "cabinet making" as follows: McNally and Finlay with fifty, Gola with forty-five, Glenwood with thirty-two, and Sherry Brothers with an unknown number. The numbers could be less.

13. Coyle's apprenticeship program had been, historically, an unintended investment in the education of furniture entrepreneurs who had gone on to establish furniture companies in the region (Jacobson and Mottiar 1999).

company had more than five hundred product lines. Coyle and its investors were blind to the severe organizational disadvantage of mass batch-production methods. These lead to low throughput efficiency, low capital turns, high indirect costs, slow delivery times, and high working-capital requirements.

Blind to world-class production principles, the company's strategy was to increase sales by adding product lines to the existing batch production system. It was the same strategy pursued by North London furniture companies in the 1970s and 1980s. All failed to meet the challenge of the new competition. The North London furniture cluster went from more than twenty to two companies in a decade, ending in 1986 with a loss of some 15,000 jobs (Best 1990, table 6).[14]

The Monaghan wooden furniture manufacturers formed a cluster measured in terms of enterprise location quotients. But it was a static cluster, consisting of enterprises with autarchic business strategies and mass batch-production methods. The enterprises were not organized to compete with their global rivals in terms of either new-product development/technology management or high-volume lean-production methods. They lacked the technical knowledge, legacy skills or expertise, and awareness of the principles of production necessary to pursue either strategy. They were not alone.

Protected by natural trade barriers, these enterprises had never needed to investigate and learn from production systems abroad and were blind-sided by rival clusters of enterprises organized around more advanced principles of production. The intractability of wood as a material delayed, but did not deter, the introduction and diffusion of advanced production methods to the furniture industry. Regions in Europe that married wood-engineering technical education with legacy skills and open-system business organization were resilient and even thriving in the new global environment, and in most cases they morphed into more technologically diverse clusters.

It was a different story on the continent of Europe. Though not an industry that figures on the front pages of the business sections of news-

---

14. In *The New Competition* (Best 1990), the difference between static and dynamic clusters is illustrated by contrasting the "closed" business system of a once large furniture cluster in North London with the "open" business system of a rival cluster located in Emilia Romagna. The North London furniture manufacturers were intensely competitive with each other over prices. They were blind to their business system disadvantage. Once their markets were invaded by networked groups of flexibly specialized enterprises with collective entrepreneurial capabilities, it was too late. Coinciding with Great Britain's entry into the EU, the entire North London furniture cluster collapsed, virtually without trace.

papers, the furniture industry is and remains a major industry in Europe. The invention of the container combined with free-trade agreements created market opportunities that were seized first by Italian, German, and Danish exporters. Over the period 1970–92, Italy's exports of furniture increased fifty times and Denmark's twenty-eight times. In the period 1961–90, the average annual growth in international demand was 19 percent, surpassed only by computers and peripherals (just over 24 percent). Furniture making, a traditional craft-based industry, mutated into a modern industry that could drive regional growth, employ skilled workers, and contribute to the EU trade balance (Lorenzen 1998; Maskell 1998).[15]

The Monaghan furniture cluster pursued a low-cost strategy to meet the design-led new competition from Europe. They mistakenly saw as the competition their competitor enterprises located within their own region. Their strategy proved short-lived when high-volume producers from China entered the global market, based on application of the principle of flow.

Specializing in high-volume production, China created and rapidly grew the world's biggest furniture industry based on the synchronization principle of mass production.[16] It took two decades. In 1990 China did not feature in the top ten exporters of furniture; in 2000 it was the world's ninth-largest exporter and by 2006 the largest. Between 2002 and 2006, Chinese furniture exports increased by 30 percent annually to reach over 20 percent of global exports, double those of Italy, the second-largest exporter.[17]

The threats of the new competition were not lost on Monaghan furniture makers; they were directly impacted. They lost orders; they visited IKEA's showrooms; they attended trade shows; they visited Chinese

15. Peter Maskell found that in the 1980s the wooden furniture sector ranked seventh out of a total of eighty-five NACE manufacturing four-digit subsectors in employment (1998, 38). NACE stands for Nomenclature Statistique des Activités Économiques dans la Communauté Européenne, or the Statistical Classification of Economic Activities in the European Community, which is the industry standard classification system used in the EU.

16. IKEA in retailing and China in production brought scale to the global furniture market as never before. In 2001, with more than 50,000 furniture manufacturers employing 50 million workers, China's business model could not have been more different than that of Italy, which had 37,000 companies and 230,000 workers. Thus, whereas each furniture company has an average of six workers in Italy, each company in China has an average of a thousand workers. See *Manufacturing & Technology News* 10, no. 3 (July 3, 2003), available at www.manufacturingnews.com/news/03/0703/art1.html. See also "North Carolina in the Global Economy," www.soc.duke.edu/NC_GlobalEconomy/furniture/overview .shtml.

17. "Strategy for the Development of the Furniture Industry," www.bestsaexporters .com/articles/203-draft-strategy-for-the-development-of-the-furniture-industry.html.

companies and saw what they could do, and some made deals to import and retail Chinese furniture. They struggled to shape a strategy, but their comparative lack of production capabilities left them with very limited options. They signed contracts with Eastern European and Chinese furniture manufacturers to supply components and ancillary products to add to their product lines. This turned out to be a self-defeating strategy since it undermined instead of advanced local production capabilities. Individual action was the best they could do, given the lack of an integrated systemic view and a regional governance capability to shape and administer a unified strategy.

It is interesting to note, however, that the growth of Chinese furniture exports was not accompanied by a sharp contraction of the European wood-processing industry. Although the growth of European furniture output did decline between 2001 and 2003, by just under 3 percent per year, it grew at a fast rate between 1996 and 2000 and 2006–7, before declining by just under 4 percent in 2008. But, more importantly, European wood-processing clusters were morphing into dynamic new multisector clusters.[18]

In comparison to furniture manufacturers in the Third Italy, Germany, Denmark, Sweden, and Finland, a Monaghan company had no experience in leveraging engineering expertise and specialized resources from outside the company to undertake a capability-development program to meet the new production standards.[19] Had they developed such partnerships, the production-improvement programs would have created pressures within the company to make a shift from an autarchic to a focus-and-network strategy, which can be a catalyst for the emergence of cluster-dynamic processes.

18. For example, Forenel is an abbreviation of FORestry, ENgineering, and ELectronics and captures the idea that the Finnish forest and related engineering and electronics (Forenel) cluster is a unique combination of elements from all three (see Kuusisto et al. 2005). Finland's economic policymakers, business enterprises, and educators together crafted a multisector system integration capability in technology management combining forestry, engineering, and electronics to supply a large range of wood engineering–derived products and services at the global level. The dynamic increasing returns characteristics of the Forenel cluster is reminiscent of the evolutionary principles of increasing differentiation, descent with adaptation, and mutual adjustment processes that are applied in chapter 3 to making sense of Greater Boston's industrial ecosystem.

19. For example, the consultancy Gerhard Schuler, located near Stuttgart, Germany, advised numerous companies worldwide on implementing a variant of JIT production methods and associated accounting systems, such as activity-based costing, to wood processing.

The development of a production-improvement program is not a quick fix; it can be likened to a journey to transform a company's production system from top to bottom. Strikingly, near to the ailing cluster of furniture manufacturers there was already a state-of-the-art enterprise that had undertaken the journey.

The Bose Corporation, a global leader in loudspeakers and ancillary audio equipment, was founded in 1964 by Dr. Amar G. Bose, then professor of electrical engineering at MIT. Its turnover in 2010 was $2 billion, and it has five facilities, including its headquarters in Framingham, Massachusetts. It opened its manufacturing site in Carrickmacross, Ireland, in 1978, attracted in part by the region's furniture-making tradition. In the words of Pat McAdam, Bose director in Ireland, importing cabinets was not economical since it involved transporting "container loads of air." The idea was to get local suppliers to make the high-specification cabinets, which for acoustical reasons are made of wood.

As it turned out, Bose was not successful in finding woodworkers that had experience in making wood products at the tight tolerances demanded for audio systems. Nevertheless, Bose developed a state-of-the-art manufacturing plant that employed 185 in 2010. Much of the specific woodworking expertise was obtained from a Bose facility in Canada that had developed good woodworking practices over the years.

The Carrickmacross plant has three CNC (computer-numerical control) woodworking machines, each of which takes the place of about seven traditional machines such as drills, planers, routers, and saws. Much of the tooling is done in an in-house machine shop.[20] Furthermore, the Bose plant recycles waste wood products into an environmentally clean boiler system to provide all its heat energy requirements.

The cabinet-making and electronic assembly plant is a model lean manufacturing facility including a high-performance, self-directed work-team organizational system. It is also unionized. The director stated that productivity has advanced by 50 percent since the company began its lean manufacturing journey in 2007. All the features of the Toyota Production System are on display, including JIT; SMED, or single-minute exchange of die; Kanban, a visual information and scheduling system; and 5-S *kaizen* continuous-innovation work organization (Best 1990, chap. 5; 2000, 15–22).

20. Commonly the tooling for CNC machines can approach half the cost of the machines, and in-house tooling capability can be critical to new product development and innovation.

Unfortunately, Bose is an isolated example of world-class manufacturing practices that represents a missed opportunity that most companies in the region could have used as a model. We were informed that no indigenous company had ever sought to visit the facility. Instead this is a case of indigenous enterprises not learning the organizational sources of competitive advantage from foreign-sector production facilities. But it also points to a flaw in the Irish government's separation of enterprise development into a foreign sector run by the IDA and an indigenous sector run by Enterprise Ireland.[21]

STRANDED REGIONS: THE POVERTY OF REGIONAL STRATEGY

The work that we did on the border region provided insights that have wider application to the task of getting indigenous enterprise strategy right. The weakness of regional development policy in both Ireland and Northern Ireland has left many of their internal regions, as well as the cross-border region, economically detached or stranded. These more peripheral regions do not have the characteristics attractive to large-scale FDI (e.g., urban population centers, third-level education establishments, high-grade transport and communications facilities). Consequently, their development is much more dependent on indigenous enterprise growth. Major infrastructural improvements have eased Dublin-Belfast, Dublin-Cork, and Dublin-Galway communications, but these city-based growth centers interact only weakly. Elsewhere in Ireland, the structural characteristics of less advanced counties and regions derive mainly from their peripherality and low level of urbanization.

In the Republic of Ireland, regional policy was revisited in the early years of the last decade, with the eventual publication in 2002 of the *National Spatial Strategy for Ireland: 2002–2020*. However, it was ironic that this publication followed the major policy decisions taken during the three major EU Regional Development Fund programs of 1989–93, 1994–99 and 2000–2006, when the economic infrastructure of the Republic of Ireland was updated to accelerate the pace of convergence to a higher

21. Bose closed its Carrickmacross plant after nearly four decades of operation. As reported in *thejournal.ie*, January 22, 2015: "Unfortunately, this area has been ignored for too long by successive Governments. Monaghan has only had two visits by the IDA in the past 5 years and many will remember that Bose was the last significant employer attracted to this region by the IDA in the late 70s." See "Shock in Monaghan as Bose Closure Sees 140 Jobs Axed," www.thejournal.ie/bose-closure-loses-140-jobs-1897065-Jan2015/.

EU-type standard of living. Logically the formulation of the strategy should have come first. The timing of the publication unintentionally revealed the lack of importance that Irish policymakers attached to regional strategy.

One of the by-products of the since abandoned *National Spatial Strategy* was that individual counties (the smallest units of governance in Ireland) were required to produce county development plans. These were usually drawn up with the assistance of specialized firms of consultants rather than produced by policymakers in the county itself. After reviewing many examples, some patterns become clear. Although each such plan contains a SWOT analysis, the intention is often to portray the county as a highly desirable location and an attractive base for inward investment. Understandably, county development plans tend to be seen more as marketing opportunities than as vehicles for self-critical analysis and realistic forward thinking.

Perhaps the most surprising aspect of the county development plans is the brevity with which they usually treat the studies of the existing county production base. For example, the Monaghan Development Plan, published in 2002 and regularly reviewed and updated since then, has no separate section covering the important county manufacturing base or, indeed, of its base of market service enterprises, but it does have detailed treatments of the environment, the level of social inclusion, provisions for a healthy and safe community, arts and culture, and sports and leisure. Somehow, production gets written out of the story!

The development plans throughout do not address the production and business organization conditions that are the inputs to effective models of economic governance elsewhere. The business associations likewise are not forums for constructing industrial strategies that address the production system challenges required to transform the regional economies. It is hard to escape the conclusion that existing interrelationships among the various agencies and actors are a mode of economic governance that is a barrier to industrial innovation and economic development.

In Northern Ireland, strategic thinking and economic data about subregions are almost completely absent from policy documents. For example, the Northern Ireland economic strategy that was published in November 2011 (Northern Ireland Executive 2011) makes no mention of subregional development challenges and, more surprisingly, very little mention of the economy of the Republic of Ireland, which lies to its immediate south. We found that officially published Northern Ireland economic statistics make it impossible to explore how—say—the economies of the Newry-Mourne region or of the region centered on Derry City are performing relative to other Northern Ireland subregions or relative to Northern Ireland as a whole. There is a range of socioeconomic indicators of population, unemployment, poverty, and so on. But there are none of the kinds of data that would be needed if the economic strategy for Northern Ireland as a whole were to be augmented by treatment of subregional black spots.

In the case of Enterprise Ireland, in the Republic of Ireland, there are lots of supportive enterprise programs being rolled out in diverse sectors and local businesses and many success stories. The *Action Plan for Jobs 2013* (*APJ*), with its myriad reforms and sectoral policies, fits well into this domestic context. There is a strategy, indeed many strategies, implicit in Enterprise Ireland and *APJ* activities, but they tend to get lost in the details.

With Ireland faced with the need to create jobs to reduce unemployment, the temptation is to focus on separate sectors and individual technologies. The *APJ* is organized along these lines, identifying eleven separate sectors. Of course, attention is paid to collaborative issues: "Companies increasingly need to collaborate to compete, requiring engagement in networks, clustering activities and in building strategic relationships with HEIs [higher education institutions], research institutes, partners and suppliers within and across sectors" (APJ 2013, 111). But in the *AJP* this appears as a mere exhortation. In reality, it is the crucial element in building a successful indigenous enterprise strategy and needs to be brought center stage. Knowing what enterprises are present in any regional economy is the start. But the fact that clusters of similar manufacturing activities exist in a region does not tell us if the constituent firms are focusing on core capabilities and partnering for complementary capabilities in a way that creates an organic and highly competitive entity referred to as an entrepreneurial industrial district.

The emphasis in the quote above is on what companies need to do. But if this is the case, why have they never done it before, and is exhortation enough to get them to start collaborating and clustering? As noted above, successful industrial policy frameworks adopted by European rivals have integrated and not separated the foreign and domestic development agencies and have established multilevel economic governance systems that combine bottom-up with top-down functions.[22]

22. The indigenous sector was less export-oriented than the foreign sector, and very dependent on one export market, the United Kingdom. Consequently, it was severely af-

Ireland's High Tech: Clusters without Entrepreneurial Firms

In chapter 3 we examined the internal dynamics that push rapidly growing high-tech firms to expand production by establishing branch plants abroad. Globalization meant that large investments in high tech could generate returns by leveraging technology platforms with offshore production, marketing, and sales facilities. For companies like Boston Scientific, much of the enterprise growth in employment is out of state and offshore but not outsourced. Nevertheless, the crown jewels of the company, its technology platform, design and development, and early-stage manufacturing, remained rooted in Massachusetts. This was not simply for control or governance purposes, important as they are, but because of the region's comparative advantage in technology-platform and business development. Technology-platform and new-product development often involve technology integration and new technology combinations and often occur at the intersection of preexisting clusters.

The Irish IDA created a pull factor to meet the push factor needed to create a platform for export from rapidly growing high-tech firms such as Boston Scientific. Together, a globalization and localization interactive dynamic was set in motion to build Ireland's competitive advantage in the supply of low-cost manufacturing capabilities to meet the demands of rapidly growing high-tech entrepreneurial firms. Both Greater Boston and Ireland benefited from international specialization within a cross-border production system. It enabled MNEs to leverage fixed costs of R&D and investing in a technology-development platform to benefit from economies of scale in production. Here we look more closely at the benefits of the specific functional specialization and localization relationship for Ireland.

It would be hard to overstate the success of the specialization dynamic by which multinational enterprises created well-paying jobs and export earnings in Ireland. Modern production capabilities were introduced on a scale that was large enough to drive national growth in a country without any significant previous industrial manufacturing history. Ireland, unlike high-tech enterprises in the United States, did not have a government-funded S&T infrastructure supporting armaments, space, and life-science

fected by the contraction of domestic demand that followed the period of austerity. This illustrates the theme that effective domestic macro policy depends on an assessment of the state of the nation's productive structures. The Nordic policymakers have a long history of taking for granted a structural competitiveness approach to industrial development (Mjøset 1992; Senghaas 1985).

industries. Rather than science and engineering departments, Ireland's early higher education tradition was geared more to literature and the humanities (Cookson, 2010).

With the support of the Irish government and Regional Economic Development Funds from the EU, the IDA invested in material and human-resource infrastructures tailored to the specific management requirements of the MNEs. The IDA growth strategy, with support from the Irish government and Structural Funds from the EU, tailored infrastructures and tax policies to turn Ireland into an export platform for hundreds of world-leading technology enterprises, including fifteen of the world's twenty-five biggest medical-device companies and eight of the top ten global drug companies (Jack 2010). In the 1990s Ireland grew at a historically fast rate and moved rapidly up the international league tables in income per capita. The economy was transformed. By 2009, foreign multinationals accounted for 88.4 percent of Ireland's manufactured exports and 94 percent of exports of internationally traded services (Forfás 2010).

The government's industrial strategy was successful in attracting MNEs to establish export-platform subsidiaries in Ireland. But has it been successful in establishing localized innovation capabilities within either subsidiaries or domestic enterprises? In this section we go inside Ireland's most prominent high-tech clusters in search of entrepreneurial firms as business units of MNEs. In high-tech sectors, entrepreneurial enterprises are the coordinators of the innovation process linking basic, developmental, and applied research with new-product design, design for manufacturability, and product performance by which competitive advantage is achieved. The capability-development process of entrepreneurial firms is the demand side of the R&D market. The supply of R&D resources does not turn into industrial innovation without coordinated production-capability development.

CLUSTERS OF AUTARCHIC ENTERPRISES

In chapter 3 the vTHREAD enterprise database was used to better understand the links between the entrepreneurial firms and cluster-dynamic processes that lie behind the creation of the region's competitive advantage in a series of high-tech sectors. Unfortunately, the technology taxonomy used to classify the data set of companies and their products that was constructed and organized to populate the vTHREAD longitudinal database of high-tech companies is unique to the data-collection methodology of CorpTech in Massachusetts. No such data set exists in Ireland, in either the public or the private sector, that could be used to organize a longitudinal data set of the activities of high-tech companies in Ireland. To search for individual entrepreneurial firms in the indigenous population of Irish enterprises we used the FAME database. But unfortunately, FAME is not organized around a finely granulated technology taxonomy of firms and products.

Lacking both an engineering-informed taxonomy and longitudinal data on the evolution of MNE branch plant activities, we can make inferences only from what company data are available. Fortunately, academic researchers have constructed data sets of high-technology clusters in Ireland that can be interpreted in terms of the dynamic-capabilities perspective. We use studies by academic researchers from data supplied by private data sources, trade associations, and governmental agencies such as the Office of National Statistics, IDA, Enterprise Ireland, the National Science Foundation, Forfas, trade associations, and private business directory databases such as FAME and Kompass that were designed for marketing purposes.

PHARMA/BIOPHARMA

Chris Van Egeraat and various co-authors have reported on the subsidiary evolution in the Irish pharmaceutical industry in a series of publications. Employment in the industry grew strongly, from just over 1,300 in 1972 to nearly 19,500 in 2003, by which time pharmaceuticals had become one of Ireland's leading industrial sectors. However, only 1,401 were employed in indigenous companies.[23]

In 2003 the 95 subsidiaries of foreign companies accounted for 93 percent of pharmaceutical employment and virtually all employment in the drug-substance subsector. Indigenous operations remained relatively small, with only seven indigenous companies employing more than 50 staff (Van Egeraat and Breatnach 2012; Van Egeraat and Barry 2008, 7). Interestingly, Ireland does seem to have developed some interesting indigenous companies that help design or configure new pharma factories,

23. A decade later, the pharmaceutical sector employed about 17,600 workers in eighty-eight companies in 2013; another report in 2010 estimated that the broader biopharma-pharmachem sector employed 25,300 (InterTradeIreland 2015, 50). "The indigenous pharmaceutical industry segment is relatively small, particularly since Elan was partly acquired by foreign interests, with only a few new indigenous small dedicated biotechnology companies, such as Opsona and Merrion Pharmaceuticals, active in pharmaceutical drug discovery."

although, if anything, this may erode Ireland's pharma manufacturing base as these firms increasingly sell their services abroad (Eoin Sullivan interview, May 20, 2016).

Van Egeraat and Curran report little to no evidence of localization, agglomeration, or cluster dynamics. They write:

> The case of the Irish pharmaceutical industry serves to show that the kind of spatial planning-driven satellite industrial platforms in the context of late-developing countries do not automatically start generating substantial localisation economies and crucial technological spillovers, not even in the largest concentration worldwide after nearly 40 years of existence. In the context of underdeveloped research infrastructures and low levels of entrepreneurship, a transformation into self-perpetuating industrial concentrations will require more than spatial planning policy. (2013, 355)

The major concentration in Cork, Ireland's second-largest city, is of enterprises that all produce similar products that have not changed over the decades. The region does not have the properties of an innovative industrial ecosystem, which have remained concentrated in the home bases of the firms involved.

MEDICAL DEVICES

Ireland has long been home to around fifteen of the world's top twenty-five medical technology companies, including Abbott, Baxter, Boston Scientific, Guidant, Johnson & Johnson, Medtronic, and Stryker. Medical technology in Galway was initiated with the arrival of C. R. Bard and the manufacture of coronary- and vascular-disease products in 1982 (CISC 2010, 24).

Three decades later the medical devices industry employed over 22,000 people (14 percent of the total engaged in manufacturing) and accounted for 20 percent of total manufacturing value added (CSO 2014). Of the 112 firms recorded in relevant NACE category 325, 71 were foreign-owned and accounted for 95 percent of employment. In 2012 Ireland became the largest global exporter of cardiovascular and diagnostic devices, primarily drug-eluting stents (InterTradeIreland 2015, 62). Much of this activity is localized in Galway.

However, a review in 2004 of the medical-technologies sector for the Irish government, conducted by the Industry Advisory Group, reported little evidence that the foreign medical-technologies companies in Ireland had changed from being a manufacturing base for producing proprietary products for export. The report cited low levels of R&D activity in foreign-owned activities in Ireland with a distinct absence of research. "Where it does occur, R&D largely involves continuous process improvements with few companies developing products of the future." The report stated that R&D is deterred by the long life cycles of many of the products manufactured in Ireland and "inadequate understanding of the manufacturing process" (Industry Advisory Group 2004, 15–16).[24]

More recently, researchers at the Centre for Innovation and Structural Change (CISC) at the National University of Ireland, Galway, have investigated the region's medical-device cluster and documented its history, evolution, and the extrafirm support agencies (Ryan et al. 2010, chap. 2; see also Giblin and Ryan 2010 and Ryan and Giblin 2012). The results from the perspective of capabilities and innovation are not encouraging: "As the economic model of attracting FDI based on cost competitiveness and grant incentives has now become relatively inadequate in Ireland, the challenge is to make the successful transition to a new model based on endogenous development" (Ryan et al. 2010, 31).[25]

The CISC researchers cite two lone examples of indigenous companies that fit the entrepreneurial firm model of cumulatively and collectively advancing a distinctive technology platform with the capability to develop a stream of new products. Creganna seized the opportunity and took full advantage of the arrival of Boston Scientific in 1994 to reposition itself to design and engineer catheters that surround Boston Scientific's cardiovascular stents. Creganna leveraged this relationship to eventually supply the global medical-devices industry and, in the process, became a mid-sized company of over 500 employees as a global provider of "outsourced design and manufacturing services to the medical device industry."[26] Creganna found it necessary to establish a base in the Greater

24. "Many foreign-owned companies in Ireland are assembly plants attracted to Ireland in the past by low rates of tax, generous grants and relatively low wage rates. As a result, they tend to have inadequate understanding of the manufacturing process which generally inhibits R&D activity" (Industry Advisory Group 2004, 15).

25. The CISC team undertook a project to develop Lucerna, a national database of companies, to apply the capabilities and innovation perspective to Ireland. It was the first effort to construct a longitudinal database of technology-driven companies and their products at the national level. The challenge was to construct a comprehensive data set of companies and products to populate a historical database to characterize the specialization and differentiation dynamics of regionally co-located companies (Ryan et al. 2010).

26. According to the Creganna website: "It is ranked as one of the top 10 global providers of outsourced design and manufacturing services to the medical device industry. We serve over 400 customers in 30 countries worldwide from a global operational network

Boston area to access business- and technology-development enabling relationships.

The second example is Crospon, established in 2006, which was formed by an executive team with individuals who had acquired experience from their employment going back to the earliest arrivals of foreign medical-devices companies. The concept was to build a company to develop proprietorial imaging catheter devices for measurement and sizing of the stents required after dilation to aid surgery in the esophagus and stomach. Crospon's distinctive technological capability involves a three-way convergence of IT (in this case, a licensing agreement with HP), medical technology, and pharmaceuticals (Ryan et al. 2010, 30). Crospon subsequently opened an office in Silicon Valley.

Creganna and Crospon are two examples of the entrepreneurial firm model. But their rarity also indicates the more general lack in Ireland of cluster-dynamic processes that foster entrepreneurial firms and drive up a region's or nation's indigenous innovation capability. They also offer a salutary lesson on the limitations of Ireland's national development policy frameworks.

Denmark's medical-technologies cluster offers a sharp contrast to Ireland's. Denmark's cluster has roughly the same number of employees (20,000+) but has 250 companies working solely with medical devices (out of a total of 1,000 companies with med-tech-related activities). More than 95 percent of Danish medical devices are exported, and there is a substantial export surplus. Two-thirds of the companies in the industry have fewer than 50 employees. But a number of companies are much larger and are R&D-intensive (Denmark Ministry of Foreign Affairs 2014). Medical-devices clusters located elsewhere exhibit a range of product categories and many globally competitive mid-sized enterprises (Best 2006).

SOFTWARE

Anita Sands begins a survey of the Irish software industry with this sentence: "The Irish software industry constitutes the first example of a successful high-tech indigenous industry in Ireland" (2005, 41). This is undoubtedly correct. In the early 1990s, 365 firms employed fewer than 8,000 persons. Between 1991 and 2001 employment grew from 7,798 to 31,500, the number of foreign firms from 74 to 140, and indigenous soft-

spanning the US, Europe and Asia." See "Creganna Medical: Who We Are," www.creganna.com/company/.

ware companies from 291 to 760. According to Sands, "The indigenous sector accounts for 760 (84 per cent) of the 900 companies and employs just under half the industry's workforce, yet it accounts for only nine per cent of the industry's revenues and eight per cent of its overall exports" (Sands 2005, 43–45).[27]

Although the software industry is the first successful indigenous Irish high-tech industry, it represents a huge missed opportunity. It is not capital-intensive, and its manufacturing operations are not complex. John Sterne describes five generations in the evolution of the Irish software industry from its beginnings in the late 1960s and the mix of foreign and domestic companies that led each. In his words:

> Over the past quarter century, the country has shown how software development can thrive as a cottage industry. Hundreds of small companies have launched and exported specialized products. Individual businesses open and close all the time. Role models emerge and fade away. It is still a rare event for a software company to survive for a full decade under the same name and the same leadership. Collectively, however, the Irish industry keeps expanding, capitalizing on its accumulation of development skills and its store of international contacts. (2004, 290)

Sterne purposefully stretches the term "cottage industry" to capture the prevalence of microfirms, many with five or fewer members. Unlike in traditional cottage industries, in the software sector two or three people can develop a product with global applications. But it is also an industry in which small open economies can grow very big indigenous firms. In Israel, the extreme case, sales of the four biggest firms exceed $3 billion, three times the entire indigenous Irish software industry (Breznitz 2005, 72).

A major difference between the Irish and Israeli software industries is that Israeli software companies benefit from a large domestic market. Irish software companies have not benefited from a cumulative dynamic of growing domestic entrepreneurial enterprises in other sectors. New-product development in most sectors involves software engineering, and new-sector development involves the emergence and growth of both hardware and software firms (see the example of network switches in chap. 3).

---

27. SkillSoft, at 322, Norkom, at 773, and Trintech, at 997, were three of the twelve indigenous companies on the Top 1000 EU R&D Investment scorecard for 2009 and together employed 1,651 persons and invested €712 million in R&D. In 2015 none of the three was still present, as one moved its headquarters out of Ireland and two were acquired by foreign firms (see below).

Ireland has individual examples of multiple forms of innovation processes, too few of which were leveraged or scaled. For example, for each of the five generations Sterne describes an example of an internationally successful indigenous software-tools company. He also describes an example of how a foreign enterprise, DEC, fostered the emergence of a globally successful indigenous high-performance technical computing group, "a rarified subset of the international software community" (2004, 115).

Staff in Digital's Irish organization successfully lobbied the Massachusetts headquarters to pursue market opportunities in new ways of licensing and delivering software. According to Sterne, "They studied the software needs of major customers and devised support services, not only for Digital products but also for other vendors' applications." When Digital phased out computer assembly in Galway in 1993, the software side had grown to 350 people and "had matured into one of the few successful US-owned concentrations of Irish development talent." It continued to thrive despite the closure of the hardware operations. As the group's experience and technical capabilities grew, so did its opportunities for new complex customer applications. It delivered software-technology products to the French Atomic Energy Commission in order to install the most powerful computer in Europe, and later it delivered "a 12,000-processor monster to the US Department of energy." Sterne writes: "Projects like these raised the profile of the high performance technical computing group in a rarefied subset of the international software community." The software center continued under Compaq, and when Compaq merged with HP, "the headcount stood at 500, including some 200 software engineers" (2004, 113–15).

This is an Irish example of a Penrose–like growth dynamic. Unfortunately, it is a very rare example. But it gives us insight into the sources of success of Israel and the Nordic economies in leveraging FDI to build indigenous innovation capabilities, as explained below.

From 1971, when DEC set up a production facility in Galway, it pursued a strong domestic market role and in the process created partnering opportunities for emerging learning firms. Mentec, one of more than a dozen original equipment manufacturers with which DEC partnered, built a team to pick up the "threads of products that Digital was not promoting. One of those was the J-11 processor." Mentec licensed the chip to build a series of single-board computers for customers to embed into process control systems, telecommunications equipment, and the electricity infrastructure. Success depended on lobbying DEC headquarters to maintain the supply of the J-11s (Sterne 2004, 55–56).

The Mentec experience is an Irish example of the Penrose–like growth dynamic that creates interstice opportunities for small- and medium-sized firms that are not large enough for the lead firm to pursue. While the Irish IDA was fully aware of the developmental roles played by DEC in terms of fostering technology development in indigenous enterprises, it did not design a development policy framework in which indigenous innovation was at the core. This is the basis of the claim that software development, in particular, represented a huge missed opportunity with respect to economic governance.

Critical Assessment

From a dynamic-capabilities perspective, the above three high-tech sectors (pharma/bio-pharma, medical devices, and software) reveal a striking similarity. The population of MNE branch plants in Ireland has not fostered the emergence and growth of a significant number of indigenous entrepreneurial firms. Moreover, the branch plants are not organized individually or collectively to do so. Internally, they have remained a remotely managed production and business system, organized to make and export products designed at their home base.

Ireland's policymakers have not solved the challenge of growing midsized, technology-driven companies. The lack of firms that invest heavily in R&D has serious consequences for attractive career opportunities. As shown in table 5.1, Denmark and Finland are also small open economies with roughly the same population as Ireland but with many multiples of Ireland's 12 companies on the European Commission's 2009 EU Industrial R&D Investment Scorecard. Finland's 58 companies employed 25 percent of the labor force, or 535,000; Denmark's 47 employed 14 percent, or 311,000; and Ireland's 12 employed 3.4 percent, or 61,000. Denmark's total of 47 indigenous enterprises on the Top 1,000 R&D scorecard invests five times as much and employs five times more than Ireland's 12 entries. In the life sciences (medical technologies, pharmaceutical, biotech) Denmark had 19 domestic companies on the European Commission's 2009 EU Industrial R&D Investment Scorecard compared to Ireland's 3 (Elan, 1,683 employees; Trinity Biotech, 757 employees; and AGI Therapeutic, 9 employees).

Promising high-tech start-ups in Ireland have emerged but rarely grow into sustainable mid-sized enterprises. They are either acquired by other firms or otherwise do not flourish, at least locally. Software examples include SkillSoft, which has headquarters in both Nashua, New Hampshire, and Dublin, but it began life in Ireland.[28] Norkom was founded in Dublin in 1998 but in 2011 was acquired by BAE Systems, a multinational corporation.[29] Trintech was sold in 2010 to a US firm. Datalex has gone through hard times but remains a Dublin-based e-commerce software enterprise specializing in the travel industry.[30]

For Michael Hennigan, editor of *Finfacts*, the sale of Trintech marked

> the last of the great hopes of the 1990s for the development of a significant Irish technology sector.... Trintech was among firms such as Iona Technologies, Baltimore Technologies, Parthus, Riverdeep, Datalex and Cognotec, which gave hope in the 1990s that an indigenous Irish high-tech sector could evolve, but all these firms have either been subsumed into American businesses, gone bust or are operating on respirators. (*Finfacts Ireland*, October 18, 2010)[31]

Populations of entrepreneurial firms do not just happen. Their internal capability-development processes are enabled by access, as needed, to extrafirm infrastructures for development finance, human resources, and S&T partnerships. Entrepreneurial firms are incubated, grow, and evolve within unified industrial ecosystems.

The industrial ecosystems of Ireland and the peripheral regions of the United Kingdom are fragmented and disorganized when contrasted with those that enabled the successful growth and transformation experiences described in earlier chapters. Germany provides a benchmark for the economic coordination of extrafirm infrastructures to enable a population of SMEs to innovate and thrive.

The Schumpeterian concept of innovation focuses attention on the role of financial institutions in the creation of future values. In the language of structural competitiveness, an enabling financial subsystem is an integral component of a region's or nation's industrial ecosystem. En-

---

28. See "History of SkillSoft Public Limited Company," www.referenceforbusiness.com /history2/86/SkillSoft-Public-Limited-Company.html.

29. See "Norkom," https://en.wikipedia.org/wiki/Norkom, accessed November 17, 2017).

30. See Newenham 2017.

31. Hennigan criticizes Ireland's policymakers for stubbornly persisting in a development strategy that was not working: "Finfacts has in the past commented that this inconvenient record was ignored by policymakers hell-bent on realising dreams of creating a European Silicon Valley in Ireland and funding the fairytale aspiration that large-scale funding of university research would be the solution to mass unemployment." See "Trintech Sold to US Firm for Knockdown Price of $93M," www.finfacts.ie/irishfinancenews/article _1020800.shtml.

trepreneurial firms are the pivotal links in the innovation process chain, connecting basic, developmental, and applied research with new-product design, design for manufacturability, and product performance by which competitive advantage is achieved.

Here the term "financial ecosystem" is used to capture the co-evolution dynamic between a region's or nation's business system and its development-finance system. Taiwan and Singapore fund business-capability development through Ministries of Trade and Industry. Israel relied on the Department of Defense, in the first instance; royalty-based finance; World Bank funds; and US financial institutions (Breznitz 2007).

Dan Breznitz describes the uniquely globally sourced financial system that co-adapted with the emergence of Israel's distinctive competitive advantage in supplying product R&D innovations to MNEs with marketing and manufacturing capabilities. Breznitz contrasts Israel's financial system's success in growing a globally successful software industry with the failure of Ireland's system after an equally promising start.[32]

Drawing from the success of sustained growth experiences, we find a common feature. The due-diligence methodology of the funding agency, whether private or public, is based on a strategy and structure assessment of the enterprise's future value proposition. Implicit are a Schumpeterian concept of competitive strategy and a Penrose/Babbage-informed concept of structure anchored by fundamental principles of production and organization.

Banking institutions and policymakers in Ireland, as in the United Kingdom, have long been influenced by laissez-faire economic perspectives in which business-organization and production-capability development are left to the market. Although inconsistent with the noninterventionist perspective, all governments in both countries conduct ad hoc industrial policymaking in the form of creating grants, subsidies, tax-code concessions, and material infrastructures in response to intense political lobbying behind the scenes. Lacking focus on the drivers of indigenous innovation, a due-diligence methodology for dealing with future value investment proposals, and extrafirm infrastructures like those of the

---

32. Breznitz (2007, 34–35) argues that Ireland's Enterprise Ireland has not employed horizontally neutral policies with regard to technologies and sectors, and consequently Ireland lacks the institutionalized processes of risk sharing that are required for early-stage technology development. EU structural funds were allocated to Enterprise Ireland to foster the creation of a venture capital industry but, according to Breznitz, unintentionally blocked it.

German model of economic governance, policymakers fall back on subsidies to individual enterprises and, in the process, undermine an entrepreneurial business culture.

A Final Comment: Macro Implications of Dual Structures

We began this chapter with the question of why the crash of the Irish economy was so catastrophic as to foster a return to widespread emigration immediately following the island's spectacular success in raising living standards from among the lowest to among the highest in the EU. Although analysis has focused on the effects of the dual structure of the economy on indigenous innovation, it is readily acknowledged that an account of macroeconomic policy is integral to a full explanation. In fact, they work together.

The dual structure provides a context for distinguishing two phases of high Irish growth. The first, the original Celtic Tiger period extending from 1986 to 2000, was soundly based on the systematic expansion of the exporting manufacturing and tradeable sectors, dominated by MNEs. The second phase, continuing into the mid-2000s, was unsustainably driven by a construction bubble and excessive fiscal easing. The short-term returns to speculation in the second phase deflected attention away from the tradable sectors and the unmet challenge of developing the production side of the domestic economy.

The macroeconomic implications of not addressing the structural challenges were delayed but profound. During the second growth phase, the exchequer relied heavily on tax revenues associated with property churning, which collapsed with the bubble. A series of austerity budgets imposed a dramatic drop in domestic demand that seriously contracted activity in the nontradable sectors (Bradley and Untiedt 2012). Unemployment rose rapidly, driven by a contraction of employment in the domestic-service sectors, both public and private. However, the nontradable sector's limited resilience to shocks was obscured by the sustained export performance of the foreign sector.

The Irish economic problem was not the lack of an interventionist government. The IDA was astute in its early identification of new technology waves emanating from the United States. It was a creative shortcut to establishing globally competitive production units in Ireland, a country without any significant industrial engineering legacy. The IDA was supported by other agencies of government, including a free-trade environment, adoption of the euro, and low-tax macroeconomic fiscal policies. In addition, the availability of generous EU development assistance during the period 1989–2007, in terms of Structural Funds, was used to improve transportation infrastructure and to establish a national tier of regional technology colleges to develop a curriculum and build a staff to educate a new generation of students to match the human-resource needs of the MNEs.[33]

The failure to develop a policy framework to address the challenge of the dual structure of the economy had unforeseen macroeconomic policy implications. The dual economy structure within the Irish economy mirrors the EU split between core and periphery economies. The development policy frameworks within the core economies are informed by a structural competitiveness macroeconomic perspective and a complementary regional economic policymaking governance system based on the concepts of the capability triad. This is not the case in the periphery.

33. It should be noted that the cost of the bank bailout of recent years greatly exceeded the totality of structural funds received over the period 1989–2013!

CHAPTER EIGHT

New Production Systems

JAPAN AND CHINA

CAPABILITY TRIADS are shaped and operate within a dynamic global system. Consequently, over time, the strategic external context for policy-making is subject to fundamental change—rarely more so than in the present times. China's share of global nominal GDP surged from 2 percent in 1980 to 15 percent in 2016; its ranking in global GDP increased from ninth in 1978 to second in 2016. Japan, with less than a tenth of China's population of nearly 1.4 billion, is the world's third-largest economy. The combination of the rapid growth and size of these two economies has transformed the global context. In this chapter we examine the production systems and strategic policymaking frameworks of both economic transformations.

Japan's New Competition

The production capacity of the global economy has changed nearly beyond recognition over the past five decades. More than a dozen countries have grown annually at 7 percent or more for twenty-five years or more. Following the experience of Japan, manufacturing exports of the four "tiger" economies (Korea, Taiwan, Hong Kong, and Singapore) increased from under $5 billion in 1962 to $715 billion in 2004 (*Growth Commission* 2008, 23). This was before China and India, the world's two most populous nations, shifted from autarchic governance structures to embrace globalization and to galvanize their growth dynamics.

In a separate publication co-authored by Mohamed El-Erian, chair of President Obama's Global Development Council (2012–17), and Nobel laureate Michael Spence, the chair of the Growth Commission that was commissioned by the World Bank to explain the rapid-growth experiences of East Asia, the authors state: "At this stage of economics we do not have models that capture ... the parallel processes of learning and accumulating intangible assets that go along with measurable capital accumulation and income growth" (El-Erian and Spence 2008, 88). They conclude that "at a fundamental level economic development is about the building of individual and institutional capabilities ... but do not as yet model well" (2008, 94). The report does not examine or explain the process of "building ... institutional capabilities": The concept of "parallel processes" of learning and accumulating intangible assets in the form of productive structures and "soft" infrastructures is at the heart of the production-systems perspective and the capability triad development policy framework.

The extension in global markets combined with the transfer of world-class manufacturing practices and technologies to new regions has fundamentally altered established patterns of competitive advantage. But the regions that grew were not empty receptacles of technology transfer. Starting with Japan, the new competitors developed and executed production-transformation strategies to seize and institutionalize the opportunities of globalization. The execution of strategies entailed the localization of production and business organizational capabilities in sync with skill-formation institutions.

The Japanese development strategies were informed by a sectoral analysis of where the country fit within the international division of labor and of the organizational changes that would be required to advance to more productive activities and sectors. Although accessing the world's pool of technology was a goal, it was only a dream without the production capabilities and complementary business-organizational capabilities to acquire, apply, assimilate, and modify technologies. Strategies for industrial transitions had to be informed by long-term investments in capability development and skills.

Figure 8.1 is a representation of the sectoral composition of national production in terms of production systems and underlying principles. Each pole is associated with the production capabilities required to achieve competitive advantage in a related set of products. Movements of the diamond in an upward and left direction represent a sectoral shift of production activities from less to more technology-, skill-, and knowledge-intensive applications. Industrial development involves transitioning from a sector composition heavily weighted at the south and east poles in the direction of the west and north poles.

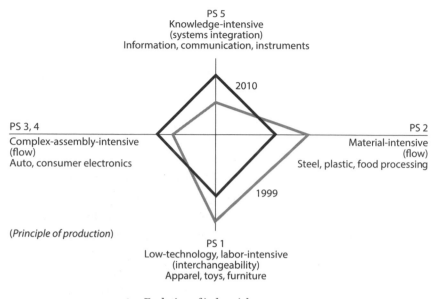

PS 5
Knowledge-intensive
(systems integration)
Information, communication, instruments

2010

PS 3, 4
Complex-assembly-intensive
(flow)
Auto, consumer electronics

PS 2
Material-intensive
(flow)
Steel, plastic, food processing

1999

(*Principle of production*)

PS 1
Low-technology, labor-intensive
(interchangeability)
Apparel, toys, furniture

FIGURE 8.1. Evolution of industrial structure, 1999–2010.
Source: Adapted from Japan Economic Survey, Economic Planning Agency, 1974–75,
cited by Magaziner and Hout (1980), 7. *Note:* PS = Production System.

Taiichi Ohno, the chief engineer and architect of the Toyota Production System, understood and described the significance and simplicity of the Ford system better than anyone since Charles Sorensen, chief engineer and architect of the Ford production system (see chaps. 2 and 6). In Ohno's words: "The basis of automobile production as a modern industry is the mass-production system that Ford himself practiced" (1988 [1978], 93). Ohno quotes from Sorensen to capture the "beginning and evolution" of the Ford system in terms of the first operational application of the principle of flow as the means to eliminate the waste of inventory and achieve economies of speed. It required the reorganization of production to pursue synchronization of the cycle times for each activity. Successful identification and elimination of the single longest cycle time was an endless process that resulted in increased throughput efficiency throughout the system. System integration was the organizing rule, not local optimization or maximization of individual work effort. According to Ohno: "The key to the Toyota Way and what makes Toyota stand out is not any of the individual elements—but what is important is having all the elements together as a system. It must be practiced every day in a very consistent manner, not in spurts."[1]

1. *Taiichi Ohno Infographic*, published by Neil Beyersdorf at linkedin.com/in/neil beyersdorf/.

Taiichi Ohno, 1912–1990. *Source:* Toyota Material Handling Europe (CC BY-NC-ND 2.0).

It was Sorensen's team at Ford who conducted the first experiments and followed them with the organization of the plant layout and production system in accord with the simple rule of engineering each activity to equalize cycle times. To this day, the common view is that the secret to Ford's system was economies of scale and the moving assembly line. But, as discussed in chapter 2, mass production to the process engineer is not about economies of scale or the moving assembly line: it is about equalizing the cycle times for each activity for each part in a multipart production process. Ohno and Toyota extended single-piece flow to multiple products on the same line; they were revolutionary in adopting methods of endless reorganization of production activities down to the shop floor to increase throughput and design quality into the process (Best 2001, chap. 2).

The production-capabilities spectrum shown in box 8.1 offers a benchmarking framework for objectively locating a region's production plants in the global production order and characterizing the development policies and action plans required to transition to more advanced performance standards.[2] The criteria are derived from a literature and quality award

2. In Box 8.1 we set out the full spectrum of production "capabilities," starting from the simplest (craft production, characterized as pre-flow and pre-interchangeability) and ending with the most complex and evolved (open systems and design modularization). Although one moves across the spectrum over time, from the first to the tenth, this can happen at different times for different products and in different countries. Thus less advanced

Box 8.1. Production-capabilities spectrum

1. Pre-flow, pre-interchangeability: Craft production, by itself, offers no basis for flow. Each drawer is custom fit. The task is to develop product-engineering skills. Jamaica and Honduras.

2. Interchangeability (*PS 1*): Product engineering is employed without process engineering, resulting in low inventory turns and working capital productivity. Cyprus and Slovenia in the 1980s.

3. Single-product flow (*PS 2*): Plants have economies of speed for a single product or range of products with dedicated lines. Workers are not multiskilled; each attends to a single machine. Training does not include continuous-improvement, rapid-changeover, or blueprint-reading skills. Multinational corporation (MNC) electronics production in Indonesia.

4. Single-product flow with continuous improvement (*PS 3*): This involves problem-solving work by *self-directed* work teams. Common training programs include Plan-Do-Check-Act diffused by the Japanese Union of Scientists and Engineers and the seven problem-solving tools of total quality management at the shop-floor level.

5. Single-product flow with process innovation (*PS 3*): Personnel include maintenance and process-control technicians with skills to identify, fix, and redesign machinery and production lines. Bottleneck analysis determines priorities. This may involve reconfiguring product design parameters at the main office as required by design for manufacturability. Singapore in the mid-1980s, Malaysia MNCs in the early 1990s.

6. Multiproduct flow (*PS 3*): The Toyota Production System. *Kanban*, just-in-time production, and single-minute exchange of dies are introduced in large plants. High throughput and flexibility are combined. Cellular production with self-directed work teams.

7. Multiproduct flow and product development (*PS 4*): Japan and Taiwan both excel at concurrent engineering and design for manufacturability. Skills include reverse engineering, prototype development, and pilot runs.

8. New-product design and technology fusion (*PS 4*): Japan's Toshiba and Canon are leaders in linking development to operations at the plant level and linking research in generic technologies to product development. Core technologies are developed, often via fusion in generic technology labs. Technology management involves worldwide sourcing of the existing technology base in pursuit of novel applications.

9. Systems integration and disruptive innovation (*PS 5*): 3M, HP, and Motorola use cross-disciplinary teams to identify new-technology drivers for product development. Disruptive or breakthrough innovations are pursued but within an organizational context of process integration and high-performance work systems. Hardware and software integration drives product concept development.

10. Open systems and design modularization (*PS 5*): Standard interface rules and diffusion of design capability support focus-and-network strategies. This fosters technology-deepening R&D and technodiversification.

Source: Best (2001, 55).

that emerged in the 1980s and 1990s to benchmark world-class manufacturing processes.[3] The Japanese forsook the "scientific management" of F. W. Taylor for the "statistical quality control" paradigm of W. Edwards Deming (1982).[4] The purpose of Taylorist information collection was to design worker activities to minimize direct labor costs for a standard product and frozen production process. The purpose of Deming's information-gathering tools was to educate and empower workers to continuously upgrade their production methods and product quality. Deming's message was that improving quality, reducing indirect labor, and increasing productivity are positively related and were the basis for structural competitive advantage within the context of early postwar Japan. In 1960 Deming became the first American to be awarded the Second Order of the Sacred Treasure by the Japanese. The attached citation states that the Japanese attribute the rebirth of Japanese industry to Deming (Walton 1986, 15). The Deming Prize became the most prestigious award a company can receive in Japan.

Regions in which firms and sectors in complex-process production activities at the west pole of figure 8.1 are the drivers of growth reveal a range of "lean manufacturing" management practices and organizational capabilities such as flow analysis, cellular manufacturing, self-directed work teams, and manufacturing performance metrics that enhance the production objectives of cheaper, better, faster, and more flexible. A similar

---

countries like Jamaica will still have many craft processes. Countries like Indonesia will have progressed to many single-product flow processes. However, Malaysia will already have evolved to single-product flow with process innovation. Japan, which is further advanced, will have implemented firms with new-product design, continuous improvement, and technology fusion. At the most advanced stage, many firms in the United States will have evolved into open-systems, early-stage technology development and design modularization. A simplified version of the full production-capabilities spectrum is shown in table 8.1. There, we show five main production systems and link them to a series of underlying characteristics such as examplar firms, the nature of the performance breakthrough, the production principle, the application, the production-capability advance, the technology-management vehicle, and the interfirm organization.

3. Representative examples that characterize world-class manufacturing include Deming 1982; Ishikawa 1985; Imai 1986; Womack, Jones, and Roos 1990; Watson 1993; and quality award programs such as the Deming Prize, the Baldrige Award, and the Shingo Prize.

4. Deming remarked that what he took to Japan was the "theory of the system" (personal conversations, 1992). He meant, in part, that much of American business enterprise was functionally departmentalized into profit centers to achieve local optimization without regard to interdependencies and that the Japanese management system came to embody the idea of reorganizing specialized activities in ways that accounted for their interrelationships.

W. Edwards Deming, 1900–1993. *Source:* Photo reproduced with
permission courtesy of the American Statistical Association.

examination of the firms and sectors in knowledge-intensive activities at
the north pole of figure 8.1 reveals a range of production capabilities that
include technology integration teams; systems integration (starting with
hardware and software); open-systems networking; industry or university
partnering models for integrating product development and R&D, decentralization, and diffusion of design, and technological diversity; new-
firm creation; and a business-development infrastructure.

To sustain growth, enterprises must transition into new sectors applying the same capabilities or make the transition to the next-higher level
of production capabilities. Once, and if, a critical mass of firms makes the
transition, a new range of opportunities opens as the region or nation be-

comes competitive in more technically and organizationally advanced activities, processes, and products.[5]

The production-capabilities spectrum (see box 8.1) spells out organizational improvements that can be incorporated into work-organization improvement programs at the shop-floor level. It identifies the specific production challenges to advancing a region's productivity at any point in time but company by company. These challenges can focus industrial policy initiatives and make them operational. A number of organization-change methodologies have been developed and widely imitated.[6]

The production system framework illustrates a simple business policy idea: a competitive strategy and production system are bound together. Any business whose managers work to advance performance outcomes that do not put in place the requisite production capabilities will not be able to compete against firms that have done so. Competing based on rapid new-product development without having a production system in which manufacturing and design are integrated will produce only frustration. Competitors that have integrated design and manufacturing will be equipped to introduce new technologies smoothly in support of new product concepts on a regular basis.

Table 8.1, Production System Models, captures the interdependence of production and business organization. The rationale underlying the table is as follows. Each production system is defined in terms of one of four principles of production: interchangeability, flow, multiproduct flow, or systems integration (column 4).[7] The original application (column 2) of

---

5. Nakame Akamatsu (1962), a Japanese proponent of a unique theory of industrial development reminiscent of Jacobs (see chap. 4), described a process common to development literature but added an interesting twist. Countries would move from imports to import substitution to exports as they learned from foreign technologies. He described the process in terms of three waves of flying geese for each product. Imports would be represented by the first gaggle of geese in flying formation: increase, peak, and falloff; production would be represented by the second gaggle: increase, peak, and decline; and exports by the third gaggle, again representing an inverted V pattern. He said that these patterns are occurring first in "crude" products and later in "refined" products, then in final goods and later in capital goods. Where a country is at any point in time is determined by the balance of forces between the level of development and wage rates. Higher development leads to higher wages and a loss in exports of easier-to-produce goods.

6. Representative examples of change methodologies include those described in Goldratt and Cox 1984; Hayes and Wheelwright 1984; Schonberger 1986; Japan Management Association 1987; Suzaki 1987; Weisbord 1987; Kobayashi 1988; Harmon and Peterson 1990; Reid 1990; Sekine 1990; Shiba, Graham, and Walden 1993.

7. For example, the principle of flow can be applied to single products, as in the case of Ford; extended to multiple products on the same assembly line, as in the case of the Toyota Production System; or extended to encompass new product development, as in the case of

Table 8.1. Production System Models

1 Production systems	2 Exemplar	3 Performance breakthrough	4 Production principle	5 Application	6 Production capability advance	7 Technology management vehicle[a]	8 Interfirm organization
PS 1	Armory	Standardization	Interchangeability	Product parts	Product engineering	Specialist machine	Open networks
PS 2	Ford	Cost (economies of time)	Flow	Single product	Throughput efficiency (synchronization)	Exogenous (R&D lab pipeline)	Vertical integration
PS 3	Toyota	Flexibility and quality (inventory turnover)	Flow	Multiple products	Incremental innovation (cellular manufacture)	Process innovation (shop-floor incremental) AR	Closed network
PS 4	Canon	New product cycle-time	Flow	New products, technology adoption	New product development	Applied R&D (design + manufacture) DR + AR	Closed network
PS 5	Intel	New technology cycle-time	Systems integration	Technology innovation (multiple technologies)	New technology development	Technology integration teams (R&D + manufacture) BR + DR	Open networks

[a] R&D = research and development; AR = applied research; DR = developmental research; BR = basic research.

each principle in history enabled a new competitive advantage based on an order of magnitude increase in performance standards (column 3). The form and institutional practices of innovation are structurally linked to each production system and business model (column 7).

The *kaisha* business model involves an extension of the production principle of multiproduct flow (the Toyota Production System) to new-product development (NPD).[8] Reducing the time to introduce next-generation products into the market depends on the production capability to introduce new technologies with each NPD cycle. Driving down NPD cycle times is not a consequence of a management directive; it is a consequence of a team-centered model of work organization. The supervisor-centered model of work proved ill suited to competing based on driving down cycle times for NPD (Best 1990, 2001).

The strength of the new business model was in continuous improvement or incremental innovation. But *kaizen* was more than self-directed work teams (or "lean production") and the development of the inclusive management philosophy of the quality movement. It also altered the constitution of research, development, and associated engineering activities in production.

It was a small organizational step from the self-directed work-team model of work organization to the integration of developmental research with production. As shown in figure 8.2, developmental research triggers new product concepts that are progressively reinvented via feedback effects with applied research (AR). The *kaizen* work organization enables the integration of applied research and production. The systematic introduction of new product concepts involves linking applied research with technological research carried out in company laboratories, which, in turn, taps into worldwide technology knowledge bases.

The new model extended the technology/market dynamic into production: developmental research became interactive with technological research on the core technologies that define a company's uniqueness in the marketplace.[9] The business model involves the integration of production

---

Canon. Each of these applications, shown in column 5, is expressed in an advance in production capabilities identified in column 6. Each of the production systems is elaborated in Best (2001, chap. 2).

8. *Kaisha* is the Japanese word for "company" used by researchers to represent the Japanese business organizations that established world-class standards for high-volume production, built continuous improvement change processes in operating units, and achieved cheaper, better, faster performance standards. See PS 2–4 in Table 8.1.

9. For an organizational chart of Toshiba that illustrates the integration of applied research and operations, see Yamanouchi (1995, 217).

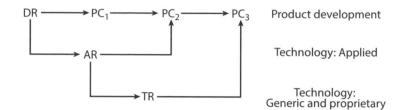

FIGURE 8.2. Incremental innovation: Japan PS 4.
Source: Adapted from Methé (1995). Note: PS = Production System;
DR = developmental research; PC = product concept; AR = applied research;
TR = technological research (new technological knowledge).

into the technology and market dynamic of the entrepreneurial firm. The manufacturing engineering challenge was profoundly changed. A design engineer's task is not finished with a new product design: he or she must design the product jointly with manufacturing personnel for purposes of manufacturability. In the case of the *kaisha,* this often means that an engineer stays with an NPD project from the initial design phase to prototyping to pilot runs and on through ramp-up to full-scale production.

The organizational capability to assimilate new *product* technologies rapidly led, in turn, to an organizational capability to assimilate new *process* technologies rapidly. Thus the development of rapid NPD cycle-time capability was simultaneous with the development of rapid technology-diffusion capability. An example is the diffusion of CNC equipment and the reinvention of the Japanese machine-tool industry. The diffusion of numerical-control machine tools grew from approximately 10 percent to 70 percent of the market between 1974 and 1981 (Kodama 1986).[10] Ironically, the numerical-control machine tool was developed in MIT's Servomechanism Laboratory under a contract with the US Air Force (Noble 1977; Forrant 1997). Its pace of diffusion throughout the United States, however, was very slow.

The success of the new model of technology management in converting new technologies developed elsewhere into a stream of new products led to the dismantling of many industrial laboratories in America. All too often, investments in R&D laboratories by functionally departmentalized American corporations were not being translated by their own manufacturing facilities into new products and commercial success.

10. The typical technology adoption times were twenty-five to fifty years for the cumulative market adoption of new technologies to reach 50 percent (Freeman 1982 and 1991; Kodama 1986).

But the integration of production and developmental research also represented a distinctive perspective on knowledge and knowledge creation, including the relationship between science and technology. Production, in the second approach, is a laboratory for creating, advancing, combining, and diffusing technological knowledge. Myers and Rosenbloom (1996), following Kline (1985), argue that science and technologies are the enablers, rather than the drivers, of the innovation process:

> Science is depicted in two constituent parts: bodies of "stored knowledge" and processes of research. Each part enters the innovation process across its breadth. Thus science and technology interact with innovation in multiple ways, including learning from previous market engagements, continuing enhancement of innovative capabilities through the creation of new tools and instruments, and acquisition of new knowledge from the external technical infrastructure. The innovation process in this view is primarily a learning process in which knowledge has a central role as the key ingredient and the principal output. (Myers and Rosenbloom 1996, 214)

This concept of production as producing both goods and ideas resonates with the idea of the entrepreneurial firm as a learning firm. The superior technology-management capabilities constituted in part by the incremental-innovation model put the big business model of innovation under pressure. But it also undermines the implicit assumption that technology is applied science. The incremental model of innovation presumes, instead, that technology is an independent body of knowledge that can be initiated in the sphere of production as well as in R&D laboratories.

However, this is not the end of the story. Japan's development policy framework was hugely successful in sectors in which enterprises could pursue a strategy of reorganizing the production system to compete in cost, quality, and time. Although the Japanese economy was transformed, Japan's annual growth rate of 8.4 percent in the period from 1955 to 1973 declined to 3.5 percent from 1973 to 1990. Japan's GDP reached a peak of $5.4 trillion in 1995, a level surpassed only once in the ensuing two decades.[11]

The Japanese industrial system became squeezed between two production-system developments elsewhere. First, a series of lower-cost followers imitated Japan's success in manufacturing by institutionalizing

---

11. See "GDP Annual Growth," http://data.worldbank.org/indicator/NY.GDP.MKTP .KD.ZG?locations=JP.

the same principles of production and organization to compete with Japan in global markets. South Korea, Taiwan, Singapore, and Hong Kong all invested heavily in science and engineering education and had access to lower-wage labor pools. Consequently, Japan no longer had a monopoly in "world-class manufacturing" practices such as JIT and TQM that it pioneered in mass production sectors such as autos and consumer electronics constitutive of Production System (PS) 4 sectors of figure 8.1. Second, Japan has not been successful in transitioning to PS 5, yet a third major model of innovation in which the United States continues to excel. This is the terrain of "systems integration," a model of innovation in high-tech regions such as Silicon Valley and Greater Boston.[12]

The Japanese development policy framework was not designed to foster regional open-system business models embedded within regional industrial ecosystems in which product-design and technology-development functions are decentralized and diffused across localized populations of enterprises. The structural competitive advantage of PS 5 is in systems integration innovation in contrast to incremental innovation. Systems integration operates at both the technological and the organizational levels (chap. 3 of this book; Baldwin and Clark 2000; Best 2003b; Prencipe, Davies, and Hobday 2003). Incremental innovation in the standard *kaisha* business model is linked to integral product architecture in which design is centralized and supplier networks are closed but extensive.[13]

China's Socialist Market Economy

Counterpoised with the slowing of Japanese economic growth in the last two decades of the twentieth century was the transformation of China from a closed to an open economy and its emergence as a major competitor in global markets. The ratio of China's foreign trade (exports plus im-

12. In contrast, the *kaisha*, closed-network business model (PS 4 in table 8.1) is not based on the principle of systems integration; it does not involve the management of feedback effects between production and basic research. It is a one-way street, with a pull into the production of technology and innovation rather than a push. This is not surprising. JIT production is all about pulling materials through the production system, not pushing.

13. David Sainsbury explains the decline in Japan's growth in terms of a policymaking failure to transition from institutions that had fostered incremental innovation to sectors that required breakthrough innovation. In his words: "The institutions which did so well in the era of Japan's industrial takeoff were dysfunctional once Japan's economy had matured. But Japan did not abandon them, and what had been a strength became a weakness" (2013, 51; see also Ha-Joon Chang [2003] for an analysis of the institutional foundation of markets).

ports) to GDP rose from 10 percent in 1978 to 33 percent in 1990, 49 percent in 2002, and 67 percent in 2006 (WB 2008, cited in Nolan 2015, 16 and 37). In the half decade it took the West to recover to levels of GDP preceding the global financial crisis of 2007–9, Chinese GDP increased by 50 percent.

Deng Xiaoping, the leader of China from 1978 to 1989, is widely acknowledged as the architect of China's strategic reorientation from a closed to an open economy.[14] Business organization is integral to Deng's "socialist market economy" perspective, which breaks with the classic dichotomy of either plan or market to distinguish socialism from capitalism. Constructing a socialist market economy entailed a policy framework designed to achieve rapid growth by the "liberation and development of productive systems" (Caeiro 2004). Deng maintained that it was a "fact" that Western managerial enterprises had driven rapid organizational change and technological advance and had created high levels of productivity and income in contrast to the limited productivity and income growth of autarchic policy regimes and central planning modes of organizing production and business.

Perhaps he was influenced most by Japan's business-led interactive growth dynamic of export-market creation and domestic production-capability development, which depended on shifting from a closed to an increasingly open economy. The Penrose–like market-opportunity and capability-development growth dynamic proposition was that international trade agreements would create export-market opportunities for enterprises in low-wage economies to become production-capability-developing organizations. The strategic implication for China was to seek opportunities in the global marketplace and start, as Japan had done, by building competitive advantage in labor-intensive, price-sensitive sectors. In time, with investment in productive structures and skills, Chinese enterprises could move up the production-capability spectrum to target higher-value activities and sectors progressively vacated by Japan and the four tigers as their wages increased.

What distinguished Deng's socialist market economy perspective was the tenet that SOEs (state owned enterprises) could, in time, be a successful alternative to both the Japanese *kaisha* and Western models of business organization. Ever the realist, Deng was fully aware that China's SOEs did not possess a legacy similar to that leveraged by Japan's *kaisha*

14. "Deng Xiaoping Is Dead at 92; Architect of Modern China," *New York Times*, February 20, 1997.

Deng Xiaoping, 1904–1997. *Source:* (CC-BY-SA).

in the 1960s to initiate the global-market and indigenous-capability development growth dynamic. Deng made several visits to Singapore, which led to a development policy framework that broke not only with classical socialism but with the *kaisha* model.

Deng's policy departure was to invite foreign MNEs to locate affiliates in special economic zones to re-export finished or semifinished products or services.[15] The purpose was, first, to generate exports and foreign exchange but, second, to learn firsthand business management, production engineering, and work organization methods from Western enterprises and to introduce advanced production technologies into China.[16] Thus Deng's vision was to use FDI as a means of creating a learning environ-

15. Special economic zones are explained at "Special Economic Zone" in https://en.wiki pedia.org/wiki/Special_economic_zone, accessed November 19, 2017.

16. See Magaziner and Patinkin (1989) for an early discussion of Singapore's strategic development policy framework, informed as if by the capability triad concept.

ment to transfer production and organizational practices in order to construct a modern Chinese SOE business model. Participation in global production networks was the means.

The FDI re-export growth strategy was hugely successful. From 1979 until 2010, China's average annual GDP growth was 9.91 percent.[17] The timing was propitious; globally the outward stock of FDI rose from $2.1 trillion in 1990 to $19 trillion in 2009 (UNCTAD 2010, cited in Nolan 2015, 38).

Deng's business development strategy has had far-reaching and unforeseen consequences in both China and the West. Most of the growth in high-technology exports from China has continued to be driven by wholly owned foreign firms. The growth of China's re-export production system has not, to date, fostered the emergence of Chinese high-technology SOEs; instead, Western-headquartered enterprises have seized the opportunity to construct global production networks by offshoring manufacturing in China's special economic zones.

Peter Nolan (2012) estimated that in 2010 foreign multinational firms accounted for two-thirds of the value added in high-technology production in China, for 55 percent of China's total exports, and for 90 percent of its exports of high-technology products. More specifically, George Gilboy (2004, 39) estimated that wholly owned foreign-enterprise industrial machinery exports increased from 17 percent of $4.2 billion in 1993 to 62 percent of $83 billion in 2003; from 15 percent of $0.7 billion of computers, components, and peripheral exports in 1993 to 43 percent of $41 billion in 2003; and from 15 percent of $12.3 billion of electronics and telecommunications equipment exports in 1993 to 43 percent of $89 billion in 2003.

China, although the beneficiary of the interdependent structural changes in the two nations' production systems, is not complacent. China does not aspire to function indefinitely as an offshore manufacturing re-export platform for wholly owned foreign enterprises. But the Deng-inspired roadmap that informs China's strategic development policy framework has not changed. It remains radically different, ambitious, long-term, and strategic.

Two long-term goals integral to Deng's political economy have not been achieved but nevertheless continue to inform policy. The first was to establish high-tech SOEs with the technological and organizational capabilities to compete with Japanese, South Korean, and Western enterprises. The second reflects a long-held technology gap concern. With their eyes on America's scientific and technological leadership, post-Maoist

17. "Historical GDP of China," https://en.wikipedia.org/wiki/Historical_GDP_of_China.

Chinese leaders even before Deng had elevated S&T to one of the "Four Modernizations" (goals first set forth by Zhou Enlai in 1963), along with agriculture, industry, and the military (Gittings 2005).

The goals are interdependent. The first defines a "socialist market economy." The second was articulated by Deng as "science and technology are primary productive forces" during a meeting with Czech President Husak on September 5, 1988. Earlier, on March 13, 1985, the Central Committee of the Communist Party of China announced a "decision on the reform of science and technology systems," which read that "modern science and technology are the most active and decisive factors of the productive forces in the new society. The whole party must attach great importance to and give full play to the great role of S&T" (see *People's Daily Online*, 2008).

It is doubtful that Vannevar Bush, Ralph Flanders, or Colonel Doriot, as architects of Greater Boston, or Frederick Termin, in his conception of Silicon Valley, would have disagreed with either Deng's or the party's emphasis on the productive role that S&T can play in the emergence and growth of innovative firms and economies. But none of the former would have agreed that SOEs or top-down state planning are consistent with an innovative high-tech economy.

Up to this point China has not successfully instituted an indigenous innovation system that links advances in S&T research with indigenous business applications to create structural competitive advantage in emerging high-tech industries. We can also be certain that China is not following the American model of an S&T infrastructure linked to a private-enterprise, open-system business model. This is the domain of the principle of system integration applied to both technological innovation and business organization illustrated by the north pole of Japan's Economic Planning Agency's original sectoral transition framework shown in figure 8.1 and described as PS 5 in table 8.1. In the example of Greater Boston, the region has evolved a structural competitive advantage in early-stage technology development in which basic research fosters the emergence of new high-tech sectors as explored in chapter 3. As in Silicon Valley, a system of interrelationships cross-penetrates government, academic, and enterprise spheres in ways that form industrial experimental laboratories with unique innovation and business-development capabilities. It is highly dependent on bottom-up, open-system dynamics (Best 2001, chap. 3).

But China may be getting close to creating its own path to indigenous technological innovation. It has been engaging in a wide range of economic governance strategies, experiments, and policies. FDI remains an integral component of China's roadmap. So, too, does the art of active policymaking to craft sector strategies in order to achieve state goals. Minus the FDI component, China's development-policy framework is reminiscent of that of the United States during World War II. In both, the central government formulated policy instruments for production restructuring and business development to direct financial agencies to channel investment funds to the restructuring of existing sectors and the creation of new ones and to establish administrative control systems to coordinate decentralized production facilities across the nation. But whereas the mobilization agencies that implemented the US government's wartime development goals were disbanded at the end of the war, their functionally equivalent policies, programs, and agencies are integral to China's peacetime strategic-development policy framework.

Based on a close examination of telecommunications and textiles Roselyn Hsueh (2011) describes the methods by which China uses liberalization, including special rights under the World Trade Organization, as an instrument of state power. As China exercises greater control over sectors with strategic value, it relinquishes controls over less strategic but already globally strong sectors.

China's sector strategies involve policies to meet the challenge of increasing wages and costs of production not by migrating away from less to more complex activities and sectors as predicted by the "flying geese" model. Instead the government initiated policies to transition from labor-intensive to advanced-manufacturing methods including automated production processes in high-volume sectors. In 2013 China became the world's biggest market for industrial robots (Manjoo 2017). To facilitate its transition to world leader in the application and production of robotics, China's president, Xi Jinping, called for a "robot revolution" in 2014 (Bland 2016).

The policy measures included the requirement that new plants established by MNCs engage in R&D and deploy global state-of-the-art manufacturing technologies and production methods; in return, MNCs could participate in the rapidly expanding Chinese market and receive support in the form of investment in hard and soft infrastructures.[18] Ford's state-of-the-art assembly plant in Hangzhou, in east-central China, is an example. Keith Bradsher (2017b) quotes Mark Fields, the chief executive of

18. Hout and Ghemawat (2010) describe a plan unveiled in 2006 by which the Chinese government requires foreign firms to partner in building advanced technology development capabilities within SOEs in return for access to Chinese markets.

Ford Motor: "We're basically building an R&D center here in China, and test track, that is on par with other parts of Ford." The facility does not simply use robots extensively; it is next door to a robot-producing factory originally owned by Kuka, a big German manufacturer of industrial robots that was purchased by a Chinese company. Innovations in the robotics industry, as in the machine-tool industry in an earlier age, diffuse technological advances across sectors.

The relative fortunes of American and Chinese solar-panel producers offer a stark contrast. While photovoltaic cells were invented at Bell Labs and initially commercialized in the United States, only 6 percent were produced in this country by 2008 (Pisano and Shih 2012, 8). Between 2007 and 2008, China's solar-power production capacity expanded more than tenfold; the number of Chinese companies among the top-ten solar-panel makers increased from zero to six, including the top two; and prices dropped by close to 90 percent. The US makers were decimated (Bradsher 2017a). Bradsher describes Chinese government policies to make this happen, which included pushing state-owned banks to provide loans at low interest rates and encouraging local governments to subsidize them with cheap land. If the solar-panel industry is a model of what is to come in China, it means they are creating world-leading enterprises with a first-mover advantage in rapidly growing technologically advanced sectors.

The Costs of Theoretical Blindness

Western policymakers too often misread China's rapid growth success as "a race-to-the-bottom" strategy, but a production-centric analysis suggests that China has in fact been pursuing and implementing a long-term "race-to-the-top" policy framework (Sainsbury 2013). Japan and China established and executed different but successful strategic policy frameworks to build manufacturing export platforms with the production, new-product development, and technology-management capabilities to turn America's leadership in S&T to national advantage. Economics in the standard paradigm is blind to competition across production systems and the role of strategic policymaking in their construction. The consequences have yet to be fully comprehended.

CHAPTER NINE

America's Fragmenting Capability Triad

If we could first know where we are, and whither we are tending, we could then better judge what to do and how to do it.

—ABRAHAM LINCOLN, "THE HOUSE DIVIDED" SPEECH, 1858

The Capability Triad and Governance Structures

The capability triad as an economics of production and businesses organization takes us beyond the standard policymaking framework to consider the multiple dimensions of economic governance that were needed in the historical experiences of successful transformation. Without governance of this type and on this scale, America's capability triad risks fragmenting.

First, the policy framework distinguishes between a narrow and a broad concept of macroeconomic policymaking. The narrow concept focuses on tactical adjustments in fiscal and monetary policies within a framework of *market* competitiveness. For the broad concept, macroeconomic stability is a necessary but not a sufficient condition for development and prosperity within a framework of *structural* competitiveness. John Bradley uses the experience of Germany to capture the broad concept:

> The German economy is strong not merely because it enjoys enviable financial and fiscal stability. Its strength comes from the competitiveness and dynamism of its enterprise sector, particularly in the range of small and medium-sized companies of its *Mittelstand*, which are highly

innovative, export oriented, provide a large number of jobs and are extremely productive. (2013, 8)

As noted earlier, Keynes explicitly assumed Ricardo's production model of diminishing returns and set aside matters of structural competitiveness in *The General Theory of Employment, Interest and Money*. He had good reason. The incorporation of productive structures would have diverted attention from the principle of effective demand as a persuasive theoretical framework to convince policymakers to use discretionary government expenditures to reduce involuntary unemployment and end the Great Depression. The unintended consequence was that Keynesian economics became a theory of macroeconomic stabilization and was incorporated into the standard account as a special case.

Thereafter the *market competitiveness* policy presupposition resumed its dominance in theory, model building, policymaking, and economic commentary. Production, in the standard paradigm, continued to be conceptualized in terms of Ricardo's diminishing returns in spite of the massive advance in production capabilities from those of Ricardo's land-based model and the strategic opportunities of enterprises to develop production and technological capabilities to drive costs down by cumulative innovation.[1]

Second, the capability triad framework incorporates the mediating role of extrafirm infrastructures that target production-capability and business-system development.[2] Avinash Dixit's encyclopedia entry for "economic governance" focuses on infrastructure:

Economic governance consists of the processes that support economic activity and economic transactions by protecting property rights, enforcing contracts, and taking *collective action* to provide appropriate

1. As noted above, Paul Krugman received the Nobel Prize in 2008; his lecture was titled "The Increasing Returns Revolution in Trade and Geography." As he had written earlier, the assumption of diminishing returns persisted contrary to the reality of economies of scale because, in his words, "Economics tends, understandably to follow the line of least mathematical resistance. We like to explain the world in terms of forces we know how to model, not in terms we don't. In International economics, what this meant from Ricardo until the 1980s was an almost exclusive emphasis on comparative advantage, rather than increasing returns, as an explanation for trade" (Krugman 1991, 6).

2. As argued in chapter 4, the capability perspective of Penrose and Chandler takes us partway. But they did not examine links between institutions of economic governance in the form of extra-firm infrastructures and capability development processes with the firm. Babbage's "new system of manufacturing" goes further by linking the innovation success of engineering intensive enterprises with access to scientific knowledge.

physical and organizational infrastructure. These processes are carried out within institutions, formal and informal. The field of economic governance studies and compares the performance of different institutions under different conditions, the evolution of these institutions, and the transitions from one set of institutions to another. (2008; emphasis mine)

Although Dixit's entry does not include examples of "appropriate physical and organizational infrastructure," the historical case studies presented here do so from a production-system perspective. For example, the realization of America's World War II Arsenal of Democracy involved an expansion in economic governance in the form of the creation of "mobilization" agencies to transform the nation's economy in pursuit of a national strategy to integrate mass-production capabilities with the establishment of technologically advanced weapons systems. It included the establishment of a national S&T infrastructure and the DPC to finance the plant and equipment for the use of private firms (see chap. 2) and facilitated the emergence of regional high-tech industrial innovation systems.

Infrastructures figure prominently in the evolution of open-system business models in the "collective entrepreneurial industrial districts" of the Third Italy (Best 1990), Greater Boston's innovation system, and the *Mittelstand*-based economy of Germany. Here we find regional institutions of economic governance and, in the cases of Germany and Greater Boston, multilevel governance structures.

Third, leadership was able to react strategically to internal and external threats to a region's or nation's livelihood. President Roosevelt, Ralph Flanders, Ludwig Erhard, Kenneth Whitaker, W. Edwards Deming, and Deng Xiaoping crafted transformative policies that broke through inertia and "business as usual" to foster capability triad growth dynamics.

Fourth, policies that address production-capability advance, enterprise growth, and skill upgrading separately and in isolation will not be successful. A requirement of successful development policy is that government policies be almost seamlessly blended into the detailed, transparent, and theoretically informed mechanics of change processes within groups of independently managed private firms. The instruments are in the form not of subsidy bribes or tax bludgeons but of services by extrafirm infrastructural agencies with specific missions and the ability to convert business leaders to shared transformative aims, as illustrated in the chapters on the United States in World War II and postwar Massachusetts and Germany.

Fifth, stewardship is the social glue that links the elements of the capability triad. Its relevance to economic performance is a major difference between the market-centric and the production-centric worldviews. With the integration of organization and time into economics, a number of inherently social processes that require stewardship to both develop and preserve are introduced. The value-creation process of the entrepreneurial firm, for example, requires investment in capability development to sustain an enterprise's competitive advantage. The benefits of management policies that foster enterprise stewardship accrue to the collective but dispersed benefit of all the individuals in the enterprise going forward. Consequently, the requirement of stewardship for enterprise development takes us beyond the motivational assumption of economic man in which the pursuit of private interest will lead, as if by an "invisible hand," to the public good.[3]

These economic governance themes restate the main message of the book: the capability triad provides a more comprehensive guide to the design and implementation of truly transformative policies. The various case studies have hammered home this lesson. However, capability triads are shaped and operate within a dynamic global system. Consequently, over time, the strategic external context for policymaking is subject to fundamental change.

Economics, as in the standard paradigm, provides a single, ahistorical theory that can be applied to all contexts. The economy is conceptualized as self-organizing, and the role of government is seen to create the conditions for the invisible hand of the price system to align the individual pursuit of the private interest with public purpose. This denies the reality of the economic success stories explored in this book, including the role of leaders in crafting and building organizational capabilities that underlie production performance and shape a region's or nation's structural competitive advantage. Until recently, the lack of awareness of how growth happens in standard economics and policymaking institutions has not been damaging to US economic performance. But with the rise of Japan and China, the costs of theoretical blindness have become painfully obvious. Western policymakers too often misread Japan's growth slowdown as evidence of policymaking failure and China's rapid growth success as a race to the bottom, but a production-centric analysis suggests that

---

3. While denying the efficacy of appealing to the social over the private interest, even Milton Friedman appeals to the social interest to preserve the common good (Best and Connolly 1982 [1976]: 26–27).

China has learned lessons from Japan's rapid growth experience and is in fact pursuing and implementing a long-term race-to-the-top policy framework.

Both nations have successfully taken full advantage of America's S&T infrastructure, which was built cumulatively over nearly two centuries. The next section examines two previous times in US history before the World War II experience when American presidential leadership informed policies and infrastructural investments that advanced the nation's structural competitive advantage. Subsequent sections examine the contradictory impact of World War II industrial planning on the performance of the American economy, including the rise of what President Eisenhower termed the military-industrial complex and others the "contract state."

Unless the United States finds new ways to enhance its structural competitiveness and manufacturing capabilities, its industrial future is at risk. The book closes by reflecting on the threat to the United States and its prosperity of persisting in misreading the ways to achieve transformative growth.

Building a National Science and Technology Infrastructure

President Roosevelt's call for an Arsenal of Democracy was the third such call of an American president to negotiate a technoeconomic transformation agenda to meet a grand challenge. The first was the call by President Thomas Jefferson to build a production system to manufacture arms to defend the nation against the military threat of Great Britain; the second was the call by President Abraham Lincoln to build and consolidate a socially inclusive industrial order based on democratic principles, free enterprise, and science-based agriculture under threat from breakaway states and the spread of slavery; the third, described in chapters 2 and 3, was Roosevelt's call to create an industrial production system with the innovation capabilities necessary to convert existing industries and drive new ones to supply the arms required to win the war against the Axis powers of World War II.

Faced with diverse challenges, each president instituted new development processes that connected governmental, industrial, and scientific/ educational spheres while respecting the distinctive roles and purposes of each. New domains of engineering expertise, scientific knowledge, productive structures, and innovation dynamics emerged in all three transformative experiences.

Championed by President Thomas Jefferson, the principle of inter-changeability was the organizing idea of the emergent "American system of manufacturing" as an alternative to the United Kingdom's "craft" pro-duction system (Best 1990, chap. 1). First implemented at the US govern-ment armory in Springfield, Massachusetts, it entailed the introduction of product engineering as a methodology for breaking down every part into its requisite productive activities and subjecting each activity to simplification, elimination, improvement, and/or mechanization.[4] The government armory's procurement program fostered the creation of the world's first machine-tool industry based on the diffusion of precision en-gineering practices, itself a precondition for standardization and the later emergence and diffusion of mass-production methods.

Earlier Jefferson had orchestrated the establishment of America's first engineering program by founding the US Military Academy at West Point (McDonald 2004).[5] It led to the *codification of the new engineering prin-ciples* into a curriculum by which engineers could be educated en masse. West Point's engineering curriculum significantly influenced the creation of subsequent engineering departments at Cornell, Harvard, Yale, and other colleges.[6] For the first half of the nineteenth century West Point grad-uates were responsible for engineering the bulk of the nation's early rail-way lines, bridges, harbors, and roads (McMaster 1951, 6; Brubacher and Rudy 1997; Endler 1998, 12).

The widespread diffusion of the American system of manufacturing based on the principle of interchangeability was driven by the creation of a large machining, tooling, and instrument-making sector that propa-gated the new precision engineering expertise to a series of emergent consumer goods sectors. The scale of the machine-tool sector enabled the new-product development and technology-management capabilities of the volume producers in the rapidly growing American industrial sys-tem. Without a machine-tool industry, the number of enterprises able to compete in terms of products as distinct from prices would have been structurally limited. And without entrepreneurial enterprises the forces

4. The emergent principle of product engineering can be found in the first chapter of Adam Smith's *The Wealth of Nations* (see chap. 4). It was as if turned into government policy in the Springfield Armory three decades later.

5. Congress formally authorized the establishment and funding of the US Military Academy on March 16, 1802.

6. See "A School for the Nation: West Point in the Making of America," Smithsonian National Museum of American History, Washington, DC, http://americanhistory.si.edu/westpoint/history_1a.html.

that drove the focus-and-network, open-system, cluster-dynamics processes would have been limited. These processes are sources of innovation and productivity improvement of the types examined in chapter 4.

The creation of the US Land Grant university system by President Lincoln with the passage of the Morrill Act of 1862 created an agricultural and an engineering university in nearly every state. It brought science and engineering to agriculture and established the partnership between agricultural colleges, the US Department of Agriculture, and farmers, providing an extension service to every county in America combined with a national system of experiment stations. In response to the challenge of allied food shortages during World War II, the extension service worked with farmers to increase food production by 38 percent in 1944 over the 1935–39 average. The long-term productivity trend has persisted, and now only 2 percent of the US labor force remains in agriculture, although the United States is the world's largest exporter of food products.[7]

From a capability triad perspective, it would be hard to overstate how much the Morrill Act contributed to a process that transformed American capitalism. The establishment in every state of an engineering university and an agricultural university empowered state governments to pursue development policy frameworks that localized America's S&T infrastructure. In the words of Julia Wrigley (1986, 169): "US corporate leaders promoted university training for engineers and helped design courses of study that produced the types of trained men they wanted; state governments obliged by underwriting vast expansions of the university system."[8] David Noble (1977, xxii–xxiii) describes the major overhaul of technical education for engineers in the late nineteenth and early twentieth centuries to argue that "the history of modern technology in America is of a piece with that of the rise of corporate capitalism."

The third transformative development-policy framework undertaken by presidential leadership built on the first two to create a unique well-funded national innovation system in the United States. Once again, the relationships among government, industry, and academia were permanently altered, and each institutional sphere was transformed in the process. Federal spending on R&D, including the underwriting of a huge increase in the education of scientists and engineers, became America's de facto industrial policy. The combination of federal and industrial labs

7. See Wright (1990) for an analysis of how industrial policy works through investment in engineering in natural resource industries.

8. In Britain the universities moved only very hesitantly into engineering education (Sanderson 1972, 39–46).

with labs in the research-intensive university system fostered an unrivaled science community in the United States. Nowhere else did industrial enterprises enjoy such a broad and deep pool of science and engineering graduates and basic research capability into which it could dip for talent and research assistance.

Building the American Industrial Planning System

Critical to meeting the production targets of Roosevelt's Arsenal of Democracy was the creation of an industrial planning capability to coordinate and control production in the privately managed business world. The president's economic governance options were limited. He could not simply grant dirigiste powers over the economy to the military, to big business, or to a government department for both practical and political reasons. The military's armaments-planning capability was virtually nonexistent (Lacy 2011). Cartels, by which business and economic coordination was long organized in the Axis powers, were historically outlawed by anti-trust legislation. No government agency had the expertise or the legitimacy to devise a central planning apparatus to dictate the management of production. Ideologically, the United States had a strong and active populist opposition to centralized power in all three spheres.

The president turned to business leaders experienced in creating the multidivisional business model that had emerged in 1920s and 1930s America. Many of these leaders had internalized the principles, methods, and practices by which American big business established an administrative planning system to run large organizations in the car, steel, electric power, petroleum, telecommunications, and retail sectors of the economy. It was in these large-scale organizations that nonmarket modes of governance had been created to pursue growth strategies based on product diversification and production rationalization (Chandler 1961, 1977; Best 1990, chaps. 2–3; Field 2011). A key innovation of the M-form was to combine centralized strategic planning with decentralized operations. In the words of Chandler and Galambos: "With diversification came decentralization of authority within the firm. This organizational innovation enabled managers to cope with the demands for both systematic management and vigorous entrepreneurship; decentralization was itself a basic innovation which Schumpeter could not foresee when he wrote *Capitalism, Socialism and Democracy*" (1970, 211).

While it has features of the M-form, the government policy involved creating a new management stratum that combined civil servants with corporate technocrats into a permanent military-industrial planning structure. Its unique structural characteristics can be traced to the president's challenge to organize and develop an economic mobilization campaign that would motivate an entire population to participate fully and productively in building an "Arsenal of Democracy." The administrative instruments of coordination and control of the nation's production units evolved rapidly over the course of the war. While the WPB had sweeping economic powers at the apex, it was not in charge of the other twenty emergency mobilization agencies, each of which was independently governed by a civilian board appointed by the president; furthermore, none of the emergency agencies managed production units, which remained in the control of private enterprises.[9]

The PRP, a priority-based system, was introduced by the WPB to be adopted on a voluntary basis at the end of December 1941. The PRP was a reporting system tracking inventories and consumption among metal-using plants that consolidated schemes for metals control (Lacy 2011, 104). It involved applying statistical and forecasting techniques to production data created and collected at the level of the economy that mimicked the accounting and data collection methods developed by large firms to coordinate and control the flow of materials through their own organizations.

The PRP was used during most of the successful mobilization period. Nevertheless, Jim Lacy (2011) described it as a nightmare: it required more than 20,000 bureaucrats to process the paperwork that industry was forced to forward on a quarterly basis. It was the forerunner to the CMP, which, according to Charles Hitch, provided "the basic mechanism for integrating strategy, production, and the flow of materials.... It attempt[ed] to organize all war plants in the United States (more than 100,000) in much the same way that a large, industrial corporation organizes its operating plants" (Hitch 1943, cited in Cuff 1987, 1–2).[10] As R. E. Smith wrote:

> The above system has the merit of confining decisions at the highest
> level to broad questions and decentralizing the detail.... The basic

9. Each of the emergency mobilization boards had a civilian-dominated board that nonetheless included the actors critical for crafting its mission and for implementation of its objectives.

10. The WPB's Planning Committee, headed by Nathan, was put in charge of replacing the PRP with a more efficient production control accounting system: "Beginning with its first meeting on 30 September [1942], this committee and its principal subcommittee—working behind locked doors in a series of meetings and conferences rarely equaled in intensity of purpose—hammered out the plan which was to organize and integrate the nation's economy for the duration of the war" (Smith 1991 [1959], Kindle locations 17540–541, 17495).

distribution of materials between the military, basic economic, Lend-Lease and other exports would be made by the War Production Board ... but the actual scheduling and directing of materials, particularly in the military field, would be taken over by those responsible for procurement and production, which cannot be carried out without control of the flow of materials in accordance with their schedules. (Smith 1991 [1959], chap. 25)[11]

The CMP was understood and actively welcomed by industries operationalizing the capability triad. To quote from *Iron Age*: "The government is going to decide what it wants from industry and when it wants it. Industry is going to inform government how much material is needed for the government's requirements and how much can be produced. The government is going to keep the books and thus maintain its demands within industrial capacity and materials supply" (*Iron Age*, November 12, 1942, 76, cited in Cuff 1987, 2).

The organizational concept was, according to Cuff, "to combine central policy making at the apex with decentralized responsibility through claimant agencies and their primary contractors, with materials accounting techniques providing one means of retaining overall control." He continues: "Ironically as a result of CMP, more central industrial control had become available to governmental administrators in the U.S. economy than to the governments of its major enemies" (Cuff 1990, 111). But it was in its postwar evolution that the CMP's transformational impact was institutionalized. In fact, it was introduced only in July of 1943, after the major increase in production had occurred (Cuff 1985, 51).

Although the WPB, and all the other emergency mobilization agencies were terminated at the end of the war, the CMP was not. The CMP evolved into Programming, Planning, Budgeting Systems and was diffused by the "policy experts" community. It was the administrative forerunner to the creation of a permanent industrial planning capability with the Pentagon at the apex. It also came to shape relationships and a methodology between other branches of government and other industries.

11. In the US Army's official history, R. Elberton Smith (1991 [1959]) attributes the success of the CMP to three things: "(1) the estimates of material requirements were, as far as possible, derived from approved production programs specifically geared to the war effort; (2) it assured the completion of important end products by providing supplies of controlled materials to all subcontractors associated with a given prime contract; and (3) it decentralized detailed operations to the agencies responsible for conceiving and administering the several production programs" (Smith 1991 [1959], Kindle locations 79506, 17525–529).

Roosevelt did not appeal to any school of economics for guidance, but he did use economic statisticians. As described in chapter 2, the economic statisticians at the WPB combined forecasts of potential national output capacity based on national income and product accounting with production bottleneck analysis to target government supply-side interventions and to schedule and synchronize the interorganizational flow rate of aggregate output.

Thus aggregate supply and demand were administratively synchronized to grow output in line with the three- to four-year quarterly projections made by the Kuznets, Nathan, and May and formalized in the WPB's Victory Program. But this could not have been accomplished without the development of an interorganizational management capability. "The Plan was the outcome of a genuine collective intellectual and institutional effort; and the management process it involved gave an on-the-job training in national administration to an entire generation of public and private, military and business technocrats" (Cuff 1987, 1).

Training in the new system was formalized. In approximately three months some 3,600 Army officers or employees and 8,287 War Department contractors were trained under the Army's Field Operations Training Program (Smith 1991 [1959], Kindle locations 17658–17660). The result was the institutionalization of a new bridging layer of middle management to strategically direct and administer the creation and growth of a new economic governance structure. The consequences for the economic performance of postwar business and industrial organization would be far-reaching within a global economy populated by the emergence of rapidly growing new competitors.

The Left's Critique: The Warfare State

Traditionally in peacetime the government had not been the dominant customer of major corporations. This changed in the postwar era of permanent industrial planning. Implementing the Arsenal of Democracy production targets turned the government from the only customer of many of America's biggest business enterprises into a permanent customer after the war.

The detonation of an atomic bomb by the Soviet Union in 1949 and the outbreak of the Korean War in 1950 brought about what Hounshell calls "a scientifically and technically oriented arms race that rivaled the R&D projects of World War II" (1996, 47). In the words of Kevles: "For almost a quarter century after 1945, defense research expenditures rose virtually exponentially, even in constant dollars, accounting through 1960 for 80 percent or more of the entire federal R&D budget. In 1950, it was estimated that there were 15,000 defense research projects; in the early 1960s, perhaps 80,000" (1978, 466, cited in Hounshell 1996, 48).

The emergence of the permanent government-contractor transformed the American economy and governance system into what H. L. Nieburg labeled the "contract state." The list of the prime aerospace contractors soon included GE, GM, AT&T, Westinghouse, Chrysler, Ford, Socony Mobil, Firestone, Philco, and Goodyear (Nieburg 1966, 173). In the emergent "contract state" a small number of government officials could oversee a contract with a private company employing many thousands while preserving the ideology of the "private enterprise" system.

Ironically, at a juncture in the evolution of American capitalism at which a government with a much-expanded role in the organization of the economy had changed its modus operandi, the market-centric image of a perfectly competitive, self-organizing business system competing on the basis of price once again became the dominant theoretical and "official" policymaking paradigm (Bernstein 2001). Although the gap between theory and reality was not an issue within the economics profession, it took a president to call attention to the "unwarranted influence" of the "military-industrial complex."

As commander of the Allied forces in World War II, General Dwight D. Eisenhower would have been intimately involved with and knowledgeable of the powerful new production capabilities of the US economy. As we saw in chapter 2, the feasibility debates pitted the economic statisticians on the WPB against military leaders over Allied military strategy options. President Eisenhower, in his Farewell Address to the Nation in 1961, described the downside of the transformation of the parameters of the postwar American political economy and governance more authoritatively and accurately than anyone before or since:

> Until the latest of our world conflicts, the United States had no armaments industry. American makers of plowshares could, with time and as required, make swords as well. But we can no longer risk emergency improvisation of national defense. We have been compelled to create a permanent armaments industry of vast proportions. Added to this, three and a half million men and women are directly engaged in the defense establishment. We annually spend on military security alone more than the net income of all United States corporations.

Now this conjunction of an immense military establishment and a large arms industry is new in the American experience. The total influence—economic, political, even spiritual—is felt in every city, every Statehouse, every office of the Federal government. We recognize the imperative need for this development. Yet, we must not fail to comprehend its grave implications. Our toil, resources, and livelihood are all involved. So is the very structure of our society.

In the councils of government, we must guard against the acquisition of unwarranted influence, whether sought or unsought, by the military-industrial complex. The potential for the disastrous rise of misplaced power exists and will persist. We must never let the weight of this combination endanger our liberties or democratic processes. We should take nothing for granted. Only an alert and knowledgeable citizenry can compel the proper meshing of the huge industrial and military machinery of defense with our peaceful methods and goals, so that security and liberty may prosper together.[12]

The military-industrial establishment proved resistant to Eisenhower's warnings. The extended global reach of the Pentagon was part of the process. In the 1920s the US armed forces were stationed in only three countries abroad. During World War II the number grew to thirty-nine. By the 1960s the United States had over 2,900 military bases spread out over sixty-four countries (Best and Connolly 1982 [1976], 175–76). The military-industrial complex is a unique industry in that it thrives on foreign competition. In 1980, two decades after Eisenhower's famous Farewell Address to the Nation, the world spent $450 billion on armaments, of which over half was spent by the Soviet Union and the United States as each responded to purported "missile gaps" with aircraft and missile defense systems only to follow with succeeding generations and new rounds of government contracts. This sum exceeded the total income received by the poorest half of humanity. For comparison, development aid given by rich nations to poor was about $20 billion.[13]

Paul Baran and Paul Sweezy's *Monopoly Capital: An Essay on the American Economic and Social Order* was published in 1966, five years after Chandler's *Strategy and Structure* in 1961. Both books described

12. "Dwight D. Eisenhower: Farewell Address," www.americanrhetoric.com/speeches /dwightdeisenhowerfarewell.html.
13. Data on spending for armaments and development aid are from Independent Commission on International Development Issues (1980, 117).

processes by which large bureaucratic organizations came to dominate the economy in terms of shares of output and employment. But whereas Chandler, along with Penrose, identified processes of enterprise capability development, Baran and Sweezy focused attention on the emergence of monopolistic structures by which big business combined with big government to twist national investment priorities, market structures, and employment patterns. Corporate power, not consumer choices or democratically accountable government agencies, determined the nation's consumption priorities and physical infrastructure systems.

Harry Magdoff and Sweezy (1975) argued that the success of the New Economics of Keynesian demand-management theory in the post–World War II era rested heavily on military expenditures. Out of the total federal purchases of $1.5 trillion between 1946 and 1971, $1.1 trillion were defense-related spending (including debt payments for previous wars, veterans' benefits, space exploration, and the Atomic Energy Commission). Without this spending, unemployment rates in the postwar period would have approximated those of the Great Depression. Thus in 1970 there were 2.9 million members of the armed forces, 1.2 million civilian employees in the Defense Department, and 3 million employees in defense industries. This total, over 7 million, included only those directly dependent on military spending. If we assume a multiplier of 1, a conservative estimate, another 7 million were indirectly dependent on military spending. If the 7.9 million unemployed in 1970 are added to these first two categories of military-dependent employees, the total comes to 22.2 million workers, or about 26 percent of the labor force, a figure slightly higher than the highest level of unemployment during the Great Depression. Without extensive military expenditures, then, it is not clear that Keynesian policies would have eliminated the unemployment of the Great Depression or even maintained tolerable levels of employment in the 1960s.

For Baran and Sweezy the rise and growth of the military-industrial complex was but one example of a sector strategy promoted by an informal cartel of corporate giants, supported and enabled by government agencies to amass unaccountable economic power under the ideological cover of the hegemonic free-market paradigm. They extended the theme of regulatory capture by business groups to the design of subsidy systems to correct for "market failure" legitimized by the free-market perspective (Stigler 1971).

The impact can be great. A recent study by the International Monetary Fund estimates that fossil-fuel companies benefited from global subsidies of $4.9 trillion (6.5 percent of global GDP) in 2013, a sum that is greater than the total health spending of all the world's governments (Coady et al. 2015). This vast sum is largely the product of polluters not paying the costs imposed on governments by the burning of coal, oil, and gas; roughly a quarter is from pre-tax subsidies.

The "monopoly capital" variant of the industrial planning system, combined with the huge increase in federal spending on R&D, propagated a business culture dependent on government contracts and/or subsidies. By so doing, it supported a hierarchal, functionally departmentalized business model in which research laboratories were separated from product design and development and both from manufacturing. The status hierarchy of engineers mirrored and reinforced the sequence of activities along a linear chain of innovation. This population of enterprises suffered from the emergence of competing business systems and models of innovation from abroad. At the same time, the monopoly capital story does not explain the sustained structural competitive advantage of America's high-tech regional innovation systems exemplified by, but not limited to, Silicon Valley and Greater Boston. We turn next to a comparison of two very different high-tech regional economies and models of innovation within the same national S&T infrastructure.

The "Iron Triangle" versus the Triple Helix

As illustrated in chapter 3, the government was also deeply involved in the emergence and rapid growth phases of the open-system business model of Silicon Valley and Greater Boston. The new enterprises that were established along Boston's Route 128 in the formation period had two features in common: distinctive technology capabilities and government support. Analogously, in a history of the companies that laid the business foundations of Silicon Valley, Stuart Leslie states that "it may not be too much of an exaggeration to say that the Department of Defense was the original 'angel' of Silicon Valley" (2000, 50). Paul Forman (1987, 164–65) writes that in 1960 the federal government paid for 70 percent of the R&D conducted by the electronics industry. Nevertheless, Silicon Valley and Greater Boston were organized around an open-system focus-and-network business model, which was unlike the conventional functionally departmentalized autarchic business model of firms that became permanent prime contractors to the government in the postwar era.[14]

---

14. The vTHREAD database described in chapter 3 is interrogated to compare and contrast the structural competitive advantages of Greater Boston and Silicon Valley in

The most extreme form of the closed-system business model emerged across the Potomac River from the nation's capitol. Paul Ceruzzi (2008) describes the transition of prewar Washington, DC, from a town without industry, with adjacent counties of Northern Virginia in which dairy farming was the major sector, to the third-largest high-tech region in the United States. In the year 2000, two-thirds of the region's 426,000 high-tech jobs were in the twenty-seven-mile corridor stretching from the Pentagon to Dulles International Airport. Strikingly, the region's enterprises do not engage in production. They specialize in research management and paper; in Ceruzzi's words: "The military's weapons are built and tested elsewhere; the Pentagon's principal product is paper (or its modern equivalent PowerPoint slides)" (2008, 17).

Many of the endless and anonymous office blocks along the corridor are filled with "tenants [that] did not want anyone to know who they were or where they were located" (74). Ceruzzi casts light on this dark corner of American business where public scrutiny is avoided by classified research, the companies that inhabit it, and what they do. It is an account of an "iron triangle" of military, industry, and politics and the complex of company and industry lobbyists, lawyers, politicians, civil servants, and government contracts that fund it. In a 2008 report titled "Post-Government Employment of Former DoD Officials Needs Greater Transparency," the US Government Accountability Office (GAO) found that of the almost 2,500 former Pentagon officials analyzed, almost two-thirds went on to senior positions at just seven companies—SAIC, Northrop Grumman, Booz Allen Hamilton, L-3 Communications, Lockheed Martin, General Dynamics, and Raytheon. Except for the consulting firm Booz Allen, all seven were on the Pentagon's list of top ten contractors. Together they received more than $87 billion in contracts from the DoD in 2007 (US GAO, 2008). Figure 9.1 captures the consolidation dynamics of the US aerospace industry in the 1990s.

Unlike those of Greater Boston and Silicon Valley, Greater Washington's business system did not co-evolve within a "triple helix" of government, universities, and business. Instead we find two distinctive capability triads within the same nation. As distinct from the triple-helix interactions described in chapter 3, Greater Washington's high-tech landscape is

Best, Paquin, and Xie (2004). It also informed the comparison between Greater Boston and Northern Virginia's high-tech regions, which are of similar size in employment but vastly different in business systems and innovation capability in Best (2011).

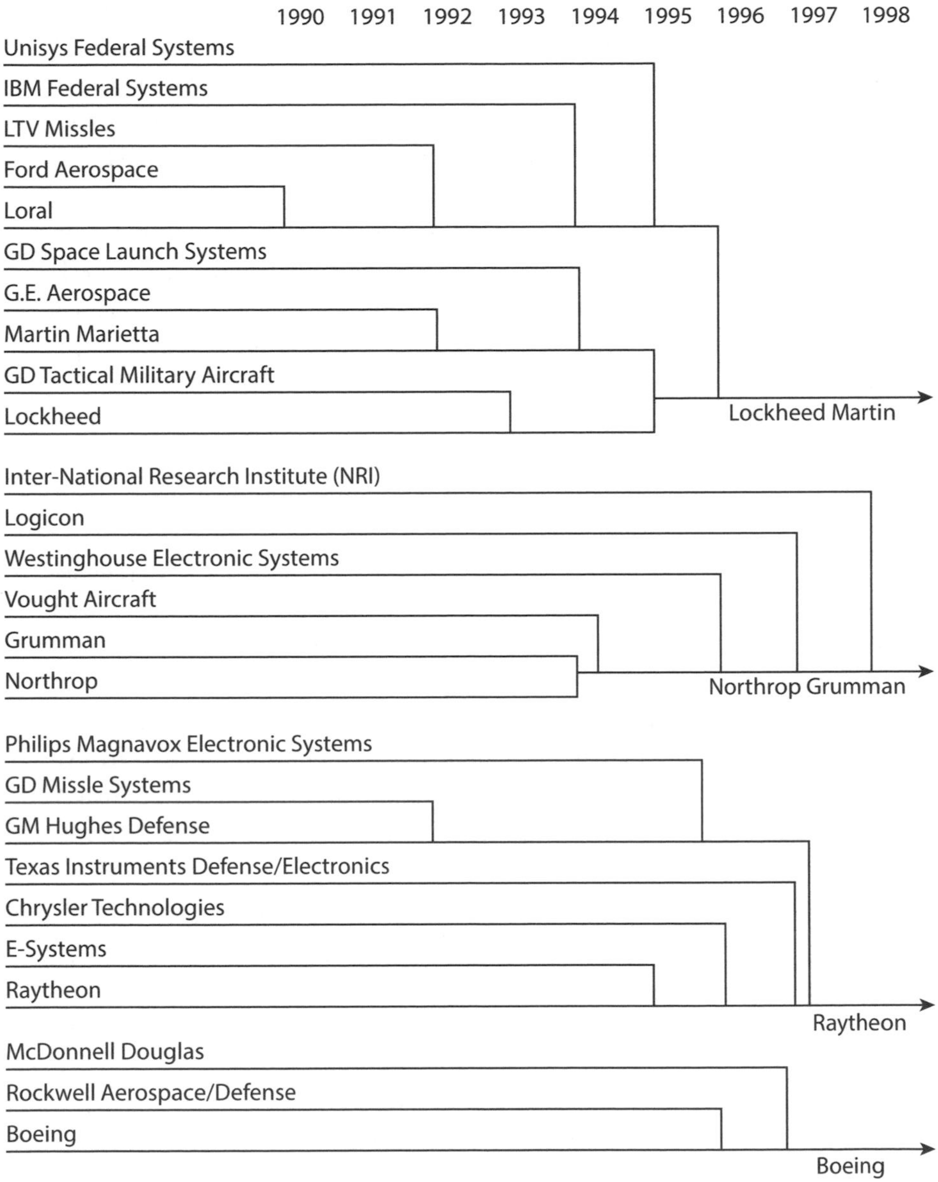

| | 1990 | 1991 | 1992 | 1993 | 1994 | 1995 | 1996 | 1997 | 1998 |

Unisys Federal Systems
IBM Federal Systems
LTV Missles
Ford Aerospace
Loral
GD Space Launch Systems
G.E. Aerospace
Martin Marietta
GD Tactical Military Aircraft
Lockheed — Lockheed Martin

Inter-National Research Institute (NRI)
Logicon
Westinghouse Electronic Systems
Vought Aircraft
Grumman
Northrop — Northrop Grumman

Philips Magnavox Electronic Systems
GD Missle Systems
GM Hughes Defense
Texas Instruments Defense/Electronics
Chrysler Technologies
E-Systems
Raytheon — Raytheon

McDonnell Douglas
Rockwell Aerospace/Defense
Boeing — Boeing

FIGURE 9.1. US aerospace industry consolidation, 1990–1998. *Source:* Adapted from *Aviation Week and Space Technology*, March 16, 1998, 25, as published in SIPRI (1999), 395.

not structured around prominent universities with faculties committed to open research and legacies of engineering expertise and enterprises.[15] What emerged, instead of an open-system population of networked enterprises and an industrial ecosystem creating and growing new high-tech manufacturing sectors, was a government-contractor business model with little commercial involvement or innovation impact.[16]

Two different innovation systems were created. A linear innovation process variant of trickle-down economics defended the massive R&D funding of prime contractors. The logic behind the science-push model is that funding science generates technological breakthroughs that usher in new products and new industries that, in turn, drive growth:

$$\text{basic research} \rightarrow \text{technological development} \rightarrow \text{product}$$
$$\text{engineering and development} \rightarrow \text{manufacture and sales.}$$

As described in chapter 3 and demonstrated in figure 9.2, the systems-integration model involves integrating technological research (TR) and basic research (BR). Technology integration teams are designed to foster the organizational capability to engage in communications across multiple technology domains and associated disciplinary languages.[17] It requires more. Technology management in production units that involve the incorporation of fundamental research into production, not as a driver but as a servant of technological advance, requires networking. As a fea-

15. The Prince William branch of George Mason University, opened in 1997, was renamed the Science and Technology Campus in 2015.

16. For example, while Virginia was at the top of the league table in per capita federal R&D, the region's corporate R&D of $3 per $1,000 in sales contrasted with $82 per $1,000 in Massachusetts and $78 per $1,000 in California in 2005; in manufacturing, exports per $1,000 GDP Virginia was at the bottom of the ten leading technology states in the United States in 2007. For these and other comparative innovation indicators, see annual publications of the Index of the Massachusetts Economy, Massachusetts Technology Collaborative, John Adams Innovation Institute. In recent years Virginia has not been included as a leading technology state.

17. Each engineering and scientific discipline has a distinctive "language." Mechanical, electrical, and software engineering methodologies, for example, are based on different units of analysis and measurement. Systems integration involves technology teams that can combine the strengths of the disciplines to develop and produce new product concepts. Internal training programs at companies like Intel rely on software tools developed for each discipline to facilitate interdisciplinary communication (see fig. 6.1, Best 2001). Nevertheless, no functional equivalent short of experience and teamwork has yet been discovered to Douglas Adams's "Babel fish," a device used to enable intergalactic communication in *A Hitchhiker's Guide to the Galaxy* (1979, 42).

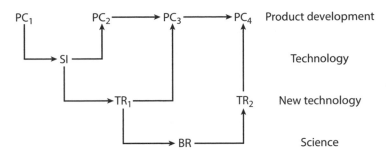

FIGURE 9.2. Systems-integration innovation: US PS 5. *Source:* Best (2001).
Note: PS = Production System; PC = product concept; SI = systems
integration; TR = technological research; BR = basic research.

ture of its systems-integration capability, Intel's technology-management process combines incremental with breakthrough innovation, and it is embedded in virtual laboratories in the form of broad and deep networks of researchers at the frontiers of scientific and technological research.

Technology-integration teams are organized to facilitate communications internally and externally. University research laboratories are an important external knowledge pool but not the only one. Intel depends on, and reinforces, an industrial district constituted by multiple design nodes, which includes a vast array of specialist producers and research institutions. In this it draws on an extended industrial high-tech district with an extraordinary capacity to conduct experiments, carry out innovations, and conduct research. In fact, Silicon Valley project teams are continuously combining and recombining within a population of 6,000 high-tech firms. Thus technology-integration teams are the hubs of extended research networks in districts like Silicon Valley. They extend beyond the firm, enabling project teams to participate in a highly innovative milieu for technology management.

The challenge of rapid technological change continually generates technical challenges and the search for solutions. Teams "dip down" into the scientific and technological bodies of knowledge that are available in the universities and "industrial districts."[18] This involves identifying where specialized knowledge and expertise can be located. Companies form long-term relationships with university research groups and other technology-oriented firms to access it.

18. The metaphor "dip down" to describe the process illustrated in figure 8.2 was suggested to me by Arthur Francis of Bradford University.

Greater Washington's "contract state" goes to the dark side of the wartime industrial planning legacy. It lacks the open system governance structures that constitute Greater Boston's Capability Triad.

America's Industrial Future?

The 1973 "oil price shock" triggered by the OPEC oil embargo brought worldwide attention to the price-setting power of Saudi Arabia as the largest oil exporter. Oil prices spiked from $20 to over $50 per barrel and then again in 1979 to $100 per barrel.[19] The US stock market crashed in 1973–74. and the Bretton Woods currency accord officially ended. This began the era of stagflation and the shift of economic policymaking from Keynesian macroeconomics to market fundamentalism. Alan Greenspan, a disciple of Ayn Rand, became chairman of the Council of Economic Advisors from 1974 to 1977 before his reign as chairman of Federal Reserve Bank from 1987 to 2006. Greenspan's tenure marked a shift in the nation's de facto economic policymaking authority to the Federal Reserve Bank and Wall Street bankers.

These events, for good reason, received much attention. But they were not the whole story. Less observed but equally transformative was a shift in business organization. The business model that had served the nation's working class so well underwent a structural change beginning in 1973, as shown in figure 9.3. No longer were wages increasing in sync with gains in productivity. The nation's economic performance was entering into a new slow-growth, stagnant-wage era. Another indication of the structural change in the nation's business system was the surge in the CEO-to-worker compensation ratio from 20 to 1 in the late 1960s to over 300 to 1 in the 2000s, as shown in figure 9.4.

Manufacturing employment's share of total US employment declined steadily from near 25 percent in 1970 to 9 percent in 2011 (Bailey and Bosworth 2014, fig. 1). After 2000, the absolute level of US manufacturing employment fell by one-third, to under 12 million in 2012 (Bailey and Bosworth 2014, fig. 2). China's entry into the World Trade Organization in 2001 had an immediate impact: "In 2000, only about one-third of the large deficit with Asia was accounted for by trade with China, but since then China has greatly increased its share, rising to 72 percent by 2012"

19. Although US oil production began its historic decline from a peak of 9.5 billion barrels a day in 1970 to under 6 billion barrels at the turn of the century, oil imports increased from 1.3 billion barrels per day to over 9 billion barrels at the turn of the century.

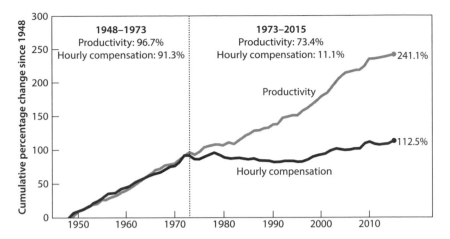

FIGURE 9.3. Productivity growth and hourly compensation growth, 1948–2015.
Source: Adapted from and based on Economic Policy Institute analysis of data
from the Bureau of Economic Analysis and the Bureau of Labor Statistics.

(Baily and Bosworth 2014, 4). In the mid-1970s, the US overall trade balance began a decline from a surplus of approximately 1 percent GDP to a
deficit of–3 percent in 1986, followed by a recovery, before plunging again
to a deficit of between 3 and 5 percent in the 2000s (Pisano and Shih
2012, 4).

Offshoring of American manufacturing to China has been the consequence of mutually reinforcing policies in both countries. The Chinese
government's policy of enticing MNCs to locate manufacturing affiliates
in special economic zones has combined with the business policy of vertically integrated corporations to spin off "noncore" activities in response to
competitive and financial-market pressures. Offshoring and outsourcing
are policy responses of once vertically integrated corporations to the "lean
manufacturing" revolution begun in Japan, the erosion of the infrastructures and industrial ecosystem that had once existed, and US government
regulatory changes that have created financial pressures for business leaders to sacrifice investments in plants and equipment or risk hostile take-
overs by "activist" investors (Lazonick 2014).

The absolute drop in manufacturing put America's innovation capability at risk. In an examination of manufacturing offshoring Gary Pisano
and Willy Shih go inside the complex array of technologies in high-tech
products that have been developed in the United States to find that many
are now embedded exclusively in offshore manufacturing systems. The
assumption that the United States can prosper as an "innovator without
manufacturing is a dangerous one," they believe (2012, xii). They argue

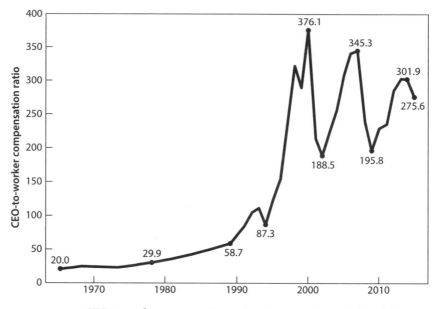

FIGURE 9.4. CEO-to-worker compensation ratio, 1965–2015. *Source:* Adapted from Lawrence Mishel and Jessica Schieder, "Stock Market Headwinds Meant Less Generous Year for Some CEOs," *Economic Policy Institute Report*, July 12, 2016, figure C.

that manufacturing is as integral to the national innovation system as are R&D, venture capital, and strong universities but that a "combination of bad decisions by businesses and inadequate policies by government is leading to an erosion of 'industrial commons'—the set of manufacturing and technical capabilities that support innovation across a broad range of industries" (xii).

An MIT Task Force on Production and Innovation recently visited more than 250 firms in the United States, China, and Germany and reported the findings in books by Berger (2013) and Locke and Wellhausen (2014). They, too, investigated the impact of the transformation of US corporate structure on the nation's innovation system. In every interview they inquired how the company got a new idea to market. They found that outsourcing of noncore business functions has resulted in "gaping holes and missing pieces in the current industrial ecosystem for the scale up of innovation" (Berger 2013). The result has been that innovative ideas in start-ups, university labs, and companies end up going abroad to reach commercial scale.

Up to this point global production networks have worked to the advantage of America's regional innovation systems, such as those of Silicon Valley and Greater Boston. But to date, most efforts to emulate the Silicon Valley model domestically, as well as abroad, have failed (Kenney 2000; Leslie 2000). These regions represent a unique system of interrelationships that cross-penetrate government, academic, and enterprise domains that collectively form industrial experimental laboratories with unique innovation and business-development capabilities. Capability triads, unlike technologies, cannot be purchased or transferred by FDI. But they are susceptible to fracture by policies that underestimate the requisite mutual adjustment processes and fall far short of a strategic national development policy framework.

Consequently, if China's industrial growth model is sustainable, the worst fears of Pisano and the MIT Task Force could come to fruition. The internal productive structures and extrafirm infrastructures that combined to grow the American economy, such as the creation of the American public school system, which was integral to the development of mass-production industries and the managerial enterprises that organized them, are both under threat. Similarly, the geographically regulated banking system that segmented financial markets to fund business development and the highly progressive income tax system that funded public investments in material and intangible infrastructures are being dismantled.

The impact of the loss of competitive advantage on employment in conventional industries and communities is reminiscent of UK industry history. When *Britain's Industrial Future* was published in 1928, the United Kingdom was still an industrial powerhouse, but the warning signs of impending decline were both clear and ignored. Although many industrial strategies were pursued in the postwar era, nothing broke the pattern, and Great Britain's share of the world's manufactured exports dropped from a quarter in 1952 to 2 percent in 2010. Will history repeat itself but in the United States? The warning signs are not hard to find, although the dynamic processes are different. This time the mindset of policymakers in America denies the role of government in fostering production and business-capability development in American history and is likewise blind to the risks of the emergence of powerful Asian competitors to the nation's economic performance.

If the critics are right, the challenge is as fundamental as was that facing Great Britain. But America will have to achieve what Great Britain did not: it will require the design and crafting of a strategic development policy framework to transform and rebuild its industrial system. For this it will have to jettison policymaking informed by the market-centric paradigm for policymaking informed by a production-centric paradigm.

Stewardship Challenges

At its simplest, stewardship is the motivation of individuals, not only leaders, to forsake personal gains to leave a company, institution, community, country, or environment in better condition for their successors than when they inherited it from their predecessors. Awareness of the role of stewardship in business development can inform and extend government policymaking options. At its simplest, the capability triad needs to be staffed.

The US World War II "mobilization" economy is an extraordinary example of the economics of stewardship. The United States was the only country that tapped into the huge productivity gains of an inclusive democratic economy that achieved buy-in from top to bottom to build companies with the productive structures necessary to meet the challenge of creating an Arsenal of Democracy. The TWI program was a revolution in management philosophy that was transferred and extended into *kaizen* and lean production by the Japanese in the postwar era. Stewardship took the form of lifelong employment. It is a prime example of the structural competitiveness paradigm.

At first glance the *Mittelstand* is simply a collection of family firms, but this ignores the range of extrafirm infrastructures, intangible and material, that mediates between and integrates the push from national policies and the pull of local/regional economic policymaking. Here infrastructural institutions are targets of economic policy instruments to shape business organization, increase knowledge-creation capability, foster sectoral transitions, and otherwise advance regional competitive advantage. It implies an economic perspective that starts with but goes beyond that of Penrose to examine capability-development processes across a population of firms and of collective action that goes beyond the theory of public goods. It takes us into the world of government stewardship of an industrial ecosystem in which innovative firms can thrive and continuously renew and upgrade the region's production system combined with macro growth policies.

Regional governments are not without policymaking instruments to meet the stewardship challenge. Again, the German social market economy is instructive. The power to convene is an instrument of economic policymaking at the regional government level. Here it does not involve the participation of the biggest firms in the same room. It involves a highly organized *Mittelstand* business system in which regional governments work with unions, education and R&D institutions, engineering consultancies, financial institutions, and mission-driven quasi-public entities to craft a joined-up approach to meet challenges from global competition, potentially disruptive technological change, and macroeconomic shocks.

Enterprise stewardship in the form of sharing the gains from innovation and productivity are reflected in Henry Ford's famous wage of $5 a day to Babbage's principles of organization to Penrose's capability development. The capability triad, triple helix, industrial ecosystem, entrepreneurial industrial district, and cluster dynamics all point to stewardship opportunities for regional economic governance. Stewardship involves organizing joint action among multiple actors with diverse interests to work together to sustain regional capabilities and address development challenges. Unlike in the case of MNEs, processes of industrial renewal cannot be directed by a management team in a central office. Governments alone have the authority to act in the regional economic interest. While a democratic government lacks the power to direct the requisite actors, it has the legitimacy to convene. Instead of policy dictates, the government must work within a complex framework by which, in the words of Bagnasco, "public policies are formulated through the direct participation of various public and private players who negotiate and reach agreements to ensure implementation" (2009, 216).

Important as it is, the stewardship responsibility of governments is not limited to economic opportunities for ensuing generations. Stewardship with respect to fostering a good society demands attention to social justice and ecological sustainability. The focus of this book on structural competitiveness is not meant to imply that the challenges of increasing inequality and global warming are of less importance. The hope is that a broader perspective of productive structures and the links connecting economic and government relationships offer policymakers alternatives to the market-competitiveness framework for addressing employment, social justice, and ecological stewardship challenges that are becoming ever more urgent. Without effectively characterizing the public good, governments cannot address the major challenges facing their communities.

We give the last word to Keynes:

> The ideas of economists and political philosophers, both when they are right and when they are wrong, are more powerful than is commonly understood. Indeed the world is ruled by little else. Practical men, who believe themselves to be quite exempt from any intellectual influences, are usually the slaves of some defunct economist. Madmen in authority, who hear voices in the air, are distilling their frenzy from

some academic scribbler of a few years back.... But, soon or late, it is ideas, not vested interests, which are dangerous for good or evil. (1936, 383–84)

This book presents some new, contested, and perhaps radical ideas in the hope that they are dangerous for good.

Abegglen, J., and Stalk, G. 1985. *Kaisha: The Japanese Corporation*. New York: Basic Books.

Abramovitz, M. 1956. "Resource and Output Trends in the United States since 1870." *American Economic Review* 46, no. 2, May.

———. 1986. "Catching Up, Forging Ahead, and Falling Behind." *Journal of Economic History* 46, no. 2: 385–406.

———. 1993. "The Search for Sources of Growth: Areas of Ignorance, Old and New." *Journal of Economic History* 53, June.

Abramovitz, M., and P. David. 1973. "Reinterpreting Economic Growth: Parables and Realities." *American Economic Review* 63: 428–39.

Adams, D. 1979. *A Hitchhiker's Guide to the Galaxy*. London: Pan Books.

Adeney, M. 1988. *The Motor Makers: The Turbulent History of Britain's Car Industry*. London: William Collins Sons.

Adner, R. 2012. *The Wide Lens: A New Strategy for Innovation*. New York: Penguin Books.

Aerospace Industries Association of America. 1945. *Aerospace Facts & Figures*. Washington, DC. This is an annual statistical series, dating back to 1945, about developments in the aerospace industry.

Aghion, P., and P. Howitt. 2006. "Appropriate Growth Policy: A Unifying Framework." *Journal of European Economic Association* 4, nos. 2–3: 269–314.

Akamatsu, K. 1962. "Historical Pattern of Economic Growth in Developing Countries." Institute of Asian Economic Affairs, *The Developing Economies* 1, no. 1: 3–25.

Alecke, B., C. Alsleben, F. Scharr, and G. Untiedt, G. 2006. "Are There Really High-Tech Clusters? The Geographic Concentration of German Manufacturing Industries and Its Determinants." *Annals of Regional Science* 40: 19–42.

Allen, R. 1983. "Collective Invention." *Journal of Economic Behavior and Organization* 4: 1–24.

Amsden, A. 1989. *Asia's Next Giant: South Korea and Late Industrialization*. New York: Oxford University Press.

Anderson, P., K. Arrow, and D. Pines. 1988. *The Economy as an Evolving Complex System*. Vol. 5. Santa Fe Institute: Studies in the Sciences of Complexity. Reading, MA: Addison-Wesley.

Ante, S. 2008. *Creative Capital: Georges Doriot and the Birth of Venture Capital*. Boston: Harvard Business Press.

APJ (Action Plan for Jobs). 2013. *Action Plan for Jobs 2013*. Dublin, Ireland: Ministry for Jobs, Enterprise and Innovation.

Arrow, K. J. 1962. "The Economic Implications of Learning by Doing." *Review of Economic Studies* 29, no. 3: 155–73.

Arthur, B. 1999. "Complexity and the Economy." *Science* 284: 107–9.

Asher, H. 1956. *Cost-Quantity Relationships in the Airframe Industry*. Santa Monica, CA: RAND Corporation.

Ashish, A., and A. Gambardella., eds. 2005. *From Underdogs to Tigers: The Rise and Growth of the Software Industry in Brazil, China, India, Ireland, and Israel*. Oxford: Oxford University Press.

Aston, B., and M. Williams. 1996. *Playing to Win: The Success of UK Motorsport Engineering*. London: Institute for Public Policy Research.

Babbage, C. 2005 (1832). *On the Economy of Machinery and Manufactures*. Cirencester, England: Echo Library.

Bagnasco, A. 2009. "The Governance of Industrial Districts." In *The Handbook of Industrial Districts*, ed. Giacomo Becattini, Marco Bellandi, and Lisa De Prisa. Cheltenham, England: Edward Elgar,216–28.

Baily, M., and B. Bosworth. 2014. "US Manufacturing: Understanding Its Past and Its Potential Future." *Journal of Economic Perspectives* 28, no. 1 (Winter): 3–26.

Balassa, B. 1965. "Trade Liberalisation and 'Revealed' Comparative Advantage." *Manchester School* 33, no. 2: 99–123.

Baldwin, C., and K. Clark. 2000. *Design Rules: The Power of Modularity*. Cambridge, MA: MIT Press.

Baran, P., and P. Sweezy. 1966. *Monopoly Capital: An Essay on the American Economic and Social Order*. New York: Monthly Review Press.

Bardon, J. 1992. *A History of Ulster*. Belfast: Blackstaff.

Barnett, C. 1986. *The Audit of War*. London: Macmillan.

Battelle. 2012. *Battelle/Bio State Bioscience Industry Development 2012*. Columbus, OH.

Becattini, G. 1978. "The Development of Light Industry in Tuscany: An Interpretation." *Economic Notes* 2–3: 107–23.

Becattini, G., and F. Coltorti. 2006. "Areas of Large Enterprise and Industrial Districts in the Development of Post-War Italy: A Preliminary Survey." *European Planning Studies* 14, no. 8: 1105–38.

Becattini, G., M. Bellandi, and L. DePropis, eds. 2009. *A Handbook of Industrial Districts*. Northampton, MA: Elgar.

Beinhocker, E. 2007. *The Origin of Wealth: Evolution, Complexity, and the Radical Remaking of Economics*. London: Random House.

Bellandi, M., and E. Santini, E. 2016. "Resilience and the Role of Arts and Culture-Based Activities in Mature Industrial Districts." *European Planning Studies* 25, no. 1.

Bellani, M. 2008. "The Governance of Clusters: Progressive Reactions to International Competitive Challenges." In *Networks, Governance and Economic Development: Bridging Disciplinary Frontiers*, ed. M. Aranguren, C. Iturrioz, and J. Wilson. Cheltenham, England: Edward Elgar: 249–67.

Berg, M. 1980. *The Machinery Question and the Making of Political Economy, 1815–1848*. Cambridge: Cambridge University Press.

Berger, S. 2013. *Making in America: From Innovation to Market*. Cambridge, MA: MIT Press.

Bernstein, M. 2001. *A Perilous Progress: Economists and Public Purpose in Twentieth-Century America*. Princeton, NJ: Princeton University Press.

Best, M. 1990. *The New Competition: Institutions of Industrial Restructuring*. Cambridge, MA: Harvard University Press.

———. 1992. "Restructuring the Wood Processing Industry of Honduras." Vienna: United Nations Industrial Development Organization.

———. 1995. *Competitive Dynamics and Industrial Modernisation Programmes: Lessons from Japan and America*. Annual Sir Charles Carter Lecture. Belfast: Northern Ireland Economic Council.

———. 2000. *The Capabilities and Innovation Perspective: The Way Ahead in Northern Ireland*. Belfast: Northern Ireland Economic Council.

———. 2001. *The New Competitive Advantage: The Renewal of American Industry*. Oxford: Oxford University Press.

———. 2003a. "Lowell's Industrial Regeneration: Dynamic Technological Capabilities." *Business and Economic History On-Line* 1: 1–50. http://thebhc.org/sites /default/files/Best_0.pdf.

———. 2003b. "The Geography of Systems Integration." In *The Business of Systems Integration*, ed. Andrea Prencipe, Andrew Davies, and Mike Hobday. Oxford: Oxford University Press, 205–32.

———. 2005. "Regional Specialization and Cluster Drivers: Medical Devices in Massachusetts." *Business and Economic History On-Line* 3: 1–35. www.thebhc.org /sites/default/files/best.pdf.

———. 2006. "Massachusetts Medical Devices: Leveraging the Region's Capabilities." *MassBenchmarks* 8, no. 1: 14–25. www.massbenchmarks.org/publications/issues /vol8i1/o6v8i1.htm.

———. 2011. "Review of *Internet Alley: High Tech in Tysons Corner, 1945–2005*, by Paul Ceruzzi (Cambridge, MA: MIT Press). *Business History* 53, no. 6 (October): 976–80.

———. 2012. "The Obscure Firm in *The Wealth of Nations*." In *Handbook on the Economics and Theory of the Firm*, ed. M. Dietrich and J. Krafft. Cheltenham, England: Edward Elgar, 29–41.

———. 2016. "Regional Capabilities and Industrial Resiliency: Specialization and Diversification Dynamics in Lowell, Massachusetts." In *Global Economic Crisis and Local Economic Development: International Cases and Policy Responses*, ed. J. Begley, D. Coffey, T. Donnelly, and C. Thornley. New York: Routledge, 47–77.

Best, M., and W. Connolly. 1982 (1976). *The Politicized Economy*. Lexington, MA: D. C. Heath.

Best, M., and R. Forrant. 1996. "Creating Industrial Capacity: Pentagon-Led versus Production-Led Industrial Policies." In *Restoring Full Employment*, ed. Jonathan Michie and John Grieve Smith. Oxford: Oxford University Press.

———. 2000. "Production Matters: The Prospects for Economic Development in Jamaica." Working paper, Center for Industrial Competitiveness, University of Massachusetts, Lowell.

Best, M., and J. Humphries. 1986. "The 'City' and Industrial Decline." In *The Decline of the British Economy*, ed. B. Elbaum and W. Lazonick. Oxford: Oxford University Press: 223–39.

———. 2003. "Edith Penrose: A Feminist Economist?" *Feminist Economics* 9, no. 1: 47–73.

Best, M., A. Paquin, and H. Xie. 2004. "Discovering Regional Competitive Advantage: Massachusetts High Tech." On-line publication of the Business History Association. www.thebhc.org/sites/default/files/BestPaquinXie_0.pdf.

Best, M., and R. Rasiah. 2003. *Malaysian Electronics: At the Crossroads*. Vienna: United Nations Industrial Development Organization. https://www.researchgate.net/publication/302909435_Malaysia_Electronics_At_the_Crossroads.

Best, N. 1990. *A Celebration of Work*. Edited and with an introduction by William G. Robbins. Lincoln: University of Nebraska Press.

Bland, B. 2016. "China's Robot Revolution." *Financial Times*, June 6.

Blundel, R. 2013. "Beyond Strategy: A Critical Review of Penrose's 'Single Argument' and Its Implications for Economic Development." *European Journal of the History of Economic Thought* 22, no. 1: 97–122. Published online October 23. Available at http://oro.open.ac.uk/34242/1/ORO%20-%20Blundel%20EJHET%2012%20-%20Penrose%20FINAL%20-%2027%20Aug.pdf.

Bookstaber, R. 2017. *The End of Theory: Financial Crises, the Failure of Economics, and the Sweep of Human Interaction*. Princeton, NJ: Princeton University Press.

Bradley, J. 1989. "The Legacy of Economic Development: The Irish Economy, 1960–1987." In *The Legacy of T. K. Whitaker*, ed. John McCarthy. Dublin: Glendale Press, 128–50. Reprinted in *The Economic Development of Ireland since 1870*, ed. C. O. Grada. London: Edward Elgar, 1994.

———. 1995. "Reflections on the Belfast-Dublin Economic Corridor." *Irish Banking Review*, Autumn, 15–27.

———. 2004. "Changing the Rules: How the Failures of the 1950s Forced a Transition in Economic Policy-Making." In *Ireland: The Lost Decade in the 1950s*, ed. Dermot Keogh, Finbarr O'Shea, and Carmel Quinlan. Cork: Mercier, 105–17. Also published in *Administration* 52, no. 1 (Spring.

———. 2013. "Economic Governance with Tight Constraints: Exploring Implications for the Irish Economy." IIEA Economic Governance Paper 7, IIEA, Dublin. www.iiea.com/publications/economic-governance-with-tight-constraints-exploring-implications-for-the-irish-economy.

Bradley, J., and M. Best. 2011. "Bypassed Places? The Post-Belfast Agreement Border Economy." *Journal of Cross Border Studies in Ireland* 6 (Spring): 25–44. www.crossborder.ie/pubs/journal6.pdf.

———. 2012a. "Rethinking Regional Renewal: Towards a Cross-Border Economic Development Zone." *Journal of Cross Border Studies in Ireland* 7 (Spring): 37–58. www.crossborder.ie/pubs/journal7.pdf.

———. 2012b. *Cross Border Economic Renewal: Rethinking Irish Regional Policy*. Study commissioned by the Centre for Cross Border Studies and funded under the INTERREG IVA Programme by the Special EU Programme Body. www.crossborder.ie/pubs/2012-economic-report.pdf.

Bradley, J., and G. Untiedt. 2012. "Emerging from Recession? Future Prospects for the Irish Economy, 2012–2020." HERMIN Economic Paper 4. www.herminonline.net/index.php/publications.

Bradsher, K. 2017a. "When Solar Panels Became Job Killers." *New York Times*, April 8.

———. 2017b. "A Robot Revolution, This Time in China." *New York Times*, May 12. Available at https://www.nytimes.com/2017/05/12/business/a-robot-revolution-this-time-in-china.html.

Branscomb, L., and P. Auerswald. 2002. *Between Invention and Innovation: An Analysis of Funding for Early-Stage Technology Development*. Washington DC: US Department of Commerce.

Breznitz, D. 2005. "The Israeli Software Industry." In *From Underdogs to Tigers: The Rise and Growth of the Software Industry in Brazil, China, India, Ireland, and Israel*, ed. A. Ashish and A. Gambardella. Oxford: Oxford University Press.

———. 2007. *Innovation and the State*. New Haven, CT: Yale University Press.

Britain's Industrial Future: Being the Report of the Liberal Industrial Inquiry. 1928. London: Ernest Benn. Second impression, 1977.

Broadberry, S., and Irwin, D. 2004. "Labor Productivity in the United States and the United Kingdom during the Nineteenth Century." Program(s): DAE ITI. NBER Working Paper 10364, NBER, Cambridge, MA. Available at www.nber.org/papers /w10364.

Brubacher, J., and W. Rudy. 1997. *Higher Education in Transition: A History of American Colleges and Universities*. Piscataway, NJ: Transaction.

Brusco, S. 1982. "The Emilian Model." *Cambridge Journal of Economics* 6: 167–84.

Bugos, G. 2001. "History of the Aerospace Industry." In *EH.net Encyclopedia*, ed. Robert Whaples. http://eh.net/encyclopedia/the-history-of-the-aerospace-industry/.

Bush, V. 1960 (1945). *Science: The Endless Frontier; A Report to the President on a Program for Postwar Scientific Research*. Washington, DC: National Science Foundation.

Caeiro, A. 2004. *Pela China Dentro*. Translated from the Portuguese. Lisbon: Dom Quixote.

Carrington, D. 2012. "How a Green Investment Bank Really Works." *Guardian*, May 24. www.guardian.co.uk/environment/damian-carrington-blog/2012/may/24/green -investment-bank-energy-efficiency?INTCMP=SRCH.

Casper, S. 2013 "The Spill-Over Theory Reversed: The Impact of Regional Economies on the Commercialization of University Science. *Research Policy* 42: 1313–24.

Castells, Manuel, and Peter Hall. 1994. *Technopoles of the World*. London: Routledge.

Ceccagno, A. 2012. "The Hidden Crisis: The Prato Industrial District and the Once Thriving Chinese Garment Industry." *Revue Européenne des Migrations Internationales* 28 (4): 43–65.

Center for Cross Border Studies. 2012. "Cross Border Economic Renewal: Rethinking Regional Policy in Ireland." March 30. http://crossborder.ie/cross-border-eco nomic-renewal-rethinking-regional-policy-in-ireland/.

Ceruzzi, P. 2008. *Internet Alley: High Technology in Tysons Corner, 1945–2005*. Cambridge: MIT Press.

Chamberlin, E. 1933. *The Theory of Monopolistic Competition*. Cambridge, MA: Harvard University Press.

Chandler, A. 1961. *Strategy and Structure: Chapters in the History of the Industrial Enterprise*. New York: Doubleday.

———. 1977. *The Visible Hand*. Cambridge, MA: Harvard University Press.

Chandler, A., and L. Galambos. 1970. "The Development of Large-Scale Economic Organizations in Modern America." *Journal of Economic History* 30, no. 1: 201–17.

Chang, Ha-Joon. 2003. "The Market, the State and Institutions in Economic Development." In *Rethinking Development Economics*, ed. Ha-Joon Chang. London: Anthem.

Chang Chin Nam. 2014. "Initiatives to Groom Talent in Precision Engineering." In *The Millenium: Our History*. Singapore: Economic Development Board.

Chia Siow Yue. 2000. "Singapore: Destination for Multinationals." In *Regions, Globalization and the Knowledge Based Economy*, ed. John Dunning. Oxford: Oxford University Press.

Christensen, C. 1997. *The Innovator's Dilemma: When New Technologies Cause Great Firms to Fail*. Boston: Harvard Business School Press.

CISC (Centre for Innovation and Structural Change). 2010. *Capabilities and Competitiveness: A Methodological Approach for Understanding Irish Economic Transformation*. Lucerna Project Report-2010, National University of Ireland, Galway. Contributors to the report included Michael Best, Paul Ryan, Satyasiba Das, Oner Tulum, and Majella Giblin.

Coady, D., I. Parry, L. Sears, and B. Shang. 2015. "How Large Are Global Energy Subsidies?" IMF Working Paper, International Monetary Fund, Washington, DC. Available at https://www.imf.org/external/pubs/ft/wp/2015/wp15105.pdf.

Coase, R. 1937. "The Nature of the Firm." *Economica N.S.* 4, no. 4: 331–51.

———. 1991. "The Institutional Structure of Production." Nobel Lecture.

Cobb, C., and P. Douglas. 1928. "A Theory of Production." *American Economic Review* 18 (Supplement): 139–65.

Comfort, N. 2012a. *The Slow Death of British Industry: A 60-Year Suicide, 1952–2012*. London.

———. 2012b. *Surrender: How British Industry Gave Up the Ghost, 1952–2012*. London: Biteback.

Conant, J. 1970. *My Several Lives: Memoirs of a Social Inventor*. New York: Harper and Row.

Cookson, C. 2010. "Innovation Has Big Role in Building Prosperity." *Financial Times*, special issue: *Doing Business in Ireland*, November 3, 4.

Coote, Sir Charles. 1801. *Statistical Survey of the County of Monaghan*. Dublin: Graisbery and Campbell, 154.

CorpTech (Corporate Technology Information Services). Various years. Woburn, MA.

CSO (Central Statistics Office), Ireland. 2014. *Census of Industrial Production Enterprises 2012*. Cork.

Cuff, R. 1985. "Ferdinand Eberstadt, the National Security Resources Board, and the Search for Integrated Mobilization Planning, 1947–1948." *Public Historian* 7, no. 4: 37–52.

———. 1987. "From the Controlled Materials Plan to the Defense Materials System, 1942–1953." *Military Affairs* 51, no. 1: 1–6.

———. 1990. "Organizational Capabilities and U.S. War Production: The Controlled Materials Plan of World War II." *Business and Economic History* 19: 103–12.

Cunningham, J., and W. Golden. 2009. "The Irish National Innovation System: Structures, Performance and Challenges." Working Paper 30, July, Centre for Innovation and Structural Change, National University of Ireland, Galway. https://aran.library.nuigalway.ie/handle/10379/2485.

Cusumano, M. 1985. *The Japanese Automobile Industry: Technology and Management at Nissan and Toyota*. Cambridge, MA: Harvard University Press.

Dahmén, E. 1970. *Entrepreneurial Activity and the Development of Swedish Industry, 1919-1939.* Trans. Axel Leijonhufvud. Homewood, IL: Richard D. Irwin. The English edition of vol. 1 of the Swedish-language edition published in 1950.

Darwin, C. 1979 (1859). *The Origin of Species.* New York: Random House. Originally *On the Origin of Species by Means of Natural Selection* (London).

David, P. 1998. "Common Agency Contracting and the Emergence of 'Open Science' Institutions." *The American Economic Review* 88, no. 2: 15-21.

David, P., and G. Wright, G. 1999. "Early Twentieth Century Growth Dynamics: An Inquiry into the Economic History of 'Our Ignorance.'" SIEPR Discussion Paper 98-3, Stanford Institute for Economic Policy Research, Stanford University, Stanford, CA.

Davis, L., and D. Kevles. 1974. "The National Research Fund: A Case Study in the Industrial Support of Academic Science." *Minerva* 12: 206-20.

Dei Ottati, G. 2009. "An Industrial District Facing the Challenges of Globalization: Prato Today." *European Planning Studies* 17, no. 12: 1817-35.

Delbridge, R., and F. Mariotti. 2009. *Racing for Radical Innovation: How Motorsport Companies Harness Network Diversity for Discontinuous Innovation.* London: Advanced Institute of Management Research (AIM).

Delmar, F., A. McKelvie, and K. Wennberg. 2013. "Untangling the Relationships among Growth, Profitability and Survival in New Firms." *Technovation* 33: 276-91.

Deming, W. 1982. *Quality, Productivity and Competitive Position.* Cambridge, MA: Center for Advanced Engineering Study, MIT.

Denmark Ministry of Foreign Affairs. 2014. "Start with Denmark: The Heart of Life Sciences for Research and Business." Copenhagen. http://clinicaltrialsdenmark.com/media/1324/start-with-denmark-2015_full-report-28-07-2015.pdf.

Denning, S. 2013. "Did Ronald Coase Get Economics Wrong?" *Forbes* 9, no. 25.

Department of Energy (UK). 1975, 1976a–1978. *Annual Blue Books Offshore Oil and Gas: A Summary of Orders Placed by Operators of Oil and Gas Fields on the UK Continental Shelf or Offshore (Year): An Analysis of Orders Placed.* London: Her Majesty's Stationery Office.

Department of Finance (Whitaker) (UK). 1958. *Economic Development.* Pr. 4803. Dublin.

Department of Trade and Investment (UK). 2007. *MotorSport in the UK: An Industry with a Winning Formula.* London.

Devine, W. 1983. "From Shafts to Wires: Historical Perspective on Electrification." *Journal of Economic History* 43, no. 2 June: 347-72.

Dinero, D. 2005. *Training within Industry: The Foundation of Lean.* New York: Productivity Press.

Dixit, A. 2008. "Economic Governance." In *The New Palgrave Dictionary of Economics Online,* ed. Steven N. Durlauf and Lawrence E. Blume. London: Palgrave Macmillan.

Dorfman, N. 1983. "Route 128: The Development of a Regional High Technology Economy." *Research Policy* 12: 299-316.

Dosi, G. 1982. "Technological Paradigms and Technological Trajectories." *Research Policy* 11: 147-62.

Dosi, G., R. Nelson, and S. Winter, eds. 2000. *The Nature and Dynamics of Organizational Capabilities*. Oxford: Oxford University Press.

Duguid, P. n.d.. "Untidy or Untractable? G. B. Richardson's View of Economics." School of Information, University of California, Berkeley.

Durlauf, S., and L. Blume. 2008. *The New Palgrave Dictionary of Economics Online*. London: Palgrave Macmillan. www.dictionaryofeconomics.com/dictionary.

Earls, A. 2002. *Route 128 and the Birth of the Age of High Tech*. Portsmouth, NH: Arcadia.

Easterly, W. 2001. *The Elusive Quest for Growth: Economists' Adventures and Misadventures in the Tropics*. Cambridge, MA: MIT Press.

Economist. 2012a. "Germany's Banking System: Old-Fashioned but in Favour." www .economist.com/news/finance-and-economics/21566013-defending-three-pillars -old-fashioned-favour/comments#comments.

Economist. 2012b. "Germany's Economic Model: What Germany Offers the World." April 14.

Edelstein, Michael. 2001. "The Size of the U.S. Armed Forces during World War II: Feasibility and War Planning." *Research in Economic History* 20: 47–97.

Eisenhower, D. 1961. "Farewell Address to the Nation." www.eisenhower.archives .gov/research/online_documents/farewell_address/1961_01_17_Press_Release .pdf.

El-Erian, M., and M. Spence. 2008. "Growth Strategies and Dynamics: Insights from Country Experiences." *World Economics* 9, no. 1 (January–March): 57–96.

Endler, J. 1998. *Other Leaders, Other Heroes*. Westport, CT: Praeger.

Enterprise Ireland. 2003. *Enterprise Ireland Annual Report and Accounts*. Dublin. https://enterprise-ireland.com/en/Publications/Reports-Published-Strategies /Annual-Reports/2003-Annual-Report-and-Accounts-Eng-.pdf.

Erhard, L. 1963. *The Economics of Success*. Trans. J. A. Arengo-Jones and D.J.S. Thomson. London: Thames and Hudson.

Ernst, D. 2000. "Inter-Organizational Knowledge Outsourcing: What Permits Small Taiwanese Firms to Compete in the Computer Industry?" *Asia Pacific Journal of Management*, special issue: *Knowledge Management in Asia*, August.

Etzkowitz, H. 2002. *MIT and the Rise of Entrepreneurial Science*. New York: Routledge.

Euromemorandum. 2012. *European Integration at the Crossroads: Democratic Deepening for Stability, Solidarity, and Social Justice*. www.euromemo.eu.

European Commission. 2007. *2007 Draft Capacity Map of Energy Research in EU Member States*. Brussels.

Eurostat. 2012. "Science and Technology at Regional Level." *Statistics Explained*, March 1. http://epp.eurostat.ec.europa.eu/statistics_explained/index.php/Science _and_technology_at_regional_level.

———. 2016. "Eurostat Statistics Explained." http://ec.europa.eu/eurostat/statistics -explained/index.php/Glossary:Nomenclature_of_territorial_units_for_statistics _(NUTS).

Evans, Peter 1995. *Embedded Autonomy: States and Industrial Transformations*. Princeton, NJ: Princeton University Press.

Evans, W. 1947. "Recent Productivity Trends and Their Implications." *Journal of the American Statistical Association* 42, no. 238: 211–23.

Fearon, P. 1987. *War, Prosperity and Depression: The US Economy 1917–45*. Oxford, England: Philip Allen.

Fenberg, S. 2011a. *Unprecedented Power: Jesse Jones, Capitalism and the Common Good*. Houston Endowment.

Field, A. J. 2008. "The Impact of the Second World War on US Productivity Growth." *Economic History Review* 61: 672–94.

——. 2011b. *A Great Leap Forward: 1930s Depression and U.S. Growth*. New Haven, CT: Yale University Press.

Floud, R. 1974. "The Adolescence of American Engineering Competition, 1860–1900." *Economic History Review* (new series) 27, no. 1: 57–71.

Ford, H. 2008 (1922). *My Life and Work*. New York: BN Publishing.

——. 1926. *Today and Tomorrow*. New York: Doubleday Page and Company. Reprint Cambridge, MA: Productivity Press, 1988.

Forfás 2010. Annual Business Survey of Economic Impact 2009. Dublin: Forfás.

Forman, P. 1987. "Behind Quantum Electronics: National Security as [the] Basis for Physical Research in the United States," Part 1." *Historical Studies in the Physical and Biological Sciences* 19: 149–229.

Forrant, R. 1997. "The Cutting Edge Dulled: The Post–World War II Decline of the United States Machine Tool Industry." *International Contributions to Labor Studies* 7: 37–58.

Forrant, R., and E. Flynn. 1998. "Seizing Agglomeration's Potential: The Greater Springfield Massachusetts Metalworking Sector in Transition, 1986–1996." *Regional Studies* 32, no. 3: 209–22.

Foster, R. 2007. *The Luck of the Irish*. London: Allen Lane.

Foxall, G., J. Fawn, and B. Johnston. 1992. "Innovation in Grand Prix Motor Racing, II: Extension of the Population Ecology Model." *Technovation* 12, no. 1: 1–14.

Foxall, R., and B. R. Johnston. 1991. "Innovation in Grand Prix Motor Racing: The Evolution of Technology, Organization and Strategy." *Technovation* 11, no. 7: 387–402.

Francis, J. 1871 (1855). *Lowell Hydraulic Experiments*. New York: D. Van Norstrand.

Frankel, L., J. Fulman, and J. Howell. 1988. "The Massachusetts Experience." In *The Massachusetts Miracle: High Technology and Economic Revitalization*, ed. D. Lampe. Cambridge: MIT Press: 348–57.

Freeman, C. 1982. *The Economics of Industrial Innovation*. London: Penguin.

——. 1991. "Networks of Innovators: A Synthesis of Research Issues." *Research Policy* 20: 499–514.

Freeman, C., and Louçã, F. 2001. *As Time Goes By: From the Industrial Revolution to the Information Revolution*. Oxford: Oxford University Press.

Frenkel, M., and R. Fendel. 1999. "How Important Is the Mittelstand for the German Economy?" In *Structure and Dynamics of the German Mittelstand*, ed. Christian Homburg. Heidelberg: Physica, 1–27

Frenken , K., F. Van Oort, and T. Verburg. 2007. "Related Variety, Unrelated Variety and Regional Economic Growth." *Regional Studies* 41, no. 5, 685–97.

Fromm, E., ed. and trans. 1961. *Marx's Concept of Man*. New York: Ungar.

Galbraith, J. 1952. *American Capitalism: The Concept of Countervailing Power*. Boston: Houghton Mifflin.

Galbraith, J. 1981. *A Life in Our Times*. New York: Random House.

Garnsey, E. 1998. "The Genesis of the High Technology Milieu: A Study in Complexity." *International Journal of Urban and Regional Research* 22, no 3: 361–77.

Giblin, M., and P. Ryan. 2010. "Tight Clusters or Loose Networks? The Critical Role of Inward Foreign Direct Investment in Cluster Creation." *Regional Studies*, October 9.

Gilboy, G. 2004. "The Myth Behind China's Miracle." *Foreign Affairs* 83, no. 4.

Gittings, J. 2005. *The Changing Face of China*. Oxford: Oxford University Press.

Glaeser, E. 2005. "Reinventing Boston: 1630–2003." *Journal of Economic Geography* 5: 119–53.

Goldin, C. 1998. "America's Graduation from High School." *Journal of Economic History* 58 (June): 345–74.

Goldratt, E., and J. Cox. 1984. *The Goal*. Croton-on-Hudson, NY: North River Press.

Goldsmith, R. W. 1946. "The Power of Victory: Munitions Output in World War II." *Military Affairs* 10, no. 1: 69–80.

Gordon, R. 1969. "$45 Billion of U.S. Private Investment Has Been Mislaid." *American Economic Review* 59, no. 3: 221–38.

Gould, S. 1996. *Full House: The Spread of Excellence from Plato to Darwin*. New York: Random House.

Griffiths, J. 1990. "The Industry's Unsung Track Heroes." *Financial Times*, January 26.

Grove, A. 1996. *Only the Paranoid Survive*. New York: Random House.

Growth Commission. 2008. *The Growth Report: Strategies for Sustained Growth and Inclusive Development*. Washington, DC: World Bank.

Hall, P., and D. Soskice. 2001. *Varieties of Capitalism: The Institutional Foundations of Comparative Advantage*. Oxford: Oxford University Press.

Hamowy, R. 1968. "Adam Smith, Adam Ferguson, and the Division of Labour." *Economica* 35: 249–59.

Harmon, R., and L. Peterson. 1990. *Reinventing the Factory*. New York: Free Press.

Hartman, E. 1970. *Adventures in Research: A History of Ames Research Center 1940–1965*. Washington, DC: National Aeronautics and Space Administration.

Hayes, R., and S. Wheelwright. 1984. *Restoring Our Competitive Edge*. New York: John Wiley.

Heanue, Kevin. 2008. "Measuring Industrial Agglomeration in a Rural Industry: The Case of Irish Furniture Manufacturing." Working Paper Series WPRE30. Rural Economy and Development Programme, Teagasc, Athenry, County Galway, Ireland.

Heim, C. 1987. "R & D, Defense, and Spatial Divisions of Labor in Twentieth-Century Britain." *Journal of Economic History* 47, no. 2: 365–78.

Hekman, J. 1980. "The Product Cycle and New England Textiles." *Quarterly Journal of Economics*, June: 697–717.

Hennigan, M. 2010. "Trintech Sold to US Firm for Knockdown Price of $93M." *Finfacts Ireland*. www.finfacts.ie/irishfinancenews/article_1020800.shtml.

Henriksen, I., and K. H. O'Rourke. 2005. "Incentives, Technology and the Shift to Year-Round Dairying in Late Nineteenth-Century Denmark." *Economic History Review* 58, no. 3 (August): 520–54.

Henry, Joseph. 1873. *Annual Report of the Smithsonian*. Washington, DC: Smithsonian Institution.

Henry, N., and S. Pinch. 2001. "Neo-Marshallian Nodes, Institutional Thickness, and Britain's 'Motor Sport Valley': Thick or Thin? *Environment and Planning A* 33: 1169–83.

Hicks, J. 1939. *Value and Capital*. Oxford: Clarendon Press.

Higgs, R. 1992. "The U.S. Economy in the 1940s." *Journal of Economic History* 52, no. 1: 41–60.

———. 1999. "From Central Planning to the Market: The American Transition, 1945–1947. *Journal of Economic History* 59, no. 3 (September): 600–623.

Hirsch, F. 1977. *The Social Limits to Growth*. London: Routledge and Kegan Paul.

Hitch, C. 1943. "Controlled Materials Plan." Records of the War Production Board, file no. 147, National Archives, Washington, DC.

Hobday, M. 1995b. *Innovation in East Asia: The Challenge to Japan*. London: Edward Elgar.

Hodgson, G. 1993. *Economics and Evolution: Bringing Life Back into Economics*. Ann Arbor: University of Michigan.

Hodgson, G. 2004. *The Evolution of Institutional Economics*. London: Routledge.

Hoisl, K. 2011. "Adaptation at Full Speed—Regulatory Changes in Fast Moving Industries Adaptation at Full Speed." Paper presented at the Danish Research Unit for Industrial Dynamics (DRUID) 2011 conference, Copenhagen Business School, Rebild, Denmark.

Hounshell, D. 1984. *From the American System to Mass Production, 1800–1932*. Baltimore: Johns Hopkins University Press.

———. 1996. "The Evolution of Industrial Research in the United States." In *Engines of Innovation: U.S. Industrial Research at the End of an Era*, ed. R. Rosenbloom and W. Spencer, 13–86. Boston: Harvard Business School Press.

House of Lords. 2008. "The Future of EU Regional Policy." HL 141, Stationary Office, London.

Hout, T., and P. Ghemawat. 2010. "China vs. the World: Whose Technology Is It?" *Harvard Business Review*, December: 95–103.

Hsueh, R. 2011. *China's Regulatory State*. Ithaca, NY: Cornell University Press.

Hu, Z., and M. Khan. 1997. "Why Is China Growing So Fast?" *Economic Issues* no. 8. Washington, DC: International Monetary Fund. www.imf.org/EXTERNAL/PUBS/FT/ISSUES8/INDEX.HTM.

Huey Yuen Ng. 2016. "Business System Transformation Process: Evolution of Singapore Precision Modules and Components Sector." PhD diss., Cambridge University, Cambridge.

Hufner, F. 2010. "The German Banking System: Lessons from the Financial Crisis." Economic Department Working Paper no.788, Organisation for Economic Cooperation and Development, Paris. www.oecd-ilibrary.org/economics/the-german-banking-system-lessons-from-the-financial-crisis_5kmbm8opjkd6-en?crawler=true.

Hughes, T. 1989. *American Genesis: A Century of Invention and Technological Enthusiasm, 1870–1970*, New York: Penguin Books.

Humphrey, T. 1997. "Algebraic Production Functions and Their Uses before Cobb-Douglas." Federal Reserve Bank of Richmond, *Economic Quarterly* 83 1: 51–83.

Humphries, J. 2011. *Childhood and Child Labour in the British Industrial Revolution*. Cambridge: Cambridge University Press.

Hyman, A. 1982. *Charles Babbage: Pioneer of the Computer*. Oxford: Oxford University Press.

Iammarino, S. 2005. "An Evolutionary Integrated View of Regional Systems of Innovation: Concepts, Measures and Historical Perspectives." *European Planning Studies* 13, no. 4 (June): 497–519.

IERC (Irish Energy Research Council). 2008. *Energy Research Strategy, 2008–2013*. Dublin.

Imai, M. 1986. *Kaizen*. New York: Random House.

Independent Commission on International Development Issues. *North-South: A Programme for Survival*. Report of the Commission under the chairmanship of Willy Brandt. London: Pan Books, 1980.

Index of the Massachusetts Innovation Economy. 2011, 2012, 2016. John Adams Innovation Institute, Massachusetts Technology Collaborative, Westborough MA.

Industry Advisory Group. 2004. Medical Technologies Sector Report. Industry Advisory Group's Report to the Enterprise Strategy Group, Dublin.

InterTradeIreland. 2015. "Mapping the Potential for All-Island Sectoral Ecosystems." Newry.

Irish Academy of Engineering and Engineers Ireland. 2010. *Infrastructure for an Island Population of Over 8 Million*. Newry: InterTradeIreland.

Ishikawa, K. 1985. *What Is Total Quality Control? The Japanese Way*. Englewood Cliffs, NJ: Prentice Hall.

Jack, Andrew. 2010. "Pharma Sector Is Confident It Will Ride Out the Tough Times." *Financial Times*, special issue: *Doing Business in Ireland*, November 3, 4.

Jacob, F. 1997. "Evolution and Tinkering." *Science* 196, June 10: 1163.

Jacobs, J. 1961. *The Death and Life of Great American Cities*. New York: Random House.

———. 1969. *The Economy of Cities*. New York: Random House.

———. 1984. *Cities and the Wealth of Nations: Principles of Economic Life*. New York: Random House.

Jacobson, D., and Z. Mottiar. 1999. "Globalization and Modes of Interaction in Two Sub-Sectors in Ireland." *European Planning Studies* 7, no. 4: 429–44.

Jacobson, D., K. Heanue, and Z. Mottiar. 2001. "Industrial Districts and Networks: Different Modes of Development of the Furniture Industry in Ireland?" In *Public Investment and Regional Economic Development*, ed. D. Felsenstein et al. London: Edward Elgar.

Janeway, E. 1951. *The Struggle for Survival: A Chronicle of Economic Mobilization in World War II*. New Haven, CT: Yale University Press.

Janeway, W. 2012. *Doing Capitalism in the Innovation Economy*. Cambridge: Cambridge University Press.

Japan Management Association. 1987. *Canon Production System*. English translation, Portland, OR: Productivity Press. Originally published as *Canon no seisan kakushin*. Tokyo: 1984.

Jenkins, M., and S. Floyd. 2001. "Trajectories in the Evolution of Technology: A Multi-Level Study of Competition in Formula 1 Racing." *Organization Studies* 22, no. 6: 945–69.

Johnson, S. 2001. *Emergence: The Connected Lives of Ants, Brains, Cities, and Software*. New York: Scribner.

Jones, J., and E. Angly. 1951. *Fifty Billion Dollars: My Thirteen Years with the RFC (1932–1945)*. New York: Macmillan.

Jones, R. 1831. *An Essay on the Distribution of Wealth, and on the Sources of Taxes*, Part I: *Rent*. London: John Murray.

———. 2016. "Innovation, Research and the UK's Productivity Crisis." University of Sheffield, Sheffield, England.

Jones Lang Lasalle. 2011. *Life Science Cluster Report*. Chicago.

Kahneman, D. 2013. *Thinking Fast and Slow*. New York: Farrar, Straus and Giroux.

Kaldor, N. 1970. "The Case for Regional Policies." *Scottish Journal of Political Economy*, November, 337–48.

Kay, J. 1996. *The Business of Economics*. Oxford: Oxford University Press.

Kendrick, J. 1961. *Productivity Trends in the US*. Cambridge, MA: National Bureau of Economic Research, and Princeton, NJ: Princeton University Press.

Kennedy, J. 1963. "Remarks at a Dinner Given in His Honor by President Segni, July 1, 1963." Made available online by Gerhard Peters and John T. Woolley as part of The American Presidency Project at www.presidency.ucsb.edu/ws/?pid =9331.

Kenney, M., ed. 2000 *Understanding Silicon Valley: The Anatomy of an Entrepreneurial Region*. Stanford, CA: Stanford University Press.

Kettler, D. 1965. *The Social and Political Thought of Adam Ferguson*. Piscataway, NJ: Transaction.

Kevles, D. 1978. *The Physicists: The History of a Scientific Community in Modern America*. New York: Knopf.

Keynes, J. M. 1936. *The General Theory of Employment, Interest and Money*. London: Macmillan.

Keynes, J. M., and H. D. Henderson. 1929. *Can Lloyd George Do It?* London: Nation and Athenaeum.

Kim, L. 1997. "The Dynamics of Samsung's Technological Learning in Semiconductors." *California Management Review* 39: 86–100.

Klein, M. 2013. *A Call to Arms: Mobilizing America for World War II*. New York: Bloomsbury.

Kline, S. 1985. "Innovation Is Not a Linear Process." *Research Management* 28 (July–August): 36–45.

Kobayashi, I. 1988. *20 Keys to Workplace Improvement*. Portland, OR: Productivity Press.

Kodama, F. 1986. "Japanese Innovation in Mechatronics Technology." *Science and Public Policy* 13, no. 1 (February): 44–51.

Koestler, A., and J. Smithies. 1971 (1958). *Beyond Reductionism*. London: Hutchinson.

Koh Tsu Koon. 1995. "The Penang Strategic Development Plan." In *Penang into the 21st Century: Outlook and Strategies of Malaysia's Growth Centre*, ed. Koh Tsu Koon. Petaling Jaya, Malaysia: Pelanduk.

Kohl, H. 1989. "Forty Years of the Social Market Economy in the Federal Republic of Germany." In *German History in Documents and Images*, vol. 9: *Two Germanies, 1961–1989*. http://germanhistorydocs.ghi-dc.org/pdf/eng/Chapter9Doc14.pdf.

Koistinen, P. 2004. *Arsenal of World War II: The Political Economy of American Warfare, 1940–1945*. Lawrence: University Press of Kansas.

Kommers, D., and R. Miller. 2012. *The Constitutional Jurisprudence of the Federal Republic of Germany*, 3rd ed. Durham, NC, and London: Duke University Press.

Kostoff, R. N. 1994. "Successful Innovation: Lessons from the Literature." *Research-Technology Management*, March-April: 60–61.

Krugman, P. 1991. *Geography and Trade*. Cambridge, MA: MIT Press.

———. 1995. *Development, Geography, and Economic Theory*. Cambridge, MA: MIT Press.

———. 2000. "The Future of New England." In *Engines of Enterprise: An Economic History of New England*, ed. Peter Temin. Cambridge, MA: Harvard University Press.

———. 2008. "Increasing Returns Revolution in Trade and Geography." Nobel Lecture.

———. 2009. "How Did Economists Get It So Wrong?" *The New York Times Magazine*, September 2.

Kuhn, T. 1962. *The Structure of Scientific Revolutions*. Chicago: University of Chicago Press.

Kuusisto, J., ed. 2005. "Knowledge-Intensive Service Activities in the Finnish Forest and Related Engineering and Electronics Industries (Forenel) Cluster." The KISA (knowledge-intensive service activities) Project of the OECD Group on Technology and Innovation Policy TIP and the Committee on Science and Technology Policy CSTP. Co-authors included H. Hernesniemi, M. Lindström, A. Juntunen, and J. Hyvönen, J. www.oecd.org/sti/inno/34624034.pdf.

Kuznets, S. 1971. "Modern Economic Growth: Findings and Reflections." Nobel Lecture, December 11.

Lacy, J. 2011. *Keep from All Thoughtful Men: How U.S. Economists Won World War II*. Annapolis, MD: Naval Institute Press.

Lall, S. 2003. "Industrial Success and Failure in a Globalizing World." Working Paper no. 102, Queen Elizabeth House, University of Oxford.

Landefeld, J. 2000. "GDP: 'One of the Great Inventions of the 20th Century.' " *Survey of Current Business*, Department of Commerce, January. Washington, DC: Government Printing Office.

Landes, D. 1969. *The Unbound Prometheus: Technological Change and Industrial Development from 1750 to the Present*. Cambridge: Cambridge University Press.

Lane, F. 1951. *Ships for Victory: A History of Shipbuilding under the U.S. Maritime Commission in World War II*. Baltimore: Johns Hopkins University

Layton, E. 1992. "From Rule of Thumb to Scientific Engineering: James B. Francis and the Invention of the Francis Turbine." *NLA Monograph Series*. Stony Brook, NY: Research Foundation of the State University of New York.

Lax, E. 2004. *The Mould in Florey's Coat*. Little Brown: London.

Lazonick, W. 1979. Industrial Relations and Technical Change: The Case of the Self-acting Mule, *Cambridge Journal of Economics*, 3: 231–262.

———. 1991. *Business Organization and the Myth of the Market Economy*, Cambridge: Cambridge University Press.

———. 2014. Profits without Prosperity, *Harvard Business Review*, September: 47–55.

———. 2015. "Innovative Enterprise or Sweatshop Economics? In Search of Foundations of Economic Analysis." Working paper no. 25, Institute for New Economic Thinking, New York.

———. Forthcoming. *The Theory of the Innovative Enterprise*. Oxford: Oxford University Press.

Lazonick, W., and D. Teece, eds. 2012. *Management Innovation: Essays in the Spirit of Alfred D. Chandler, Jr*. Oxford: Oxford University Press.

Lécuyer, C. 1998. "Academic Science and Technology in the Service of Industry: MIT Creates a 'Permeable' Engineering School," *American Economic Review* 88, no. 2: 28–33.

Leslie, S. 2000. "The Biggest Angel of Them All: The Military and the Making of Silicon Valley." In *Understanding Silicon Valley: The Anatomy of an Entrepreneurial Region*, ed. M. Kenney, 44–67. Stanford, CA: Stanford University Press.

Lewchuk, W. 1986. "The Motor Vehicle Industry." *The Decline of the British Economy*, In ed. B. Elbaum and W. Lazonick, 135–61. Oxford: Oxford University Press.

Lewis, J. 2002. *Spy Capitalism: Itek and the CIA*. New Haven, CT: Yale University Press.

Lewis, M. 2011. *Boomerang: The Meltdown Tour*. London: Allen Lane.

Lichtenstein, N. 2002. *State of the Union: A Century of American Labor*. Princeton, NJ: Princeton University Press.

Lieberman, H. 1968. "Technology: Alchemist of Route 128." *New York Times*, January 8, 139.

Lilley, T., P. Hunt, J. Butters, F. Gilmore, and P. Lawler. 1947. "Problems of Accelerating Aircraft Production during World War II." Division of Research, Graduate School of Business Administration, Harvard University, Cambridge, MA.

Loasby, B. 1999. *Knowledge, Institutions and Evolution in Economics*. The Graz Schumpeter Lectures. London: Routledge.

Loasby, B. J. 2000. "Organizations as Interpretative Systems." Paper presented at the Danish Research Unit for Industrial Dynamics (DRUID) Summer Conference, Rebild, Denmark. Available at www.business.auc.dk/druid.

Locke, R., and J.-C. Spender. 2011. *Confronting Managerialism*. London: Zed Books.

Locke, R. M. and R. Wellhausen, eds. 2014. *Production in the Innovation Economy*. Cambridge, MA: MIT Press.

Long, C. D. 1944. "The American Labor Force in World War II." In *The Labor Force in Wartime America*, vol. 1. Cambridge, MA: National Bureau of Economic Research 49–57.

Lorenzen, M., ed. 1998. *Specialization and Localized Learning: Six Studies on the European Furniture Industry*. Copenhagen: Copenhagen Business School Press.

Lucas, R. 1988. "On the Mechanics of Economic Development." *Journal of Monetary Economics* 22, no. 1: 3–42.

———. 2003. "Macroeconomic Priorities." *American Economic Review* 93: 1–14.

Lundvall, B. 2002. *Innovation, Growth and Social Cohesion: The Danish Model*. Cheltenham, England: Edward Elgar.

Mac Shary, R., and P. White. 2000. *The Making of the Celtic Tiger: The Inside Story of Ireland's Boom Economy*. Dublin: Mercier.

MacKay, D. 2009. "Sustainable Energy—Without Hot Air, a Ten-Page Synopsis." www.withouthotair.com.

Magaziner, I., and T. Hout. 1980. *Japanese Industrial Policy*. London: Policy Studies Institute.

Magaziner, I., and M. Patinkin. 1989. *The Silent War: Inside the Global Business Battles Shaping America's Future*. New York: Random House.

Magdoff, H., and P. Sweezy. 1975. "Capitalism and Unemployment." *Monthly Review*, June, 1–14.

Malthus, T. 1836. *Principles of Political Economy: Considered with a View to Their Practical Application*. London: W. Pickering.

Manjoo, F. 2017. "How to Make America's Robots Great Again." *New York Times*, January 25.

March, E. 2003. "Cascade Communications "Family of Companies." Anticipating Technology Trends Research Paper, Center for Industrial Competitiveness, University of Massachusetts, Lowell, August.

Marshall, A. 1920 (1890). *Principles of Economics*, 8th ed. London and New York: Macmillan.

Martin, R., and P. Sunley. 2007. "Complexity Thinking and Evolutionary Economic Geography." *Journal of Economic Geography* 7, no. 5: 573–601.

Marx, K. 1961 (1867. *Capital: A Critical Analysis of Capitalist Production*, vol. 1. Moscow: Foreign Languages Publishing House.

———. 1972. *Grundrisse*, ed. and trans. David McClellan. New York: Harper Torchbooks.

———.1961. *Marx's Concept of Man*. Ed. and trans. E. Fromm. New York: Ungar.

Maskell, P. 1998. "Localized Low-Tech Learning in the Furniture Industry." In *Specialization and Localized Learning: Six Studies on the European Furniture Industry*, ed. M. Lorenzen, 33–70. Copenhagen: Copenhagen Business School Press.

———. 2001. "Towards a Knowledge-Based Theory of the Geographical Cluster." *Industrial and Corporate Change* 10, no. 4: 921–43.

MassBio. 2017. *Biotechnology Industry Snapshot 2017*. Cambridge: Massachusetts Biotechnology Council. Available at http://files.massbio.org/file/MassBio-Industry-Snapshot-2017.pdf.

Mastromarco, C., and M. Runkel. 2009. "Rule Changes and Competitive Balance in Formula One Motor Racing." *Applied Economics* 41 23: 3003–14. doi:10.1080/00036840701349182.

Mathews, J. 1997. "A Silicon Valley of the East: Creating Taiwan's Semiconductor Industry." *California Management Review* 39, no. 4 (Summer): 26–54.

Maxcy, G., and A. Silberston. 1959. *The Motor Industry*. London: George Allen and Unwin.

McClellan, D., ed. and trans. 1972. *The Grundrisse*. New York: Harper Torchbooks.

McDonald, F. 2011. "Bringing the House Down." *Irish Times*, March 25.

McDonald, R., ed. 2004. *Thomas Jefferson's Military Academy: Founding West Point*. Charlottesville: University of Virginia Press.

McMaster, R. K. 1951. *West Point's Contribution to Education*. El Paso, TX: McMath.

Meder, A., A. L. J. ter Wal, and U. Cantner. 2010. "Innovator Networks and Regional Knowledge Base." In Foxall, Fawn, and Johnston 1992, 496–507.

Methé, D. 1995. "Basic Research in Japanese Electronic Companies: An Attempt at Establishing New Organizational Routines." In *Engineered in Japan: Japanese Technology Management Practices*, ed. J. Liker, J. Ettlie, and J. Campbell. New York and Oxford: Oxford University Press.

Meyer, D. 2006. *Networked Machinists: High-Technology Industries in Antebellum America*. Baltimore: Johns Hopkins University Press.

Mindell, D. 2002. *Between Human and Machine: Feedback, Control, and Computing before Cybernetics*. Baltimore: Johns Hopkins University Press.

MITRE Corporation. 2008. "Fifty Years of Service in the Public Interest." https://www.mitre.org/sites/default/files/pdf/Fifty_Years_of_Service_in_the_Public_Interest_2008.pdf.

Mjøset, L. 1992. *The Irish Economy in a Comparative Institutional Perspective*. Dublin: National Economic and Social Council.

Mokyr, J. 1990. *The Lever of Riches: Technological Creativity and Economic Progress*. Oxford: Oxford University Press.

Moore, J. 1993. "Predators and Prey: A New Ecology of Competition." *Harvard Business Review*, May–June: 75–86.

Mottiar, Z., and D. Jacobson. 2000. "The Importance of Place, Space and Culture in the Development of an Industrial Agglomeration in Ireland: The Furniture Industry in Co. Monaghan." Paper no. 41, Research Paper Series, Dublin City University Business School, Dublin, Ireland.

Mowery, D., and R. Nelson. 1996. "The U.S. Corporation and Technical Progress." In *The American Corporation Today*, ed. C. Kaysen. New York and Oxford: Oxford University Press.

Mowery, D., and N. Rosenberg. 1989. *Technology and the Pursuit of Economic Growth*. New York: Cambridge University Press.

———. 1993. "The U.S. National Innovation System." In *National Innovation Systems*, ed. R. Nelson. Oxford: Oxford University Press.

Myers, M., and R. Rosenbloom. 1996. "Rethinking the Role of Industrial Research." In *Engines of Innovation*, ed. R. Rosenbloom and W. Spencer. Boston: Harvard Business School.

Myrdal, G. 1939. *Monetary Equilibrium*. Translated from the Swedish edition of 1931. London: Hodge.

———. 1957. *Economic Theory and Underdeveloped Regions*. London: Duckworth.

Nathan, R. R. 1994. "GNP and Military Mobilization." *Journal of Evolutionary Economics* 4: 1–16.

National Spatial Strategy for Ireland, 2002–2020: People, Places and Potential. 2002. Dublin: Government Publications. Available at http://nss.ie/pdfs/Completea.pdf.

Nelson, R., ed. 1993. *National Innovation Systems*. Oxford: Oxford University Press.

Nelson, R., and S. Winter. 1982. *An Evolutionary Theory of Economic Change*. Cambridge, MA: Harvard University Press.

Newenham, P. 2017. "Datalex Flying as It Aims to Leave Turbulence Behind." *Irish Times*, December 6. www.irishtimes.com/business/technology/datalex-flying-high-as-it-aims-to-leave-turbulence-behind-1.2162739.

Nieburg, H. 1966. *In the Name of Science*. Chicago: Quadrangle Books.

Noble, D. 1977. *America by Design: Science, Technology, and the Rise of Corporate Capitalism*. New York: Alfred Knopf.

Nolan, P. 2012. *Is China Buying the World*. Cambridge: Polity Press.

Nolan, P. 2015. *Re-balancing China*. London: Anthem Press.

North, D. 1990. *Institutions, Institutional Change, and Economic Performance*. New York: Cambridge University Press.

Northern Ireland Executive. 2011. *Economic Strategy: Priorities for Sustainable Growth and Prosperity*. Belfast.

OECD (Organisation for Economic Co-operation and Development). 2013. *Main Science and Technology Indicators*. Issue 1. Paris. United Nations Educational, Scientific, and Cultural Organization Institute for Statistics).

Office of Statistical Control, Army Air Forces. 1945. "Army Air Forces Statistical Digest, World War II." Retitled "United States Air Force Statistical Digest World War II." US Air Force, Washington, DC. https://ia802505.us.archive.org/5/items /ArmyAirForcesStatisticalDigestWorldWarII/ArmyAirForcesStatisticalDigest WorldWarII.pdf.

O' Gráda, C. 1977. "The Beginnings of the Irish Creamery System, 1880–1914." *Economic History Review* 30, no. 2 (May): 284–305.

Ó Riain, S. 2004. *The Politics of High-Tech Growth*. Cambridge: Cambridge University Press.

Ohno, T. 1988 (1978). *Toyota Production System: Beyond Large Scale Production*. Cambridge: Productivity Press.

O'Rourke, K. 2007. "Culture, Conflict and Cooperation: Irish Dairying before the Great War." *Economic Journal* 117 (October): 1357–79.

Ostry, J., P. Loungani, D. Furceri, D. 2016. "Neoliberalism: Oversold?" International Monetary Fund, *Finance and Development*, June: 38–41.

Overy, R. 1995. *Why the Allies Won*. London: Pimlico.

Owens, L. 1990. "MIT and the Federal 'Angel': Academic R&D and Federal-Private Cooperation before World War II." *ISIS* 81: 188–213.

Owen-Smith, J., and W. Powell. 2006. "Accounting for Emergence and Novelty in Boston and Bay Area Biotechnology." In *Cluster Genesis: Cluster-Based Industrial Development*, ed. P. Braunerhjelm and M. Feldman. Oxford: Oxford University Press.

PDC (Penang Development Corporation). 1994. *Penang Development Corporation: 1969–1994*. Pulau Pinang, Malaysia.

Peaucelle, J. 2006. "Adam Smith's Use of Multiple References for His Pin Making Example." *European Journal of Economic Thought* 13, no. 4: 489–512.

Penrose, A. 2017. *Edith Penrose: No Ordinary Woman*. Oxford: Oxford University Press.

Penrose, E. 1955. "Research on the Business Firm: Limits to the Growth and Size of Firms." *American Economic Review* 45, no. 2 (May): 531–43.

———. 1959. *The Theory of the Growth of the Firm*. Oxford: Basil Blackwell and New York: John Wiley and Sons. 2nd ed. 1980, Oxford: Basil Blackwell and New York: St. Martins. Rev. ed. 1995, Oxford: Oxford University Press.

———. 1960. "The Growth of the Firm—A Case Study: The Hercules Powder Company." *Business History Review* 34: 1–23.

People's Daily Online. 2008. "Science and Technology Are Primary Productive Forces in 1988." October 9. Available at http://en.people.cn/90002/95589/6512392.html.

Perez, C. 1983. "Structural Change and the Assimilation of New Technologies in the Economic and Social System." *Futures* 15, no. 5: 357–75.

———. 2002. *Technological Revolutions and Financial Capital.* Cheltenham, England: Edward Elgar

Pernick, R., and C. Wilder. 2007. *The Clean Tech Revolution: The Next Big Growth and Investment Opportunity.* New York: HarperCollins.

Petrin, T. 1995. "Industrial Policy Supporting Economic Transition in CEE: Lessons from Slovenia." Economic Development Institute Working Papers nos. 95–97, World Bank, Washington, DC.

Petrin, T., R. Vitez, and M. Mesl. 2000. "Sustainable Regional Development Experience from Slovenia." Paper presented at the conference Approaches to Sustainable Regional Development: The Role of the University in the Globalizing Economy," University of Massachusetts, Lowell, October 28.

Pinch, S., and N. Henry. 1999. "Paul Krugman's Geographical Economics, Industrial Clustering and the British Motor Sport Industry." *Regional Studies* 33, no. 9: 815–27.

Pinch, S., N. Henry, M. Jenkins, and S. Tallman. 2003. "From 'Industrial Districts' to 'Knowledge Clusters': A Model of Knowledge Dissemination and Competitive Advantage in Industrial Agglomerations." *Journal of Economic Geography* 3, no. 4: 373–88.

Piore, M., and C. Sabel. 1984. *The Second Industrial Divide.* New York: Basic Books.

Pisano, G., and W. Shih, W. 2009. "Restoring American Competitiveness." *Harvard Business Review*, July–August.

———. 2012. *Producing Prosperity: Why America Needs a Manufacturing Renaissance.* Boston: Harvard Business Review Press.

Porter, M. 1990. *The Competitive Advantage of Nations.* New York: Macmillan.

Prencipe, A., A. Davies, and M. Hobday, eds. 2003. *The Business of Systems Integration.* Oxford: Oxford University Press.

Prescott, E. 1986. "Theory Ahead of Business Cycle Measurement." *Federal Reserve Bank of Minneapolis Quarterly Review* 10: 9–21.

Rabellotti, R., A. Carabelli, and G. Hirsch. 2009. "Italian Industrial Districts on the Move: Where Are They Going?" *European Planning Studies* 17, no. 1: 19–41.

Randow, J., and A. Kirchfeld. 2010. "Germany's Mittelstand Still Thrives." *Business Week*, September 20.

Rao, A., and P. Scaruffi. 2013. *A History of Silicon Valley.* Palo Alto, CA: Omniware Group.

Rapping, L. 1965. "Learning and World War II Production Functions." *Review of Economics and Statistics* 47, no. 1: 81–86.

Rasiah, R. 2000. "Politics, Institutions and Flexibility: Microelectronics Transnationals and Machine Tool Linkages in Malaysia." In *Flexible Specialization in Asia*, ed. Richard Doner and Frederic Deyo. Ithaca: Cornell University Press.

Rattner, S. 2011. "The Secrets of Germany's Success." *Foreign Affairs*, July–August, 7–11.

Reid, P. 1990. *Well Made in America: Lessons From Harley-Davidson on Being the Best.* New York: McGraw-Hill.

Ricardo, D. 1817. *Principles of Political Economy and Taxation*. London: John Murray.

Richardson, G. B. 1960. *Information and Investment: A Study in the Working of the Competitive Economy*. Oxford: Oxford University Press.

———. 1972. "The Organization of Industry." *Economic Journal* 82 (September).

Ridley, M. 2009. "The Natural Order of Things." *Spectator*, 10 January. Available at www.spectator.co.uk/2009/01/the-natural-order-of-things/.

Robert, L., and J.-C. Spender. 2011. *Confronting Managerialism*. London: Zed Books.

Roberts, E. 1991. *Entrepreneurs in High Technology: Lessons from MIT and Beyond*. New York: Oxford University Press.

Robinson, A., and D. Schroeder. 1993. "Training, Continuous Improvement, and Human Relations: The U.S. TWI Programs and the Japanese Management Style." *California Management Review* 35, no. 2: 35–57.

Robinson, J. 1933. *The Economics of Imperfect Competition*. London: Macmillan.

Robson, G. 1990. *Cosworth: The Search for Power*. Yeovil, England: Patrick Stephens.

Roe, J. 1937. "Interchangeable Manufacture." *Mechanical Engineering* 59, no. 10: 755–58.

Rolt, L. 1970. *Victorian Engineering*. London: Allen Lane.

Romer, C. D. 1992. What Ended the Great Depression? *Journal of Economic History* 52, no. 4: 757–84.

Romer P. 2016. "The Trouble with Macroeconomics." https://paulromer.net/wp-con tent/uploads/2016/09/WP-Trouble.pdf.

Rosegrant, S., and D. Lampe. 1992. *Route 128: Lessons from Boston's High-Tech Community*. New York: Basic Books.

Rosenberg, N. 1963. "Technological Change in the Machine Tool Industry, 1840–1910." *Journal of Economic History* 23.

———. 1982. *Inside the Black Box: Technology and Economics*. Cambridge: Cambridge University Press.

Rosenberg, R. 1999. "Growing with the Flow: Endless Stream of Data Spawns Computer-Storage Firms." *Boston Globe*, April 14.

Ross, S. 1962. "Scientist: The Story of a Word." *Annals of Science* 18, no. 2: 65–85.

Rossi, N., and G. Toniolo. 1996. "Italy." In *Economic Growth in Europe since 1945*, ed. N. Crafts and G. Toniolo. Cambridge: Cambridge University Press: 427–54.

Ryan, P., and M. Giblin. 2012. "High-Tech Clusters, Innovation Capabilities and Technological Entrepreneurship: Evidence from Ireland." In *World Economy* 35, no. 10: 1322–39.

Ryan, P., M. Giblin, S. Das, and M. Best. 2010. "Capabilities and Competitiveness: A Methodological Approach for Understanding Irish Economic Transformation." Centre for Innovation and Structural Change, National University of Ireland Galway, Galway. Available at www.nuigalway.ie/cisc/documents/lucerna_project _final_report_june2010.pdf.

Ryle, G. 1949. *The Concept of Mind*. London: Hutchison.

Sainsbury, D. 2013. *Progressive Capitalism: How to Achieve Growth, Liberty and Social Justice*. London: Biteback.

Samuelson, P. 1944. "A Warning to the Washington Expert." *New Republic*, September 11: 298.

Samuelson, P. 1980. *Economics*, 11th ed. New York: McGraw-Hill.

Samuelson, P., and W. Nordhaus. 1995. *Economics*, 15th ed. New York: Mcgraw-Hill.

Sanderson, M. 1972. *The Universities and British Industry: 1850–1970*. London: Routledge and Kegan Paul.

Sands, A. 2005. "The Irish Software Industry." In *From Underdogs to Tigers: The Rise and Growth of the Software Industry in Brazil, China, India, Ireland, and Israel*, ed. A. Ashish and A. Gambardella. Oxford: Oxford University Press.

Saul, S. B. 1962. "The Motor Industry to 1914." *Business History* 5: 22–44.

Saxenian, A. 1994. *Regional Advantage: Culture and Competition in Silicon Valley and Route 128*. Cambridge, MA: Harvard University Press.

———. 2006. *The New Argonauts: Regional Advantage in a Global Economy*. Cambridge: Harvard University Press.

Scherer, F. 1982. "Inter-Industry Technology Flows and Productivity Growth." *Review of Economics and Statistics* 64 (November): 627–34.

Schonberger, R. 1986. *World Class Manufacturing*. New York: Free Press.

Schumpeter, J. 1934. *The Theory of Economic Development*. Cambridge, MA: Harvard University Press.

———. 1939. *Business Cycles: A Theoretical, Historical and Statistical Analysis of the Capitalist Process*. New York: McGraw-Hill.

———. 2008 (1942). *Capitalism, Socialism and Democracy*. New York: Harper and Brothers.

———. 1947. "The Creative Response in Economic History." *Journal of Economic History* 7, no. 2: 149–59.

———. 1954. *History of Economic Analysis*. London: Allen and Unwin.

Sekine, K. 1990. *One-Piece Flow*. Portland, OR: Productivity Press.

Senghaas, D. 1985. *The European Experience*. Leamington Spa, England: Berg.

Shackle, G. 2010. *The Years of High Theory: Invention and Tradition in Economic Thought, 1926–1939*. Cambridge: Cambridge University Press.

Shapira, P. 1998. "Manufacturing Extension: Performance, Challenges, and Policy Issues." In *Investing in Innovation*, ed. L. Branscomb and J. Keller. Cambridge, MA: MIT Press, 250–75.

Shiba, S., A. Graham, and D. Walden, D. 1993. *A New American TQM: Four Practical Revolutions in Management*. Portland, OR: Productivity Press.

Shiman, P. 1997. *Forging the Sword: Defense Production during the Cold War*. USACERL Special Report. Champaign, IL: US Army Construction Engineering Research Laboratory.

Shirk, S. 1993. *The Political Logic of Economic Reform in China*. Berkeley and Los Angeles: University of California Press.

Singh, A. 1995. "How Did East Asia Grow So Fast?" United Nations Conference on Trade and Development document no. 97, Geneva, February.

SIPRI (Stockholm International Peace Research Institute). 1999. *SIPRI Yearbook 1999: Armaments, Disarmament and International Security*. Oxford: Oxford University Press.

Skidelsky, R. 2013. "Meeting Our Makers: Britain's Long Industrial Decline." *New Statesman*, January 24.

Smiles, S., ed. 1883. *James Nasmyth, Engineer, an Autobiography*. London: John Murray.

Smith, A. 1976 (1776). *An Inquiry into the Nature and Causes of the Wealth of Nations*, ed. R. H. Campbell, A. S. Skinner, and W. B. Todd. 2 vol. Oxford: Oxford University Press.

Smith, M. R., ed. 1985. *Military Enterprise and Technological Change*. Cambridge: MIT Press.

Smith, N. 2011. *The Sea of Lost Opportunity: North Sea Oil and Gas, British Industry and the Offshore Supplies Office*. Handbook of Petroleum Exploration and Production, vol. 7. Oxford: Elsevier B.V.

Smith, R. E. 1991 (1959). *The Army and Economic Mobilization* (US Army Green Books). In *The U.S. Army in World War II*, the Army's official history undertaken by the Office of the Chief of Military History under Maj. Gen. Richard W. Stephens, Chief. Washington, DC: Center of Military History of the United States Army.

Snyder, L. 2011. *The Philosophical Breakfast Club*. New York: Broadway Books.

Solow, R. 1957. "Technical Change and the Aggregate Production Function." *Review of Economic Statistics* 39, August.

Sorensen, C. 1956. *My Forty Years with Ford*. New York: Norton.

Staudt, L. n.d. "Status and Prospects for Wind Energy in Ireland." Centre for Renewable Energy, Dundalk Institute of Technology, Dundalk.

Staudt, L. n.d. "Ireland's Energy Outlook," rev. 1.5. Centre for Renewable Energy, Dundalk Institute of Technology, Dundalk.

Sterne, J. 2004. *Adventures in Code: The Story of the Irish Software Industry*. Dublin: Liffey.

Stigler, G. 1971. "The Theory of Economic Regulation." *Bell Journal of Economics and Management Systems* 2, no. 1: 3–21.

Suzaki, K. 1987. *The New Manufacturing Challenge*. New York: Free Press.

Tassava, C. 2008. "The American Economy during World War II." *EH.Net Encyclopedia*, edited by Robert Whaples. http://eh.net/encyclopedia/the-american-economy-during-world-war-ii/.

Tate, Dr. James P. 1998. *The Army and Its Air Corps: Army Policy toward Aviation, 1919–1941*. Maxwell Air Force Base, Montgomery, AL: Air University Press. Available at http://en.wikipedia.org/wiki/United_States_Army_Air_Corps.

Teece, D., G. Pisano, and A. Shuen. 1997. "Dynamic Capabilities and Strategic Management." *Strategic Management Journal* 18, no. 7: 509–33.

Ter Wal, A.L.J., and R. Boschma. 2011. "Co-evolution of Firms, Industries and Networks in Space." *Regional Studies*, 45, no. 7: 919–33.

Thomson, R. 2009. *Structures of Change in the Mechanical Age: Technological Innovation in the United States, 1790–1865*. Baltimore: Johns Hopkins University Press.

Thorpe, J. 1999. *In My Own Time*. London: Politico's Publishing.

Time Magazine. 1959. "The Idea Road," July 13.

Tödtling, F. 1994. "Regional Networks of High-Technology Firms—The Case of the Greater Boston Region." *Technovation* 14, no. 5: 323–43.

Tuttle, W. 1981. "The Birth of an Industry: The Synthetic Rubber 'Mess' in World War II." *Technology and Culture* 22, no. 1: 35–67.

UNCTAD (United Nations Conference on Trade and Development). 2010. *World Investment Report*. Geneva.

UNESCO (United Nations Educational, Scientific, and Cultural Organization).

UNIDO (United Nations Industrial Development Organization). 2002. *Competing through Innovation and Learning: Industrial Development Report 2002/2003*. Vienna.

US Bureau of the Census. 1975. *Historical Statistics of the United States, Colonial Times to 1970*. Washington, DC.

US Council of Economic Advisers (1990). *Annual Report, 1990*. Washington, DC.

US Department of Commerce. 1954. *A Supplement to the Survey of Current Business*. Washington, DC.

US GAO (Government Accountability Office). 2008. "Defense Contracting: Post-government Employment of Former DOD Officials Needs Greater Transparency." May 28. www.gao.gov/products/GAO-08-485.

Van Egeraat, C., and F. Barry. 2008. "The Irish Pharmaceutical Industry over the Boom Period and Beyond." Document no. 39, National Institute for Regional and Spatial Analysis, Maynooth University, Maynooth, Ireland, September.

Van Egeraat, C., and P. Breathnach. 2012. "The Drivers of Transnational Subsidiary Evolution: The Upgrading of Process R&D in the Irish Pharmaceutical Industry." *Regional Studies* 46, no. 9: 1153–67.

Van Egeraat, C., and D. Curran. 2013. "Spatial Concentration in the Irish Pharmaceutical Industry: The Role of Spatial Planning and Agglomeration Economies." *Tijdschrift voor Economische en Sociale Geografie* 104, no. 3: 338–58.

Veblen, T. 1898. "Review of William H. Mallock, *Aristocracy and Evolution*." *Journal of Political Economy* 6 (June): 430–35.

Venhor, B. 2010. "The Power of Uncommon Common Sense Management Principles—The Secret Recipe of German Mittelstand Companies—Lessons for Large and Small Companies." Presented at the Second Global Drucker Forum, Vienna, November 18 and 19.

Vincent, J., and H. Termeer. 2000. "New England's Important Role in the Biomedical Revolution." *Boston Globe*, March 25, Op-Ed, A15.

von Tunzelmann, G. N. 1995 *Technology and Industrial Progress: The Foundations of Economic Growth*. Brookfield, VT: Edward Elgar, 1995.

Wade, R. 1990. *Governing the Market: Economic Theory and the Role of Government in East Asian Industrialization*. Princeton, NJ: Princeton University Press.

Wagner-Braun, Magarete. n.d. "Die Deutsche Girozentrale als Antwort auf Finanzprobleme des frühen 20. Jahrhunderts." In *Die DekaBank seit 1918*. Frankfurt: Institut für bankhistorische Forschung e.V.

Wallis, G., and J. Whitworth. 1969 (1855). *The American System of Manufacturs: The Report of the Committee of the United States, 1855, and the Special Reports of George Wallis and Joseph Whitworth, 1854*, ed. and intro. Nathan Rosenberg. Edinburgh: University of Edinburgh Press.

Walton, M. 1986. *The Deming Management Method*. New York: Dodd, Mead.

Watson, G. 1993. *Strategic Benchmarking*. New York: John Wiley.

WB (World Bank). 2008. *World Development Indicators*. Washington, DC.

Weisbord, M. 1987. *Productive Workplaces: Organizing and Managing for Dignity, Meaning and Community*. San Francisco: Jossey-Bass.

Whewell, W. 1831. "Mathematical Exposition of Some of the Leading Doctrines in Mr. Ricardo's Principles of Political Economy and Taxation, 1831." Paper presented

March 2 and 4, 1829. In *Transactions of the Cambridge Philosophical Society* 3, Part 1 (1830): 191–230. Cambridge: Cambridge University Press.

White, G. 1949. "Financing Industrial Expansion for War: The Origin of the Defense Plant Corporation Leases." *Journal of Economic History* 9, no. 2: 156–83.

——. 1980. *Billions for Defense: Government Financing by the Defense Plant Corporation during World War II*. Tuscaloosa: University of Alabama Press.

Whitworth, J. 1854. *New York Industrial Exhibition*. London.

WMC (War Manpower Commission). 1945. *The Training within Industry Report, 1940–1945: A Record of the Development of Management Techniques for Improvement of Supervision—Their Use and the Results*. Bureau of Training, Training within Industry Service, Washington, DC, September.

Womack, J., D. Jones, and D. Roos. 1990. *The Machine That Changed the World*. New York: Rawson Associates.

Wright, G. 1990. "The Origins of American Industrial Success." *American Economic Review* 80, no. 4: 651–68.

——. 1997. "Towards a More Historical Approach to Technological Change," *Economic Journal* 107, no. 444: 1560–66.

Wright, T. 1936. "Factors Affecting the Cost of Airplanes." *Journal of Aeronautical Sciences* 3: 122–28.

Wrigley, J. 1986. "Technical Education and Industry in the Nineteenth Century." In *The Decline of the British Economy*, ed. B. Elbaum and W. Lazonick. Oxford: Oxford University Press: 162–88.

Yamanouchi, T. 1995. *A New Study of Technology Management*. Tokyo: Asian Productivity Center. Distributed in North America and Western Europe by Quality Resources, New York.

Yang, D. 1996. *Calamity and Reform in China*. Palo Alto, CA: Stanford University Press.

Young, A. 1928. "Increasing Returns and Economic Progress." *Economic Journal* 38 (December).

Zachary, G. 1999. *Endless Frontier: Vannevar Bush, Engineer of the American Century*. Cambridge, MA: MIT Press.

Zeitlin, J. 1992. "Industrial Districts and Local Economic Regeneration: Overview and Comment." In *Industrial Districts and Local Economic Regeneration*, ed. F. Pyke and W. Sengenberger. International Institute for Labor Studies, Geneva.

A NOTE ON THE TYPE

{≈≈≈〰≈≈}

THIS BOOK has been composed in Miller, a Scotch Roman typeface designed by Matthew Carter and first released by Font Bureau in 1997. It resembles Monticello, the typeface developed for The Papers of Thomas Jefferson in the 1940s by C. H. Griffith and P. J. Conkwright and reinterpreted in digital form by Carter in 2003.

Pleasant Jefferson ("P. J.") Conkwright (1905–1986) was Typographer at Princeton University Press from 1939 to 1970. He was an acclaimed book designer and AIGA Medalist.

The ornament used throughout this book was designed by Pierre Simon Fournier (1712–1768) and was a favorite of Conkwright's, used in his design of the *Princeton University Library Chronicle*.